FAITH TO CREED

FAITH AND ORDER SERIES

Apostolic Faith in America
  edited by Thaddeus D. Horgan

Black Witness to the Apostolic Faith
  edited by David T. Shannon and Gayraud S. Wilmore

*Women and Church: The Challenge of Ecumenical Solidarity
in an Age of Alienation*
  edited by Melanie A. May

*Faith to Creed: Ecumenical Perspectives on the Affirmation
of the Apostolic Faith in the Fourth Century*
  edited by S. Mark Heim

Faith to Creed

Ecumenical Perspectives on the
Affirmation of the Apostolic Faith
in the Fourth Century

Papers of the Faith to Creed Consultation
Commission on Faith and Order NCCCUSA
October 25-27, 1989 — Waltham, Massachusetts

Edited by S. MARK HEIM

William B. Eerdmans Publishing Company
Grand Rapids, Michigan

for Commission on Faith and Order
    National Council of the Churches of Christ in the U.S.A.

Copyright © 1991 by Commission on Faith and Order, NCCCUSA
475 Riverside Dr., Room 872, New York, NY 10115-0050 (212) 870-2569

First published 1991 for the Commission on Faith and Order by
William B. Eerdmans Publishing Co.
255 Jefferson Ave. S.E., Grand Rapids, Mich. 49503

Library of Congress Cataloging-in-Publication Data

Faith to Creed Consultation (1989: Waltham, Mass.)
   Faith to creed: ecumenical perspectives on the affirmation of
the apostolic faith in the fourth century: papers of the Faith to
Creed Consultation, Commission on Faith and Order, NCCCUSA,
October 25-27, 1989—Waltham, Massachusetts / edited by
S. Mark Heim.
       p.   cm.   — (Faith and order series)
   Includes bibliographical references.
   ISBN 0-8028-0551-5
   1. Theology, Doctrinal—History—Early church, ca. 30-600—
Congresses. 2. Nicene Creed—Congresses. 3. Church history—
4th century—Congresses. I. Heim, S. Mark. II. National Council
of the Churches of Christ in the United States of America. Commis-
sion on Faith and Order. III. Title.
BT25.F35   1989
238'.142—dc20   90-22215
                                                          CIP

*Dedicated to the memory of
Albert C. Outler
scholar, ecumenist, teacher,
in recognition of his long service
to the ecumenical movement
and his unflagging zeal
"that all should be one"*

Contents

A Memory of Albert C. Outler

Albert Outler was an ecumenist whose deep devotion to the United Methodist Church was focused primarily in the direction of God's utilization of it for the next generations. From that perspective he was a loyal and constant critic of the churches—all of them—as faulty expressions of the body of Christ. His wit and exceptional cogency in precise language were often more intimidating than he intended, I believe, but for those willing and able to listen, his analyses and predictions had potential for institutional improvement. A historian who was dedicated to our learning from history, he was a teacher for anyone who came within the sound of his voice or the force of his written word. He could trade theological probings with the best scholars in all the churches and could and did convey excitement to and elicit emotional commitment from persons engaged in dialogue around him. He understood thoroughly the need for mutual clarification, the identification of misinterpretations, the press for more adequate expression of consensus, and fuller movement toward the truth. He was always on "tip toe" excitement about new revelatory learnings in areas from patristics to contemporary studies, and he was keen about their future. This volume and the consultation behind it were dear to his heart, because of their promise.

Dr. Outler was a chief participant in the United Methodist–Roman Catholic dialogues on a variety of subjects from 1966 onward, particularly on public aid to private education and the relationship of faith and good works to salvation. As, I believe, the only Protestant observer at the Second Vatican Council who read documents in the original Latin, he was also a stimulating mentor to neophyte observers and an indefatigable teacher (often into the wee hours of the night after a full day at the Vatican sessions!). He was a walking encyclopedia of Roman history as well as a sought-after confidant and counselor for the inner circles of the newly created Secretariat for Promotion of Christian Unity. He was respected, with affection, among Roman Catholics and other Second Vatican Council participants. He related well to both scholars and church officials and could "explain what happened" the previous day to those whose responsibilities kept them involved in details. He was the first Protestant president of the American Catholic Historical Association and, typically, addressed that group on "Ecumenical Uses of Church History"!

Dr. Outler did not suffer fools gladly, but there was an innate graciousness that usually overrode his frustration. His clever wit and sometimes devastating flicks of judgment were not universally appreciated, but he was heard because his analyses of power and political expediency always had solid research behind them. In more than one situation over his active years he combined the scholarly with the political in uncovering motivations and short-sightedness. For example, he was more recently an astute critic of the church-growth polemics in many of the churches. His language style was usually irrepressible and always impeccably tuned to lead the hearer or reader through complexities that he refused to treat simplistically.

He was an ecstatic researcher in the Wesleyan foundation of what is now the United Methodist Church and for years was the acknowledged chief among peers for that scholarship. An elegant professor and scintillating lecturer, he drove himself to the point of health problems in his comprehensive pursuit of long-term perfection in the Body of Christ. For though his critically alert devotion to the church of his ordination was clear, he was an ecumenist by profession. A strong participant in the World Council of Churches, he was a key figure in such statements as that of the 1961 New Delhi Assembly about Christian unity "in every place" and again as a delegate to the WCC Uppsala Assembly in 1968. A member of the working group of the WCC Faith and Order Commission, his combination of scholarship and political practicality was influential in progress toward the *Baptism, Eucharist, and Ministry* statement of 1982. For many United Methodists his 1966 study book *That the World May Believe* made the greatest single contribution in the lives of pastors and laity. Certainly it demonstrated his ability to write clearly and trenchantly for laity as well as for professional scholars. A General Conference statement adopted in 1968 on the "Cause of Christian Unity and the United Methodist Church" (printed and reprinted since under the title *On the Ecumenical Road*) came largely from his hand. In both, his basic understanding is clear that "God's own design and providence for his Covenant People" is the profoundest imperative to Christian unity, that a change of heart is crucial to ecumenical advance, and that the crucial danger to the oneness we are given by God through Jesus Christ is "the passionate fear of change and the disposition to cling to accustomed ways."

His own scholarship was open to new developments. The fact that history is full of unpredicted outcomes (even divergent from his own predictions) was a source of delight and excitement in him that did not dim in the last stage of his life. The temptation to quote from his speeches, books, and articles is well nigh inescapable, but for a short work of appreciation, where could one stop? I am led instead to quote his words to me on the occasion of my election as the first Methodist Church general secretary for ecumenical affairs in 1965. He was a vice president of the new Commission on Ecumenical Affairs that had been authorized by the 1964 General Conference and was a member of the executive/search committee. At the coffee break immediately following my acceptance speech, he put his hand on my shoulder, looked me in the eye, and, as I waited expectantly for some clear theological word of wisdom, said: "I have one bit of advice to you: never lose a chance to go to the john!" Five seconds later he was making arrangements for my presence with him at the last session of Vatican II. His practical wisdom was ever matched by his devotion to the Christian future in which "despair and faint-heartedness are denied Christians as live options, however ambivalent the prospects." In his life and works Albert C. Outler combined that ability to narrate and analyze human actions in religious affairs with the Christian vision in which the Holy Spirit's prevenience has always been finally dominant. We celebrate his marks on the church universal, on his own denomination, and on us as persons.

Ecumenical Staff Office   ROBERT W. HUSTON
The United Methodist Church

Introduction

The history of the first four centuries of the Christian church has often been viewed through lenses shaped by the myriad later divisions of Christianity. Most Christians have affirmed the substance of the doctrines of incarnation and trinity that were formulated in these centuries. But different denominational traditions have viewed the period in dramatically varied ways: as the triumph of orthodoxy or the fall of the church, as the Christian leavening of the world or the political corruption of the faith.

These conflicting perspectives—to some extent manifest within individual traditions as well as among them—have long been with us. In many Christian communions a particular view of these centuries has been passed down and received as a constituent part of denominational identity. The modern ecumenical movement has tended to soften some of the conflicts among these received views. But when discussion is focused on the Nicene Creed, an integral part of the historical sweep of these four centuries, the varied perspectives come sharply to the fore again. This book is a demonstration and a test of the extent to which Christians can converge on a common understanding of the fourth-century setting out of which the Nicene Creed comes to us and by extension on a common understanding of the faith it expressed.

This is a task that requires scholarly skills of the highest order, but it is hardly an academic project in the narrow sense of that word. For an incarnational faith like Christianity, history and theology can never be sharply divided. So too in these pages the work of the historian and the theologian converge, not simply in the traditional overlap of the "history of doctrine" but in the effort to take with seriousness the theological significance of the social and political context of the development of the creed.

"Faith to Creed: Toward a Common Historical Approach to the Affirmation of the Apostolic Faith in the Fourth Century" was the full title of a consultation held 25-27 October 1989 at the Espousal Center in Waltham, Massachusetts. It was organized by the history subsection of the Apostolic Faith study group in the Faith and Order Commission of the National Council of the Churches of Christ in the USA. The organizers planned it as a specific contribution to the broader work of the Apostolic Faith study within the World Council of Churches. It is necessary therefore to see this project in the context of this larger movement.

For the better part of this century, the Faith and Order movement has played a leading role in the search for Christian unity. It has sought to serve the churches on their three-step path toward unity. The first step is reconciliation over the church-dividing issues of baptism, eucharist, and ministry. The second is a common confession of the apostolic faith. The third step is to find a common process for decision making and acting together. Over many years, Christian churches have come to agree that there is no way to full unity that does not meet these challenges.

At Lima in 1982 the Faith and Order Commission of the World Council of Churches sent the *Baptism, Eucharist and Ministry* convergence document to the churches for their response. *BEM* represented a major movement toward the first crucial condition for Christian unity. The process of discussion and reception of *BEM* continues as a very lively part of the ecumenical agenda.[1] Precisely because of the energy generated by the

1. *Baptism, Eucharist and Ministry,* Faith and Order Paper No. 111 (Geneva: WCC, 1982). See also the continuing series of volumes, *Churches Respond to BEM,* published by the World Council of Churches, and *Baptism, Eucharist and Ministry, 1982-1989: Report on the Process and the Responses,* forthcoming from the 1989 Budapest plenary meeting of the WCC Faith and Order Commission.

BEM process, renewed attention has turned to the second question—the question of common confession.

Already at the Nairobi Assembly of the World Council of
Churches, the churches were asked "to undertake a common
effort to receive, reappropriate and confess together, as contemporary occasion requires, the Christian truth and faith, delivered
through the apostles and handed down through the centuries."
The WCC Faith and Order Commission therefore initiated a
long-term study project, "Towards the Common Expression of
the Apostolic Faith Today."[2] The first major design for this study
came from the same Lima meeting that completed the *BEM*
document. Obviously, even if the churches were to come to
agreement on the vexed issues of baptism, eucharist, and ministry, this would not constitute full and common confession of the
church's essential faith. The Apostolic Faith study process seeks
to address this even more daunting question of full unity in faith.

The World Council process identified three phases for this
work: (1) a common recognition of the apostolic faith and (2) a
common explication of the apostolic faith, which would lead
finally to (3) a common confession of this faith together. An early
consultation was held to address the apostolic faith as found in
the Scriptures and in the early church.[3] The process has also
included an attempt to gather materials from a wide variety of
churches indicating the manner in which they confess the apostolic faith today.[4]

2. See *Towards Visible Unity,* ed. Michael Kinnamon, 2 vols., Faith and Order
Papers Nos. 112, 113 (Geneva: WCC, 1982); and Faith and Order Paper No. 121,
"Minutes, Standing Commission of Faith and Order, Crete" (Geneva: WCC,
1984).

3. See *The Roots of Our Common Faith: Faith in the Scriptures and in the Early
Church,* ed. Hans-Georg Link, Faith and Order Paper No. 119 (Geneva: WCC,
1984).

4. See *Confessing Our Faith around the World I,* ed. C. S. Song, Faith and Order
Paper No. 104 (Geneva: WCC, 1980); *Confessing Our Faith around the World II,* ed.
Hans-Georg Link, Faith and Order Paper No. 120 (Geneva: WCC, 1983); *Confess-
ing Our Faith around the World III: The Caribbean and Central America,* ed. Hans-
Georg Link, Faith and Order Paper No. 123 (Geneva: WCC, 1984); and *Confessing
Our Faith around the World IV: South America,* ed. Hans-Georg Link, Faith and
Order Paper No. 126 (Geneva: WCC, 1985).

At the Lima meeting special note was taken of the Nicene-Constantinopolitan Creed of 381—the so-called Nicene Creed —as having a special place as an expression of the apostolic faith. As the most widely recognized and authoritative extrabiblical confession of faith among Christians, it seemed especially worthy of ecumenical exploration. The original hope was that through a common explication of the creed's meaning and a common recognition of the nature of its faithfulness to the apostolic witness the way might be opened for churches to confess together the same apostolic faith of which the creed is an expression.

The steering committee of the Apostolic Faith study eventually decided that the first step ought to be a common *explication* of the apostolic faith as confessed in the Nicene Creed. The result was a study document, *Confessing One Faith: Towards an Ecumenical Explication of the Apostolic Faith as Expressed in the Nicene-Constantinopolitan Creed.*[5] This document has been the focus for a series of international consultations dealing with the substance of the three articles of the creed as well as with important specific issues such as the filioque.[6]

The Faith and Order Commission of the National Council of Churches, through its subgroup on the apostolic faith, has sponsored a series of events and publications bearing on these issues.[7] A special concern in this study process was to highlight

---

5. *Confessing One Faith: Towards an Ecumenical Explication of the Apostolic Faith as Expressed in the Nicene-Constantinopolitan Creed,* Faith and Order Paper No. 140 (Geneva: WCC, 1987).

6. For reports on these consultations, see Faith and Order Paper No. 145, "Minutes, Standing Commission of Faith and Order, Boston" (Geneva: WCC, 1988); and *Spirit of God, Spirit of Christ: Ecumenical Reflections on the Filioque Controversy,* ed. Lukas Vischer, Faith and Order Paper No. 103 (Geneva: WCC, 1981).

7. See *Spirit of Truth: Ecumenical Perspectives on the Holy Spirit,* ed. Theodore Stylianopoulos and S. Mark Heim (Brookline, Mass.: Holy Cross Orthodox Press, 1986); *Christ in East and West,* ed. Paul Fries and Tiran Nersoyan (Macon, Ga.: Mercer University Press, 1987); *Confessing One Faith: Grounds for a Common Witness: A Guide for Ecumenical Study* (Cincinnati: Forward Movement Publications, 1988); *Apostolic Faith in America,* ed. Thaddeus Horgan (Grand Rapids: William B. Eerdmans, 1988); *Black Witness to the Apostolic Faith,* ed. David T. Shannon and Gayraud S. Wilmore (Grand Rapids: William B. Eerdmans, 1988); Cecil M. Robeck, "Confessing the

elements in the context of the church life of North America that would constitute a special enrichment of the study at the World Council level.

The NCCC Apostolic Faith study group planned the consultation "Faith to Creed" as a contribution to this process, a contribution intended to bring the special resources and concerns of North American churches into the worldwide conversation. This necessitated first of all a consultation that would bring together a wide variety of Christian traditions reflecting the denominational pluralism of North America churches. Second, it called for a strong representation of the so-called "free churches," both those like the Baptists who were offspring of the magisterial reformation and those like the Mennonites who stem from the Anabaptist movement. This necessarily implied attention to the convictions of Christian churches for which the Nicene Creed is neither a normative theological authority nor a living part of liturgy and worship. For these communions, the creed calls up memories of persecution and exclusion, not unity. Third, both because of the anti-Constantinian tradition in these churches that has become more widespread in the United States and because of the implications of modern social theory, it was important that close attention be paid to the sociohistorical factors that shaped the Nicene-Constantinopolitan Creed and its historical effect. Each of these elements has a special urgency in the North American context, while in other parts of the world Christian communities may bring different perspectives to the study process.

The consultation was also meant to contribute to what might be called "ecumenical history." Increasingly the history of Christianity is being written and taught without specific confessional guidelines. While this is partly the result of the contribution of the secular historical guild, it is also the product of increased dialogue among church historians. Convergence of views comes about not simply as a result of the parties involved adopting a

---

Apostolic Faith: Pentecostal Churches and the Ecumenical Movement," *Pneuma* 9 (Spring 1987); special issue on the topic "Gender and Language in the Creeds," *Union Seminary Quarterly Review,* August 1985.

thoroughly secular perspective but often because they recognize a value in the historical perspectives formed in their different theological contexts. The organizers of the consultation assumed not only that our varied theological views needed to be tested against history but that different theological orientations might illuminate aspects of the historical record itself.

The initial articles in this volume come from those in traditions that have traditionally affirmed the Nicene Creed as part of their authoritative and liturgical structure. It is often assumed that Roman Catholic and Orthodox scholars feel especially at home dealing with the patristic period, in the same way it is assumed that Protestant scholars will be most attracted to the Reformation period. However, as our contributors make clear, not only are these assumptions increasingly breaking down but the benefit of ecumenical dialogue is bringing new aspects of the patristic period into focus.

John Meyendorff's "The Nicene Creed—Uniting or Dividing Confession?" served as the keynote address for the consultation. In it one of the Orthodox Church's outstanding representatives to the ecumenical movement sketches in a masterly way his perspective on the genesis and function of the creed in the fourth century. While emphasizing clearly the importance of placing the creed within a full texture of organic unity, Meyendorff equally highlights the rich variety and diversity that were consistent with that unity in the fourth century and perhaps are still so today.

André de Halleux's paper is one of two that were not presented at the consultation. It appeared originally in *Revue theologique de Louvain* in 1984.[8] It is included here because it offers a superb overview of the background of our topic in the world Faith and Order movement and provides a complementary Roman Catholic description of the fourth-century development.

William Rusch was unable to present his paper at our meeting but had played a major role in keeping the issues discussed here on the national and international ecumenical agenda. His article surveys recent patristic scholarship and argues that a

8. André de Halleux, "Pour une profession commune de la foi selon l'esprit des Pères," *Revue theologique de Louvain* 15 (1984): 275-96.

significant consensus has arisen that offers a basis upon which ecumenical confession today can build. He outlines the way that this can be understood within his own Lutheran communion but indicates much broader possibilities as well.

If these first three pieces offer a nuanced review of the doctrinal development that has always been central to the creed's importance, indicating its relevance in our own context, Roberta Bondi's article moves us in a different direction. Drawing on her work in monastic spirituality, she reminds us that the creed was an expression of an apostolic faith that was manifest in the fourth century in many forms in addition to that of bishops gathering in imperial councils. What additional meanings and significance might we see in the creed if we brought this background into focus as well? Rosemary Jermann's contribution explores some of these same concerns, focusing on the social location in which the Cappadocian fathers developed their trinitarian formulations.

The essays by Paulo Siepierski and Eduardo Hoornaert complement this attempt to enlarge the historical context for the creed by bringing the contemporary perspective of the churches of the poor and oppressed explicitly into the conversation. Siepierski illustrates how such a perspective can illuminate new facets of our period, particularly the life of Basil of Caesarea. Hoornaert, on the other hand, offers us a methodological argument that indicates how contemporary questions become an integral part of the creed's explication. Both speak with clarity for many who wish to measure the creed's witness in terms of its ethical effect in its own century and in ours.

E. Glenn Hinson and A. James Reimer bring assessments from two traditions—Baptist and Mennonite—that have historically been indifferent or hostile to the use of the creed. Like Bondi, Hinson sees the creed as integral to a part of the church's life in the fourth century that is not often stressed—in this case, the church's mission witness. He indicates the way in which this historical context may help those who see the creed only as an expression of state power. Reimer provides a clear exposition of the traditional Mennonite view—one shared by many Christians of various denominations—that the creed is fatally flawed by its embrace of imperial power, even to the point that it repudiates the gospel preached and embodied by Christ. Proponents of this view maintain that the creed supplanted Christ's teaching and example with philosophical categories and political realism. Reimer emphasizes the elements of this critique that remain of perennial value but argues that the witness of the creed can be seen as foundational for and complementary to the ethical discipleship his tradition affirms.

Max Stackhouse, writing from a Reformed perspective, seeks to draw our eyes to the horizon on which contemporary confession of the apostolic faith must take place. He believes that the renewed energy the ecumenical movement has focused on this exploration of the fourth century is a sign of hope that the church may collectively find its voice to offer a public and constructive ethic for the societies around us, as was true in the fourth century.

Each of the papers at the consultation received vigorous responses, and the participants identified several topics arising from the papers for further extensive discussion. That dialogue is reflected in a very condensed form in an agreed summary statement that was approved at the final session of the consultation. This statement will give the reader some flavor of the concerns that were uppermost in our conversation and some indication of an agenda for future work.

In his article, Max Stackhouse acknowledges the groundbreaking work of his teacher George Williams in the area of the sociopolitical context of the creed and its associated theological debates. In many ways his work was a prototype for the kind of discussion this consultation sought to expand. It was a special honor to have Dr. Williams as a participant in the consultation, and this introduction is an appropriate place to thank him not only for his contributions to our discussion but for his patient labor over the years to bridge the denominational divisions in the study of church history.

In the course of the preparation of the consultation, we were saddened to learn of the death of Albert C. Outler. Dr. Outler's own work, particularly his pioneering advocacy of ecumenical church history, was a primary inspiration for the apostolic faith study process. A dynamic scholar of the early church, he never failed to press upon us the possibilities for unity that lay in a common reappropriation of that history. Writing several months before his death, Dr. Outler regretfully indicated that his health would not allow him to attend the "Faith to Creed" consultation. And he noted with appreciation the plans that were already under way to dedicate this volume to him in recognition of his long and distinguished service to the ecumenical movement. He closed that letter with these words: "I shall continue with you all in spirit and prayer. The ecumenical way forward now lies in the rediscovery of how much diversity was once included in the notion of 'organic unity,' together with an updating of *that* meaning in these times!" We trust that this book goes some small way on that path and are pleased to dedicate it to his memory.

I cannot close this introduction without offering thanks to several people whose efforts were essential to bringing this project to completion. Thomas Finger and Thomas Fitzgerald served as cochairs of the original consultation. Not only did they share the leadership of those sessions, but they played a central role in planning the event and in assembling its participants. Chuck Van Hof and T. A. Straayer of Eerdmans Publishing offered us editorial support and patience of a sort to be coveted by any author. Elizabeth Mellen, associate in the Faith and Order office, has done a great deal of the organizational work. Sr. Mary Peter Froelicher assisted us by translating the papers of Prof. de Halleux and Prof. Hoornaert.

At every stage the leadership of Br. Jeffrey Gros, executive director of the Commission on Faith and Order of the National Council, has been crucial. His support for this project, his tireless travels and visitation, and his ability to interest and inspire a wide range of scholars were essential in bringing it to fruition. This book is only one of the many ecumenical contributions for which he has served as midwife. Not only is he due a vote of thanks from all of us involved for his role in this specific work, but he is equally due thanks for his role in undergirding the whole study process on the apostolic faith, of which this book is one part.

Contributors

Dr. Roberta C. Bondi
Candler School of Theology
Emory University
Atlanta, Georgia

Sr. Mary Peter Froelicher SHCJ
Graymoor Ecumenical Institute
Graymoor, New York

Prof. André de Halleux
University of Louvain
Louvain-la-Neuve, Belgium

Rev. Dr. S. Mark Heim
Andover Newton Theological School
Newton Centre, Massachusetts

Rev. Dr. E. Glenn Hinson
Southern Baptist Theological Seminary
Louisville, Kentucky

Prof. Eduardo Hoornaert
Fortazela Institute of Theology and Pastoral Studies
Fortazela, Brazil

Rev. Robert W. Huston
Ecumenical Staff Office
United Methodist Church
New York, New York

Dr. Rosemary Jermann
Theology Digest
St. Louis, Missouri

The Very Rev. John Meyendorff
St. Vladimir's Theological Seminary
Crestwood, New York

Dr. A. James Reimer
Conrad Grebel College
University of Waterloo
Waterloo, Ontario, Canada

Rev. Dr. William G. Rusch
Office for Ecumenical Affairs
Evangelical Lutheran Church in America
Chicago, Illinois

Dr. Max L. Stackhouse
Andover Newton Theological School
Newton Centre, Massachusetts

Dr. Paulo D. Siepierski
Seminário Teológico Batista do Norte do Brasil
Recife, Brazil

The Nicene Creed:
Uniting or Dividing Confession?

JOHN MEYENDORFF

It is highly significant that our ecumenical movement today would become receptive to the idea of choosing a *historical* issue as the main focus of a consultation like ours. Much of the critical historical scholarship of the nineteenth century consisted in showing that in history there is nothing but change and that if any permanent affirmation is ever made by anyone, one can be sure that it reflects only the historically conditioned convictions of those who make it. This relativizing approach was applied to Scriptures, both the Old and the New Testaments, and even more definitely to statements made by the historical church.

This predominance of a "historical" approach to theology seemed quite objectionable to those who did not want to lose their beliefs in the apostolic truth as permanent and saving. Unenlightened believers often ended up rejecting historical scholarship as such. Within Protestantism (particularly American Protestantism), they moved in the direction of fundamentalism. Within Roman Catholicism during the long reign of Pius IX, the concern was not to relativize but to preserve the historical church and its permanent, institutionally definable magisterium. The decrees of Vatican I on papal authority and infallibility were

1

the results. Orthodoxy also felt these kinds of concerns. Scriptural scholarship tended toward fundamentalism, whereas the magisterium of the church was sometimes expressed through the questionable affirmation that the infallible truths were to be proclaimed infallibly by ecumenical councils *only*. Fortunately, neither of these two trends was allowed to be frozen into nonnegotiable dogmatic positions. Rather, the Orthodox Church generally identified itself as the church of Tradition, reading and interpreting Scriptures and preserving the faith not only through formal decrees of ecumenical councils but also in its liturgy, spirituality, and the living experience of the entire people of God.

It does appear therefore that the task that stands before us today is to define the place of the Nicene Creed within Tradition, understood broadly as a common reference available to all Christians.[1] An Orthodox theologian feels at home in this basically historical methodology, but major misunderstandings can arise whenever one attempts to connect Tradition to the nature of the church itself. Indeed, there is no way in which one can define Tradition without some common understanding of the church.

PRE-NICENE ECCLESIOLOGICAL PRESUPPOSITIONS

Historical methodology cannot be avoided in the study of the early church. However, historical knowledge of the early Christian communities cannot rely *exclusively* on documentary evidence, which is rather scarce. The experience and the vision of the church, which is evident in the way early Christians understood salvation in Christ—their theological perception of the new life-giving relationship between God and humanity and of human beings between themselves—must also be considered before one can understand the true nature of ecclesiology in the apostolic and postapostolic periods.

Since our focus here is on the Nicene period, I will have to limit myself to four points that are characteristic for the earlier,

---

1. Cf. *The Fourth World Conference on Faith and Order: Montreal, 1963*, ed. P. C. Rodgers and L. Vischer (New York: Association Press, 1964).

pre-Nicene times and that also provide a sometimes contrasting link with our approach to the conciliar and confessional developments in the "Constantinian" period.

1. The Christian faith has never been a matter of simple individual convictions or propositional affirmations: it is a matter of reaching through baptismal death and resurrection to a new dimension of personal existence in the communion of the risen Body of Christ. This communion is realized in the eucharist. In the early church period, the eucharist determined beliefs and patterns of conduct. It was taken for granted that the church was a eucharistic community and that "dogmas are principally *soteriological* declarations, their object is to free the original εἰκών of Christ, the truth, from the distortions of certain heresies, so as to help the Church community to maintain the correct vision of the Christ-truth and live in and by this presence of truth in history."[2]

2. The universal acceptance of the "episcopal" principle of church structure as it is described in the letters of Ignatius (ca. 100 A.D.) can be explained only by reference to a "eucharistic ecclesiology": "Where the bishop is present, there let the congregation gather, just as where Jesus Christ is, there is the catholic church" (*Smyrn.* 8.12). The model of the church is provided by the eucharistic gathering, at which Christ (or the one who was called to act as his "image") was presiding, securing the proclamation of the apostolic faith as well as harmony and unity within the community.[3] A "certain charisma of truth" (*charisma veritatis certum*, Irenaeus, *Adv. haer.* 4.26.2) was attributed to bishops, not as a magical, personal privilege coming from an apostolic succession bestowed upon them as individuals but in view of their being presidents (προϊστάμενοι) of the eucharistic assembly. "The bishop is the apostles' successor inasmuch as he is the image of Christ within the community."[4] The preservation and confession of the faith was not seen as simply a historical transmission, passed on as information from one individual to

---

2. J. Zizioulas, *Being as Communion* (Crestwood, N.Y.: St. Vladimir's Seminary Press, 1985), pp. 116-17.

3. On this, see J. Meyendorff, *Catholicity and the Church* (Crestwood, N.Y.: St. Vladimir's Seminary Press, 1983), pp. 53-55.

4. Zizioulas, *Being as Communion*, p. 116.

another, but as a charismatic way of being, an answer of the Spirit to those who had called for it, as a divine response to the invocation (*epiclesis*) of the church.

3. In the second century the church faced a major challenge from a profusion of doctrinal and mystical claims made by those who became known as *Gnostics*. It was in response to Gnosticism that St. Irenaeus of Lyons developed a conception of the church in continuity with the views of Ignatius that also provides the ecclesiological basis for the establishment of a *canon of Scripture* and a *canon of faith*. The Gnostics maintained that Christian teachings were transmitted through individuals charismatically empowered to carry on the traditions from generation to generation. The transmission was secret and the charismatic power arbitrary, and hence there was no way to determine the authenticity of the secret connections that Gnostic leaders claimed to have with the apostles. In opposing Gnosticism, Irenaeus did not deny the charismatic nature of the teaching function in the church, but he proclaimed that the *empowering* of the teachers could be neither secret nor merely individual, that it needed a public liturgical and eucharistic context, involving a community. The witness of each community had also to be checked against the universal consensus of local churches. This consensus further revealed and defined a *canon of faith* and a canon of authentic apostolic *Scriptures*. In fact, for Irenaeus the concepts of "canonicity" and "apostolicity" were practically synonymous. The way to discover authentic faith, he argued, was through the eucharistic reality in each local church, confirmed by an uninterrupted public succession in the episcopal ministry and all the churches. "Our opinion is consistent with the eucharist, and the eucharist supports our opinion," he wrote (*Adv. haer.* 4.18.5). "Having received this preaching and this faith," he continued, "the church, although scattered in the whole world, carefully preserves it, as if living in one house. . . . Neither do the churches that have been established in Germany believe otherwise, or hand down any other tradition, nor those among the Iberians, nor those among the Celts, nor in Egypt, nor in Libya, nor those established in the middle parts of the world" (*Adv. haer.* 1.10.3).

Thus, "the tradition of the apostles, made clear in the world, can be clearly seen in every church by those who wish to behold the truth. We can enumerate those who were established by the apostles as bishops in the churches, and their successors down to our time, none of whom taught or thought of anything like these mad ideas [of the Gnostics]" (*Adv. haer.* 3.3.1).

4. Preserving the right apostolic faith was not a matter of intellectual conviction or of philosophical speculation; it was a *soteriological* matter. One discovers that the earliest *credal* formulas were parts of the *baptismal* liturgy. "It was precisely the need for a formal affirmation of belief to be rehearsed by the catechumen at baptism which instigated the Church to invent creeds in the first place. . . . The true and original use of creeds, their primary *raison d'être*, was to serve as solemn affirmations of faith in the context of baptismal initiation."[5] This is why, even after all the historical evolution that followed, as the creed became an integral part of the eucharistic liturgy, the first-person singular ("I believe," πιστεύω) continued to be used, reminding each faithful that belief in Christ is a personal, free decision and remains so even as this solemn, personal baptismal commitment is renewed at each eucharistic celebration. The plural form "we believe" (πιστεύομεν) was reserved for conciliar statements expressing an agreement of faith of the episcopate. When the ancient term *symbol* (Lat. *symbolum;* Gr. σύμβολον) was used to designate a creed, it had the meaning of "sign," or "password."[6] Anyone desiring entry into the church—originally through baptism but later by simply confessing again the true faith—had to exhibit it in order to be accepted within the eucharistic fellowship of a local church.

The early church knew no administrative or doctrinal authority which would impose absolute uniformity in either the baptismal rite itself or the wording of the catechumen's confession at baptism. What is remarkable, however, is how similar—in the absence of any external power of centralization—was the

5. J. N. D. Kelly, *Early Christian Creeds*, 3d ed. (New York: Lonergan, 1981), p. 31.

6. See Kelly, *Early Christian Creeds*, pp. 52-61.

baptismal liturgy, including the credal formulae, in the entire Christian world. Practically all of the credal formulas that came down to us include elements that distinguish catholic Christianity from Gnosticism: the unity of God the Creator (*pantokrator*); the historical and visible aspects of the life, death, and resurrection of Christ; the sending of the Spirit; the eschatological resurrection. There is little formalism about the wording, but there is a clear and universal concern for a doctrinally united, universal commitment to the one faith, accepted consciously and personally, as one entered the one church.[7]

THE FOURTH CENTURY

Following what we generally call today the "conversion of Constantine," Christian theology was shaped by the intellectual and political realities of the new social context. The church faced two new tasks: it had to use philosophical categories familiar to the educated Greek converts to the faith, and it had to respond to obligations imposed on it by the patronage it was now receiving from the Roman state. Specifically, it had to provide formulas that would distinguish members of the "true" church from heretics and schismatics—formulas that would be readily understandable to the emperor and his officials, who were now dealing regularly with established "catholic" Christianity *only*.

Of course these two tasks were not entirely new for the church. A dialogue with Greek intellectuals had been started by the second-century Christian apologists. With the great Origen, Christian theology had already become "philosophical theology." In the fourth century, however, not only isolated individuals but all responsible theologians had no choice but to

7. Such historians as Kattenbusch, Harnack, Lietzmann, and others have performed an immense task in studying and classifying creeds from East and West. If most Latin creeds seem to be related to an original Roman text—which is historically understandable, since Rome was the only "apostolic" church in the West—the variations in the East allow for no "original" model. All of them are built around the same trinitarian structure determined by the baptismal use of creeds, however.

use Greek concepts and terminology, and the church itself began to use philosophical terms in its doctrinal statements. It was also producing doctrinal statements, as for instance the doctrinal statement (ἔκθεσις) of the council of Antioch (268) against Paul of Samosata. But the new alliance between the church and the Roman state clearly demanded improvisation on both sides. Neither the Empire nor the leadership of the church was practically or ideologically prepared to face the daily mechanics of the new relationship begun with Constantine. Constantine himself was interested in religious unity and was disappointed from the start to find the Christian communities divided as they were. He was informed of the teaching and disciplinary functions that belonged to bishops, so he used episcopal meetings, or councils, to solve the Donatist schism in Africa. The councils failed in their task. Divisions persisted, and Constantine was forced into taking sides himself, supporting the Catholics. The idea of having a major council in Nicaea was a next step. Disappointed as he was by failure in Africa, he assumed a personal role in running the Nicene assembly from the very beginning and even in suggesting a solution. Respectful of the role of the bishops, he became, as his biographer Eusebius puts it, "a bishop of those who were outside the church" (ἐπίσκοπος τῶν ἐκτός), convinced as he was that without unity the church would be unable to become the church of the Empire and attract the pagan majority of the population. The bishops first accepted but then soon rejected the Nicene formula of union proposed by Constantine. Divisions continued. But in response to the state's demands, the bishops began producing confessional formulas, one after another, each claiming adequacy to truth itself.

What was the *raison d'être* of all these formulas, published by so many successive councils, all supported or sponsored by Constantine or his imperial successors, between 325 and 381? C. H. Tumer once wrote that "The old creeds were creeds for catechumens, the new creed was a creed for bishops."[8] He might as well have added that the new creeds were creeds for emperors

8. Tumer, *The History of the Use of Creeds and Anathemas*, 2d ed. (London, 1910), p. 24.

concerned with Christian unity. In the fourth century the Roman state considered itself to be in charge of a united society, and the church did not object to this new role of Christian emperors. So, the state understood the credal formulae to be *uniting formulae*. The bishops, theologians, and indeed the entire church viewed the matter differently. Fully admitting the need for unity for the sake of witness and mission, they nevertheless understood "witness" solely as witness for *truth,* and they believed that truth could be expressed in words and concepts. This being the case, as a practical matter the formulas were also divisive. In a famous and humorous text, Gregory of Nyssa describes the situation: "The streets are filled with people who debate unutterable issues: the streets, the markets, the squares, the crossroads; you would ask: 'How much do I have to pay?', they philosophize about the Unborn and One-who-is-born; you want to know the price of bread, they answer 'The Father is greater than the Son'; you inquire whether the bath is ready, they proclaim: 'the Son proceeded from nothingness.' "[9]

Nevertheless, following years of such debates, what we now generally call the "Nicene Creed" emerged as a truly uniting text—accepted by the entire Christian world for centuries and (in principle) until our own time as the legitimate expression of the Christian faith. This text, as we all know, is distinct from the original creed, approved in Nicaea in 325. It is more properly called the Creed of Nicaea-Constantinople. It sanctioned a consensus reached between the various groups of Eastern theologians by the end of the fourth century and eventually was also accepted in the West.

The genesis of that text—which, of course, cannot be described here in detail—allows for important observations, directly relevant to the problem of Christian unity today.

1. *To express its faith, the church has remained faithful to the baptismal context of the early creeds.*

We know relatively little about what exactly happened at Nicaea itself in 325, since no minutes of the assembly are pre-

---

9. *Patrologia Graeca,* ed. J. P. Migne, 162 vols. (Paris: Garnier Fratres, 1857-1866), 45:556.

served. But it seems certain that the theological dispute between Bishop Alexander and his presbyter Arius was settled on the basis of a baptismal creed—perhaps the creed of Caesarea-in-Palestine, according to a motion of its influential bishop, Eusebius, or more likely a similar creed used in Jerusalem—with the addition of two key expressions stating that the Son of God was "consubstantial" (ὁμοούσιος) to the Father and that he was born "from the essence of the Father" (ἐκ τῆς οὐσίας τοῦ πατρός). The additions were apparently proposed by the emperor himself—which secured their immediate adoption—but they certainly did not come from Constantine's personal theological speculation. Constantine used some advice, most probably that of his main counselor for ecclesiastical affairs, the Spanish Bishop Ossios of Cordoba. The use of the concept of "essence" (οὐσία) involved a departure from the usual, purely scriptural language of existing creeds: church unity required now an expression understandable to those who spoke and thought in Greek. But the expression was now included in a liturgical *baptismal creed*: it was not an independent doctrinal statement.

2. *Nobody at Nicaea or in the church at large had an exact idea of the authority of the council or of the text it approved.*

Indeed, historical evidence shows that the theological debates that continued in the decades following Nicaea were concerned with *the content of the faith*, not with Nicene terminology as such. Churches continued everywhere to use their local baptismal creeds. The council itself was understood, of course, to have condemned Arianism, which taught that "there was a time when the Son was not" and that he was a "creature." But this negative condemnation of Arius did not involve commitment to any *positive* formulation, at least for a time. The great Athanasius of Alexandria—who practically single-handedly stood up for the positive content of the Nicene definition—seldom even mentioned the crucial word *homoousios* in his writings, knowing that it was controversial; instead, he insisted over and over again on the biblical and soteriological significance of the divinity of Christ: "If God did not become man, man does not become God." The struggle of Athanasius was for a gospel of salvation: mortal humanity can be saved only through real communion with the Only Immortal, God himself. But the majority of Eastern bishops were afraid of some of Athanasius's supporters—Marcellus of Ancyra, for example, whose theology seemed to imply modalism (i.e., that Father, Son, and Spirit were an identical unity, the persons being mere names). This is how they interpreted the saying that God was a single "essence" (οὐσία), and hence they preferred to forget about Nicaea, despite the fact that they agreed with the condemnation of Arius. In the West the Creed of Nicaea was not even translated until 355, and Hilary of Poitiers "never heard of the faith of Nicaea" until 356, when he was sent into exile for refusing to sign Arianizing confessions.[10]

3. *There was a general agreement that what really mattered was the meaning of the words, not the words themselves.*

Councils followed councils, and each of them adopted doctrinal formulas meant to express the relationship between the Father and the Son ("similar," "similar in all things," "of similar essences," etc.). These formulas were all coming from Eastern theologians concerned with preserving real trinitarianism, particularly Origen's formula—"three *hypostases*"—although Arian interpretations were sometimes implied in those concerns. The formulas became more and more elaborate, less and less like baptismal creeds—more, indeed, like "creeds for bishops." And in this manner they became more and more divisive (unless one formula was imposed by state force, as happened under pro-Arian Emperor Constantius [d. 361]).

4. *The solution was found eventually in a return to the brevity and simplicity of the Nicene Creed, but also in the adoption of a trinitarian understanding and terminology, giving a new meaning to Greek words.*

A first step in that direction was taken in 362 by the council of Alexandria, as Athanasius was able to return to see, following the death of Emperor Constantius. It opened the possibility of distinguishing the meaning of the two words that were at the center of the debate: *essence* (οὐσία) and *hypostasis*. The council

10. On these facts, there is a vast historical literature. For a clear summary, see Kelly, *Early Christian Creeds,* pp. 254-62.

of Nicaea (in its "anathemas") had used them synonymously, and the synonymity, based on Aristotelian logic, was accepted by all. One essence in God meant one *hypostasis* (Lat. *substantia*), and "three *hypostases*" implied essential differences between Father, Son, and Spirit. But they had to transcend Aristotelian logic and terminology if they were to express adequately the trinitarian mystery: God is *one* in essence, but speaking of the *hypostatic* or personal existence of the Father, the Son, and the Spirit is not simply another way of speaking about the One God: it is a distinctive and existentially primary way of expressing *who* the living God of Scripture is. When Nicaea said that the Son proceeded "from the essence" (ἐχ τῆς οὐσίας) of the Father, it meant to say that he comes "from the *hypostasis*" of the Father and that the person or *hypostasis* of the Father is the "origin of the Godhead." This personalistic approach to trinitarian theology was to be developed by the Cappadocian Fathers, the great Basil of Caesarea-in-Cappadocia becoming the architect of reconciliation and unity. But unity came neither through a betrayal of Nicaea nor by avoiding issues but through a creative theological progress that involved transcending the accepted meaning of Greek philosophical terms and assuming fully the soteriological and incarnational theology of Athanasius.

5. *The reconciliation was finally sealed by the adoption of a new creed, accepted together with the Nicene. The doctrine of the three* <u>*hypostases*</u> *was not included in it (it remained as an understood background of the settlement), but the text did include a theological statement on the Holy Spirit, made necessary by contemporary discussion on the subject.*

The acceptance of the new creed, known as the Nicene-Constantinopolitan, was the result of some conciliar activity, but in fact and primarily it was received by consensus. We do not know for sure whether it was actually approved at the council of Constantinople in 381, which sanctioned the Orthodox restoration in the imperial capital. In any case, that council—which eventually became accepted universally as the "second" ecumenical council—was not really very "ecumenical." It was deliberately boycotted by Alexandria, Rome, and the entire West, because these important parts of the Christian world were not ready yet for the Cappadocian settlement; they stood by the old identification of *ousia* and *hypostasis*, fearing that any departure from the identification would amount either to Arianism or tritheism. The "reception" of the Nicene-Constantinopolitan Creed took some time. It was still ignored at the council of Ephesus (431), where Cyril of Alexandria imposed a motion forbidding that any modifications or additions be made to the *original* Nicene text of 325. Finally, the creed of Nicaea-Constantinople was formally approved at the council of Chalcedon (451), side by side with the original Nicene. It was then accepted universally, even by those who had reservations about some decisions of Chalcedon (e.g., Rome rejected its "canon 28") and those who rejected Chalcedon altogether (the "Non-Chalcedonian," or "monophysite" Eastern churches). These historical processes are important for the understanding of the ways in which councils are "received," "conditionally received," or sometimes "partially rejected" by particular local churches.

6. *Once it was accepted by all as the true rallying point of trinitarian theology, the creed of Nicaea-Constantinople also became the universal baptismal creed.*

The East, particularly, considered the creed as having a fixed and final character, as confirmed by the universal consensus of the church. Each ecumenical council following Chalcedon would solemnly confirm it. There is no doubt that the Empire, which, as we have noted, needed clear formulas to affirm religious unity, contributed to that fixity. The Roman church, which found itself within the Byzantine imperial domain between the sixth and the eighth centuries, also adopted it as its baptismal creed. The popes even defended it to the extent of objecting strongly to the filioque interpolation made in Spain in the seventh century and accepted in the Frankish empire. The creed became very much a *uniting* factor, and tampering with its text was seen as the reason of the schism between East and West. In the East during the interminable christological controversies, the creed provided a common ground between Chalcedonians and non-Chalcedonians, since it clearly affirmed that "the Son of God incarnate . . . suffered under Pontius Pilate"—that being the ground of the doctrine known as "theopaschism," which affirmed the points made by Cyril of Alexandria against Nestorius. In order to proclaim theopaschism once more and emphasize that Chalcedonians and monophysites were not divided on that point, Emperor Justin II ordered in 568 that the creed be recited at each eucharistic liturgy (initially, after the Lord's Prayer, which is to say right after communion).[11] A reverse process took place in the West, when Pope Leo III sought (unsuccessfully) to stop the popularization of the filioque interpolation in Frankish lands by recommending that the singing of the creed at the eucharist be dropped altogether.[12]

The preceding review of some of the conditions under which, in the fourth century, the creed of Nicaea-Constantinople was received by most of Christendom as the normal expression of the faith is not really controversial. It is accepted by all church historians. Two remarks, however, are in order.

First, the consensus between East and West was not quite complete, as later theological developments would show. The Greeks and the Latins retained their own fundamentally distinct conceptions of the Trinity, because the Cappadocian understanding of the distinction between "essence" (οὐσία) and *hypostasis* was hardly understood in the West.

Second, a large section of recently converted "barbarian" Christendom remained formally Arian: the Goths—who had received the faith and Scriptures in their own language (Wulfila's translation), circa 360, when the empire was Arian—maintained for centuries their Arian confession as an expression of their cultural identity and their Gothic liturgy and scriptures. Only in the seventh century did Gothic Arianism disappear completely and Latin liturgy come to be accepted everywhere in the "barbarian" West.

---

11. See John of Beclar, *Chronicon* (*Patrologia Latina*, ed. J. P. Migne, 221 vols. [Paris: Garnier Fratres, 1844-1864], 72:863).

12. See Abbot Smaragdus's account of the reception of Charlemagne's envoys by the pope, ca. 810 (*Monumenta Germaniae Historica, Concil.*, II, p. 240; also in *Patrologia Latina*, 102:971).

CONCLUDING OBSERVATIONS

In the light of all these facts, how are we to answer the question raised in the title of this essay: Was the Creed a uniting or a dividing factor in the life of the fourth-century church?

If the question were addressed to a bishop in the years immediately following the Council (around 325), he would probably answer that it was, indeed, uniting, except for the one controversial word *homoousios* included in it. As controversies fired by the use of that word continued, and as more and more theologians became convinced that there was really no available substitute, all accepted with less hesitation than before the proposition that the creed was indeed a strong uniting factor. One reservation remained, however, particularly among the Easterners in 381: the *homoousios*, as well as the creed as a whole, should be understood within a *context*—the context of the catholic faith in the Trinity and the incarnation. Without that context, all credal formulas are liable to misunderstanding, they believed, and are therefore necessarily *divisive*.

In these reactions, which I presume would be characteristic of Christian bishops and theologians around 325 and 381, respectively, I sense both a similarity to and a significant difference from the likely reaction of an ecumenist today.

The similarity lies in the belief that philosophical words, credal formulas, and doctrinal statements are not ends in themselves. They can be easily serve as convenient covers for actual misunderstandings and divisions. And, convenient as they may have been for the Roman state, which needed to distinguish those it wanted to support from those it wanted to persecute, the formulas were still mere words.

The difference between the reaction to the formulas of a theologian of the fourth century and that of a contemporary ecumenist is linked to their different perceptions of the grounds of unity in the church. Fourth-century theologians believed strongly that unity of the church is inseparable from full unity in faith and that such a unity is both possible and necessary. Modern ecumenists, on the other hand, tend to be more skeptical about full doctrinal unity; they would rather try to find common denominators allowing for institutional church unity on the basis of a *doctrinal minimum* or else searching for an already existing unity transcending divided institutions, abandoning the search for formal doctrinal agreement. The problem with such ecumenical minimalism is that it overlooks what is really needed in today's divided Christendom: the *ecclesial context*, the *sensus ecclesiae*, that existed between divided parties in the fourth century and that allowed them eventually to unite. The creed was never an end in itself; it was a symbol of unity. It did not create unity but expressed it, sealed it formally. By no means was it seen as theologically exhaustive or credally "sufficient." Athanasius and his Orthodox supporters always emphasized the soteriological dimension of the divinity of Christ rather than terminology. Thus, at the council of 362 in Alexandria, knowing very well that most Eastern bishops continued to speak of "three *hypostases*" in God, Athanasius became fully aware of the *existence* of a real unity of faith whenever the preferred Eastern terminology was combined with the Nicene *homoousios*. It is then that he could proclaim that an acceptance of the Nicene symbol was "proper and self-sufficient"[13] and that those who accepted it should be received in communion without rebaptisms or reordinations. Of course this was also the attitude of Basil.[14] The end of the Arian disputes thus marked an important step in the practice of receiving schismatics and heretics into the church: whereas earlier the prevailing principle was that expressed—in his own concrete circumstances—by Cyprian of Carthage (that baptism is an entry into the church; there is only one church; those baptized into another were not baptized . . .), the history of the credal controversies of the fourth century had shown that the one church could continue to exist in spite of distinct credal positions. However, a common creed and a common commitment to the proper ecclesial context of the Christian confession constituted a condition for public communion in the eucharist within the Catholic Church.[15]

13. Athanasius, *Ep. ad Afros,* 1 (*Patrolia Graeca,* 26:1029).
14. See particularly Basil, *Ep. 204 ad Neocaes.* (*Patrolia Graeca,* 32:753).
15. On this problem, see the truly brilliant chapter "Truth and Communion" in Zizoulas's *Being as Communion,* pp. 67-122.

I believe that these observations clearly show that the attitude of the fourth-century church toward the creed was very different from Christian "confessionalism" of the post-Reformation period. The *common* trait between the two is, of course, the concern to *exclude* error and heresy. But theological affirmations (or exclusions) contained in the various Protestant *Confessions* had a motivation greatly different from the rationale of ancient creeds. The Confessions were meant to replace the teaching magisterium of the medieval Latin church, and they were also aimed at listing *all the essentials* of the faith: by accepting those essentials, one became eligible for sacramental communion and church membership. There was a concern for truth, certainly, but also a polemical intent and a desire to distinguish between "essentials" and "nonessentials." Within the American context, as many became skeptical about doctrines and dogmas and rather indifferent to doctrinal heresies, the Confessions lost much of their real authority, and "confessional" groups became "denominations."

As distinct from that process, the church in the fourth century always had the consciousness of existing *as church*. One became a member through baptism, accepting the truth, and entering into a new personal relationship with the Father in the Son through the Spirit—a relationship that entailed new life, shared with brothers and sisters in the body of Christ in anticipation of the kingdom to come. Truth was not supposed to be accepted in the form of sentences and propositions but as living fullness, *into which* each Christian was called to grow within the sacramental membership of the church. Heresy was seen as deadly dangerous, not so much because it was a poor formulation but because it prevented this living growth in the truth, which was the church's very *raison d'être*.

Actually, before the age of the Reformation, there were neither "confessional" churches nor drawn "confessions of faith." As a result of the debates of the fourth century, the church settled for the creed of Nicaea-Constantinople as a short baptismal and liturgical "symbol of faith." Of course later ecumenical councils issued statements of faith, but these were not creeds. They were not intended for liturgical use. Their intent was primarily *exclusive:* condemnation of heretical or erroneous mis-interpretations of the scriptural and credal faith. None of them was intended to be final or to canonize a terminology forever. On the contrary, the fifth ecumenical council (553) specifically allowed the christological use of Cyrillian (in fact "monophysite") terminology, provided the Chalcedonian definition was also maintained, excluding monophysite misinterpretations of Cyril. Some terminological pluralism was thus built into the Tradition itself.

In the course of such developments, both during the fourth century and later, the church basically maintained the vision of Irenaeus: local churches were in communion with one another because they were one in faith. The common creed was a major and necessary sign of unity, but unity in itself was much more than the creed: it was true *identity* in faith, life, and apostolic structure. The episcopate was seen as *one,* since each bishop, within his church, occupied the same "chair of Peter," and no other chair was endowed with the same "*charisma* of truth." The empire, with its universal claims and great power, understood that it was its right and responsibility to maintain unity between the churches. It used its own peculiar methods to achieve that goal and unfortunately also used the church to its own ends, but it constantly failed in its efforts. When Christians believed truth to be at stake, they always refused legally enforced unity. Emperors called together councils that could formally be called "ecumenical,"[16] but these were rejected by the consciousness of the church, whereas a strong theological consensus (as for instance, on the Cappadocian "neo-Nicene" understanding of Nicaea) would, in fact, secure church unity.

The lesson that contemporary ecumenism can draw from the complicated and often dramatic history of the Nicene Creed is, therefore, that credal formulas are not by themselves either uniting or divisive. They are uniting only when they express a

16. Cf. "What Is an Ecumenical Council?" in J. Meyendorff, *Living Tradition* (Crestwood, N.Y.: St. Vladimir's Seminary Press, 1978), pp. 45-62.

common ecclesial commitment and spiritual context. The creed of Nicaea-Constantinople has acquired a particularly eminent position in that respect. After its formulation, it remained for centuries the only common baptismal creed, the central message of which was supposed to be *confirmed* by all subsequent doctrinal statements made by the church. I do not think that it can serve as a uniting factor anymore if it loses that exclusivity, if its meaning is diluted and it is considered to be of equal importance to other confessions or creeds of more local and more relative significance.

The issue here, of course, is the nature of history and of Tradition. The creed of Nicaea-Constantinople implies—as, I think, the New Testament does—that the Christian gospel is "good news" about a historical person and a historical fact: about Jesus of Nazareth, "born of the Virgin Mary," who was also "true God of true God," and whose death "under Pontius Pilate" and subsequent resurrection broke once for all the determinism of death and sin. Nothing substantial can be added to this "good news"; it must either be accepted or rejected. If accepted it can and must be expressed in different languages and explained to different cultures and generations. Several New Testament authors already began to formulate it in terms of Greco-Roman philosophical thought, and this process of "explanation," often confusing and challenging, was to some extent crowned by the trinitarian settlement of the fourth century.

Accepting this settlement today implies not only that one believes in the *consistent* and constant guidance of the Holy Spirit within the church but also that one acquires a *consistent theological vision,* of which the personal divinity of Jesus is the true and necessary focus. Indeed, it is only because he was God that his victory over death was both possible and significant: it is only the paradox of a voluntary "death of God," who "alone has immortality" (1 Tim. 6:16), that can fully express the mystery of divine love as the very being of God. The truth of his humanity is of course affirmed at the same time, since he died a fully human death. Furthermore, the dignity of *our* humanity is proclaimed also, since it is seen as deserving that kind of sacrifice. If the divine, personal identity of Jesus is denied, the entire biblical story becomes a somewhat banal development of divine providence, exercised by a God who somehow remains "in heaven" and rules creation from outside.

What, then, is the Nicene Creed *saying* to us? Or, more precisely, what is it that *each one of us is saying* at his or her baptism while reciting the creed? The answer to this question is found in Matthew 16:13-16. "Whom do *you* say that I am?" Jesus asks. And Peter answers: "You are the Christ, the Son of the living God." This is the faith that makes the church to be the church. One can—and even must—express this same faith in a variety of ways, because the church is indeed universal, and the message must be carried throughout the changes of history, from culture to culture and from century to century. But the *context* of the "good news" and the apostolic "vision" of the mystery of Christ cannot be changed. It is that vision that we discover in the struggle of Athanasius for the Nicene faith and in the text of the creed itself, with its trinitarian implications and its ecclesial context. Understood in such a way, the creed is not only one of the uniting factors of past ecclesiastical history, it is the most traditionally authoritative expression of the Christian faith. If we are interested in other forms of unity, we can bypass the creed, but a unity *in faith* has really no other focus or basis.

Toward a Common Confession of Faith according to the Spirit of the Fathers

ANDRÉ DE HALLEUX

The first series of questions proposed already in 1920 for the Lausanne World Conference of Faith and Order, which convened only seven years later, was the following:

1. What degree of unity in faith would be necessary in a church reunited?
2. Is the declaration of this one faith in the form of a creed necessary or desirable?
3. If so, what creed should be used or what other formula would be desirable?
4. What are the specific uses of a creed and of a confession of faith?[1]

The text of this essay was originally presented at a colloquium in honor of Msgr. Charles Moeller entitled "Towards a Common Confession of Faith," held 1 February 1984 at Louvain-la-Neuve. Footnotes have been reduced to the essentials. A version of material with fuller documentation has been published as "The Reception of the Ecumenical Symbol from Nicea to Chalcedon," *Ephemerides theologicae Lovanienses* 61 (1985): 5-47.

This essay was translated from the French by Mary Peter Froelicher, SHCJ, Graymoor Ecumenical Institute, January 1990.

1. "Topics Discussed at the Preliminary Meeting in Geneva, Switzerland,

Thus the problem of a common confession of faith was clearly formulated by separated Christians at their very first encounter in the ecumenical movement.

The work of the fourth section of the Lausanne Conference, especially charged with the question of the creed, was dominated by the personalities of the Anglican bishops Gore and Headlam. The report, adopted *nemine contradicente*, still appears today to be remarkably balanced.

> 1. In spite of our doctrinal differences, we are united in a common Christian faith, which is proclaimed in the Holy Scriptures, to which we bear witness and which is safeguarded in the ecumenical symbol commonly called Nicean, as well as in the symbol of the Apostles; this faith is continually confirmed in the spiritual experience of the Church of Christ. 2. We believe that the Holy Spirit, in leading the Church into all truth, may permit her, while at the same time keeping her firmly bound to the witness of these symbols, our common heritage of the ancient Church, to express the truths of revelation under other forms, such as might be called for from time to time by new problems.[2]

In 1976, the mixed working group of the Roman Catholic Church and the World Council of Churches decided to study jointly a way of proceeding in the search for visible unity in the same and unique faith and in the same and unique eucharistic community, and it entrusted this study to the Faith and Order Commission of the World Council of Churches, with which Catholic members had been fully associated for a number of years. At a colloquium on the unity of faith held in Venice in 1978, a statement was issued entitled "Towards a Confession of the Common Faith."[3]

---

in August 1920, and Proposed to that Meeting for Further Study and Discussion throughout the World. First Series of Questions Proposed by the Subjects Committee. Concerning the Faith of the Reunited Church," in *Documents on Christian Unity 1920-1930*, ed. G. K. A. Bell (Cambridge: Oxford University Press, 1930), p. 17.

2. *Faith and Order: Proceedings of the World Conference at Lausanne, August 3-21, 1927*, ed. H. B. Bates (New York, 1928), p. 466.

3. *Towards a Confession of the Common Faith*, Faith and Order Paper No. 100 (Geneva: WCC, 1980).

According to this document, full ecclesial communion demands a faith professed in common not only in prayer, action, and witness but also in doctrinal formulas, which may nonetheless never be separated from the vital context of Christian experience. The statement underscored the conviction that the Holy Spirit led the church to express the elements necessary for communion in the apostolic faith during the founding period of the Fathers and the ecumenical councils, of the creeds and of the great liturgies. In this progressive explication of the rule of faith, particular mention is made of the symbol of the apostles and of that of Nicaea and of Constantinople. The statement of Venice further argues that the two principal functions of the ancient creeds—namely, to meet the exigencies of the surrounding culture and to safeguard ecclesial unity against schism and heresy—are still important today, and moreover that an appropriate translation emphasizing the existential aspects of the faith has become necessary and urgent. The document finally affirms that the ecumenical council of the future, which will reunite separated churches in a conciliar community, will have to rediscover a common confession of faith, and it recommends some provisional rules for that process.

Thus, fifty years after the Lausanne Conference and in an ecclesial and global context profoundly transformed, the Faith and Order Commission, henceforth joined by the Roman Catholic Church, persists in the attempt to resolve the tensions between tradition and renewal in a spirit of living fidelity. The effort to maintain a loyalty to tradition calls for some courage, in light of the pressure from young churches and from many young believers in the old churches for whom the ancient symbols have become incomprehensible and uselessly cumbersome. The "Common Declaration of Our Faith," issued at the meeting in Bangalore in August 1978, greets cursorily "the apostolic faith according to the Scriptures, transmitted to us through the centuries," but seems more impressed by "the confrontation with a new situation and the challenge of mission today," and it is satisfied, as regards a confession of faith, with the christological and trinitarian "base" of the World Council of Churches and with the doxology of the Pauline letter to the

Ephesians (1:3-15).[4] Along the same lines, the statement of the second "question group" of the Sixth World Assembly of the World Council, which gathered in Vancouver in 1983, expresses the hope that the unity confessed by the churches will be first of all marked by the "sharing of the same understanding of the apostolic faith and by its common confession in forms comprehensible to our contemporaries, bringing reconciliation and liberation."[5] One notices that in neither case is the focus on the ancient creeds of the undivided church.

In reaction to this tendency, Orthodox and Catholics seized the opportunity of the Sixth Centenary of the Second Ecumenical Council to present the symbol of Nicaea and Constantinople as the only means of uniting all Christians in the common confession of apostolic faith, once the obstacle of the addition of the filioque in its Latin version had been put aside.[6] And the report of a Faith and Order Commission colloquium held in Rome in October 1983 on "the apostolic faith in Scripture and in the primitive church" likewise recalls the role of the creed of Nicaea as "ecumenical symbol."[7]

The actual debate over a new reception of this ancient symbol for a common confession of faith evidently depends on the permanent value Christians of the various churches and communities are disposed to place on a text that goes back to the age of the Fathers. Opinions on the subject are no doubt infinitely varied, but one can group them into four types that I will characterize here without any pretense of identifying their effective or potential followers.[8]

4. "A Common Statement of Our Faith," in *Confessing Our Faith around the World*, Faith and Order Paper No. 104 (Geneva: WCC, 1980), pp. 81-84.

5. "Rapport du Groupe-Question," *Irénikon* 56 (1983): 391.

6. "Table ronde. Possibilité et opportunité de formuler un nouveau credo," in *La signification et l'actualité du II concile oecuménique pour le monde chrétien d'aujourd'hui*, Les études théologiques de Chambésy, 2 (Geneva: WCC, 1982), pp. 565-84.

7. See the summary of the statement by E. Lanne in *Irénikon* 56 (1983): 535-36.

8. See L. Vischer, *Confessio fidei in der oekumenischen Diskussion*, in *Confessio fidei. International Ecumenical Colloquium. Rome, 3-8 November 1980*, ed. G. Békés and H. Meyer, Studia anselmiana, 81 = Sacramentum, 7 (Rome: Pontificio Ateneo S. Anselmo, 1982), pp. 17-36.

According to some, a confession of evangelical faith that is public, doctrinal, and universal is neither necessary nor desirable. With respect to the public element, the creed would betray the aspect of interiority essential to a spiritual church, to the kingdom of God within us, to a piety of the heart that alone allows believers to recognize one another. With respect to the doctrinal element, the creed would undermine through dogmatic conceptualization an existential confidence in Christ that can be realized only through prayer, personal or liturgical, and through the involvement of witness. With respect to the universal element, the creed would absorb into an impoverishing uniformity the variety of Christian confessions through which the basic faith is now expressed.

Other Christians, while admitting the utility or even necessity of an objective and common expression of apostolic faith, contest no less the normativity of the formulas elaborated in the ancient church. They contend that the "antiquity" of the Fathers—that is to say, their temporal proximity to the origins of tradition—did not confer on them any privilege, since the Holy Spirit has never ceased to assist the church. On the contrary, the ancient ecumenical councils responded to controversies that are outdated today, and the philosophical terminology of the symbols they produced has become foreign to us. Besides, the old patristic confessions are silent about elements of revelation that appear to us essential. In this way, the ancient creeds may have become an obstacle to evangelical witness in the contemporary world and a hindrance to the unity of the church. To be credible, an ecumenical confession of the common faith today can consist only in a new creed that is exclusively scriptural.

In contrast to this second opinion, a third supports the normative character of the symbols of the patristic period, and concretely that of the liturgical creed of Nicaea and Constantinople. Inasmuch as this creed has been received for a long time by the majority of the churches, it has a much better chance of becoming the ecumenical confession of tomorrow than a new formulation would have. Any new creed would likely be considered ephemeral by many; it would be perfectly utopian to imagine that all Christians would accept it. But theological reasons must be more decisive than pragmatic motivations. The creed of Nicaea and Constantinople served to formulate the dogma of the whole church in the constitutive period when a hierarchy of ministers, a liturgy of the sacraments, and a canonical order were established that on the whole remain those of the churches of the apostolic tradition. This foundational character of the ecumenical symbol make its formulas unalterable, since they express all the essentials of the faith in the language of the Bible and the language of a perennial philosophy not restricted to a particular culture. It should suffice, therefore, for us simply to explain the old symbol, to make it comprehensible to our contemporaries, without changing one single iota of its substance.

A fourth opinion is similar to the third in admitting the normative nature of the period of the ancient ecumenical councils, but it denies that fidelity to the patristic spirit consists in simple repetition of venerable formulas. The Fathers saw only the heresies of their time, and they undertook the risk of interpreting the apostolic tradition in view of the culture of late antiquity. If we were genuinely to be inspired by their example today, we would have to work to complete and, if necessary, reformulate their confession of traditional faith, to translate it better in the face of new challenges of the modern world, using the language of our day, whatever the practical difficulties of such an enterprise might be.

The first two opinions deny patristic scholars any role in the debate over contemporary reception of the creed of Nicaea and Constantinople, but they could at least contribute to arbitrating between the other two positions. They could not present a simple solution, obviously, but they could make more precise the theological value that the Fathers attributed concretely to the ecumenical confession. Must one conclude from the ancient history of the reception of the symbol in its decisive period (i.e., during the 125 years between the councils of Nicaea and Chalcedon) that the churches are once and for all bound to a formula fixed in its literalness? Or does this history authorize—would it even recommend—an *aggiornamento* of the old confession of faith in view of new needs of the church?

From extremely complex and historical literary data, much of which still remains to be studied, one can take as the thread of inquiry the fundamental patristic axiom of the sufficiency of the faith of Nicaea. Considered in the abstract, this principle would seem to involve the conservation of verbal repetition, but its concrete significance among the Fathers of the period in question, as well as the manner in which they adapted it to the changing circumstances, distinguishes spirit from letter in the sense of a creative fidelity. We will thus sketch, in a rather schematic way, the history of the axiom in question during the two chief phases of the crucial period, first from Nicaea to Constantinople and then from Ephesus to Chalcedon.[9]

FROM NICAEA TO CONSTANTINOPLE

The principle of the sufficiency of the *Nicaenum* makes its first official appearance during the Council of Alexandria of 362, which was presided over by Athanasius. But one can comprehend its significance only by going back about twenty years to its antecedents. The formula of "the faith of the 318 Fathers of Nicaea" was contested for a long time—and not only by the Arians, since the large majority of the Oriental episcopate itself suspected there a veiled "Sabellianism." And, in fact, since the Nicene anathema seemed to identify *hypostasis* with "ousia," the *homoousion* of the symbol appeared to many to be incompatible with the three *hypostases* of the theological tradition of Origen, dear to the Orientals.

Gathered in 341 on the occasion of the dedication of the great church of Antioch, the Orientals declared, against the

9. In subsequent notes, the patristic and conciliar sources will be taken from vols. 2-4 of M. Geerard's *Clavis Patrum Graecorum* (hereafter abbreviated CPG): vol. 2, *Ab Athanasio ad Chrysostomum*, nn. 2000-5197 (Turnhout: Brepols, 1974); vol. 3, *A Cyrillo Alexandrino ad Iohannem Damascenum*, nn. 5200-8228 (Turnhout: Brepols, 1979); vol. 4, *Concilia*, nn. 8500-9444 (Turnhout: Brepols, 1980). Citation will list the CPG number followed by the name of the edition indicated there, the page or the column, and (in italics) the letter or the lines to which the matter refers.

"Sabellian" Marcellus of Ancyra and his Roman protectors, that according to "the evangelical and apostolic tradition" the Father, the Son, and the Holy Spirit are "three (things) by hypostasis and one (thing) by symphony"—that is to say, by moral unanimity.[10] The following year the Western Council of Sardica replied that it held "the tradition, faith and catholic and apostolic confession as that of one hypostasis (divine), which the heretics also call *ousia*."[11] In fact, the *Nicaenum* here found itself overinterpreted, since the Fathers of 325 had in no way intended to solve the question of the divine unity-trinity.

Faced with this exclusiveness of the "old Nicaeans," their Oriental adversaries multiplied, during the next two decades, creeds and synodal anathemas, which they had hoped to be able to substitute for the *Nicaenum*, with the support of imperial power, as the ecumenical formula of the faith. Finally, in decreeing the last of these symbols, the Council of Constantinople of 360 forbade the use in the future of the terms *ousia* and *hypostasis* on the grounds that they were not biblical and they provoked numerous scandals.[12] At the same time, the Arians began to tighten their doctrinal position in the Anomeian sense, and, while enjoying the favor of Emperor Constantius, they maneuvered the passive majority of the Oriental orthodox, on occasion by recourse to violence.

In the face of this new danger, some of these Orthodox considered making common cause with the Nicaeans against Arianism, on the condition that they be permitted to interpret the *homoousion* in the sense of *homoion kat' ousian*—that is, to conceive of the ontological relationship of the Son to the Father as a unity of *ousia* compatible with the plurality of *hypostases*. In his *De synodis*, Athanasius greeted at once, as the return of a prodigal son, these advances of the Homoiousians to the Nicaeans since their Council of Ancyra in 358.[13] The succession of synodal symbols in the preceding years having demonstrated

10. CPG, n. 2128.8, Opitz, p. 249, *11-33*.
11. CPG, n. 8561, Parmentier, p. 113, *11-14*.
12. CPG, n. 2128.15, Opitz, p. 259, *13-17*.
13. CPG, n. 2128, Opitz, p. 260, *9-11*, and p. 266, *28-32*.

the inconsistency of the heresy, the only solution to the schism proved to be that of a return to the *Nicaenum*.

The religious liberty that Emperor Julian gave back to all parties at the beginning of his ephemeral reign soon permitted the solidification of the alliance by Athanasius, returned from his monastic refuge. At the time of the Council of 362, the Nicaeans recognized that the formula of the three *hypostases* was susceptible to an orthodox reading. From now on, they urged, to "make peace" with the schismatics desirous of orthodoxy, one ought to "require nothing more than to anathematize the Arian heresy, to profess the faith professed at Nicaea by the holy Fathers and to anathematize also those who say the Holy Spirit is a creature."[14]

Concretely, this tolerance amounted to nothing less for the Nicaeans than the repudiation of the symbol of Sardica of 342, which had condemned the theology of the three *hypostases*. The Council of Alexandria henceforth qualified this confession as a "pamphlet which some repeat," and it maintained the somewhat forced interpretation that the Fathers of Sardica would have defined "that nothing more should be written on the faith, but that one be content with the faith confessed at Nicaea by the Fathers, because there is nothing lacking to it, but that it is full of piety, and that one ought not to propose a second faith, for fear that what was written at Nicaea be considered imperfect and thereby a pretext be given to those who always wish to write and define the faith."[15]

Here, then, is the principle of the sufficiency of the *Nicaenum* at the same time neatly formulated and paradoxically attributed to a council whose intolerant interpretation of "the faith of the 318 Fathers" was being overturned. The "perfection" that the Council of Alexandria recognized in this faith did not imply any exclusive attachment to the letter, since the Fathers of 362 supplemented the symbol of Nicaea with the condemnation of those who regarded the Holy Spirit as a creature. But, doing this, they understood nothing new to have been added to the *Ni-*

14. CPG, n. 2134, Montfaucon (PG), col. 797C-800A.
15. CPG, n. 2134, Montfaucon (PG), col. 800C.

caenum, because they considered the blasphemy against the Holy Spirit had made manifest an Arianism according to the spirit that was denied according to the letter.[16] In other words, it is because the anathema of the *pneumatomachoi* was found already contained powerfully in that of Arius that there was nothing lacking in the faith of Nicaea for those who understood it in the orthodox sense of the Fathers of 325, even if a later heresy arose that made necessary a further explicitation.

One can even say that the Alexandrian Council inserted the *Nicaenum* in some way into the web of Tradition, not only post-Nicene, when they repudiated the negators of the divinity of the Holy Spirit, but equally pre-Nicene, when they demanded anathematizing in the same way Valentinian, Basilides, and Mani as well as Sabellius and Paul of Samosata[17]—the great Gnostic trinitarian and christological heresies of the two preceding centuries.

The ideas clearly expressed as early as 362 on the sufficiency of the *Nicaenum* eventually became settled tradition. They justified in advance the canonization of the symbol of Constantinople, in which the development of the pneumatological article was not felt to be an addition to the Nicene faith. According to the Fathers, every confession conforming to the spirit of Nicaea (i.e., every confession that includes the principal anti-Arian formulas of the *Nicaenum*) qualifies as the "faith of the 318 Fathers." One therefore should not be surprised to find regularly cited under this name, in the fourth and fifth centuries, different symbols of particular churches that did not harmonize in detail with the pure text of the *Nicaenum.*[18] The theology of the Fathers did not have our philological scruples.

A second major witness to the theological axiom of the sufficiency of the faith of Nicaea was presented by Basil of Caesarea, who succeeded in using this principle with consummate skill in favor of the "neo-Nicene" theology of which he

---

16. CPG, n. 2134, Montfaucon (PG), col. 800*A.*
17. CPG, n. 2134, Montfaucon (PG), col. 800*A* and 804*A.*
18. See J. Lebon, "Les anciens symboles dans la définition de Chalcédoine," *Revue d'histoire ecclésiastique* 32 (1936): 834-70.

became the promoter among the circle of his Cappadocian friends. To be convinced of this, one need only read one of his letters (*Ep.* 125), which is sometimes called the synodal of Nicopolis. He made his proposal in 373, the year of the death of Athanasius, with the signature of his old master, Eustathius of Sebaste, shortly before their rupture over the pneumatological question.[19]

One notices in the exposition of Basil a direct echo of the Council of Alexandria of 362. The sole confession to be imposed, as much for the reception of heretics as for the catechizing of non-Christians, ought to be the faith of Nicaea. This latter is sufficient to itself, because all found there is "sufficiently and exactly defined, certain points for the correction of those who have suffered harm and others for the prevention of errors which should arise." If the words concerning the Holy Spirit had only been mentioned at Nicaea in passing, without any elaboration, it was because "one had not yet set in motion the question, but the opinion concerning him was found unassailable in the souls of the faithful." Only the blasphemy against the Holy Spirit of the successors of Arius now made necessary the formal anathema of those who made him a creature foreign to the divine nature.[20]

To this extent Basil remained faithful to the instructions of the Council of 362, but he somewhat betrayed their spirit when, passing to the positive interpretation of the "sense sanely manifested by the terms" of the *Nicaenum,* he laboriously tried to demonstrate that the Fathers of Nicaea confessed a distinction between the unique *ousia* and the three *hypostases.*[21] While the Council of Alexandria had been content to abandon tacitly the contrary interpretation of the Western Fathers of Sardica and to recognize the orthodoxy of the theological tradition of Origen, Basil abandoned this tolerance and reversed the reading of the *serdicense* in proposing an exegesis of the symbol of Nicaea that the Fathers of 325 had not considered. The principle of the

19. CPG, n. 2900, Courtonne, vol. 2, pp. 30-34.
20. CPG, n. 2900, Courtonne, vol. 2, 1, *1-10,* and 3, *1-21,* pp. 30-31 and p. 33.
21. CPG, n. 2900, Courtonne, vol. 2, 1, *18-50,* pp. 31-32.

sufficiency of the *Nicaenum* thus received an application that would probably have surprised its creator Athanasius.

The trinitarian formula of Basil and of his Cappadocian friends, "one *ousia* in three *hypostases*," was nevertheless soon to be dogmatized for the Orientals at the Council of Constantinople in 381 due to favorable circumstances, in part political, that it would be superfluous to recall here. This formula was not inserted as such in the symbol of Constantinople, no doubt out of respect for the formula of the *Nicaenum*, but it figures in the synodal letter, the authors of which claimed to have "validated the faith of the Fathers of Nicaea and anathematized the heresies that had arisen against it."[22]

Like Basil, the Council of 381 used the principle of the sufficiency of the Nicene faith to justify a trinitarian theology foreign to the preoccupations of the Fathers of Nicaea, even if these would probably not have repudiated it any more than Athanasius would. Thus it was not without motive that their successors of 381 chose, in preference to the pure text of the *Nicaenum*, one of another confession of faith, less strictly Nicene and stripped of the anathema that seemed to identify the *hypostasis* with the *ousia* to amplify the pneumatological article.[23] It is no less remarkable that, while adopting this different formula and completing it in that way, "the 150 Fathers" of Constantinople maintained the conviction of respecting the principle forbidding anyone to propose a second faith after that of Nicaea and ordering that "henceforth one would rather content oneself with using the words [of Nicaea]."[24]

But the *Constantinopolitanum* was never referred to under that name before the council of Chalcedon, and none of the supposed allusions to it in pre-Chalcedonian literature is incontestable. This silence of seventy years has something strange about it, involving as it does a confession presumed to constitute

22. CPG, n. 8602, Parmentier, p. 292, *13-16;* CPG, n. 8598, Benesevic, p. 95, *1-6.*

23. CPG, n. 8599, Dossetti, pp. 244-50.

24. CPG, n. 8602, Parmentier, p. 292, *13-16;* CPG, n. 8598, Benesevic, p. 95, *1-6;* CPG, n. 2134, Montfaucon (PG), col. 800C.

a solemn act of "validation" of the faith of Nicaea at the time of the great council of the Nicene restoration in the Orient. The theories worked out to explain this phenomenon cannot be discussed here.[25]

It is important to elucidate, however, the reasons for joining the symbol of Constantinople to that of Nicaea in the Chalcedonian christological definition. No doubt the motivations were partly of a political and ecclesiastical order, inasmuch as the council that elaborated the *Constantinopolitanum* also instituted, in its third canon, the privileges of honor of the see of New Rome.[26] But no doubt the theological reasons were determinative, and in order to understand them well, one has to go back to a decree of the Council of Ephesus, to approach the second major phase of the history of the ancient reception of the ecumenical creed.

FROM EPHESUS TO CHALCEDON

The authority of the "faith of Nicaea" played a key role in the Nestorian crisis from its beginning. This point must be stressed at the very outset: although Nestorius quotes regularly under this name a symbol of Antiochian type, while his adversary Cyril of Alexandria always produces the pure text of the *Nicaenum*,[27] this divergence concerning the letter had no perceptible effect in the argumentation of the two theologians. All of their polemic dealt essentially with the interpretation of Nicene christology.

According to Nestorius, the symbol begins by enumerating the names common to the divinity and the humanity—"one Lord Jesus Christ"—and only then distinguishes the *theologia*, to which is attributed the birth of the Son consubstantial with

25. But see A. M. Ritter, *Das Konzil von Konstantinopel und sein Symbol. Studien zur Geschichte und Theologie des II. Ökumenischen Konzils*, Forschungen zur Kirchen und Dogmengeschichte, vol. 15 (Göttingen, 1965), pp. 132-208.

26. CPG, n. 8600; Joannou, pp. 47-48.

27. See Lebon, "Les anciens symboles dans la définition de Chalcédoine," pp. 840-47.

the Father, and the *oikonomia*, where there is no longer any question of birth, since the one who was born from all eternity cannot be born again a second time; consequently, concluded Nestorius, the Holy Virgin cannot be called Mother of God.[28] Cyril responded that the incarnation and the inhumanization, of which the symbol speaks apropos of the *oikonomia*, necessarily implies the birth, according to the flesh, of the Word of God born of the Father, and that Mary is therefore properly *Theotokos*.[29]

The conflict having started that way, it was to be expected that the ecumenical council of Ephesus would raise the slogan of "the faith of Nicaea" as much with Cyril of Alexandria and his partisans as with their Oriental adversaries of Antioch. At the time of the first session of the Cyrillian Council (22 June 431), it was actually the "expression of the faith of the 318 Fathers" that served as doctrinal touchstone and canonical authority for the approbation of Cyril and the condemnation of Nestorius. The sequel of the procedure itself gives evidence of this: one began by reading the pure *Nicaenum* with its anathema, after which one read the second letter of Cyril to Nestorius, which the Fathers recognized to be in agreement with the symbol, and then one read the response of Nestorius to Cyril, which the Fathers declared irreconcilable with the same symbol.[30]

A month later, on July 22, the Cyrillian Council passed a decree on the sufficiency of the *Nicaenum* whose canonical collections made up the seventh canon of Ephesus.[31] A priest of Philadelphia named Charisios had denounced to the assembly a confession of "Nestorian" faith that had recently served to receive into his church the repentant schismatics. It was in addressing this "tract of impious dogmas, composed in the manner of a symbol" that the Council forbade, under pain of deposition for the bishops and clerics and anathemas for the laity, the composition and the proposition to pagans, to Jews,

28. CPG, n. 5703, Loofs, pp. 282-88; CPG, n. 5669, Schwartz, pp. 29, 27, to 30, 3.
29. CPG, n. 5217, Schwartz, p. 29, 11-26.
30. CPG, n. 8675.4-6, Schwartz, pp. 12-36.
31. CPG, n. 8800, Joannou, pp. 61-63.

and to heretics of "another faith than that defined by the holy Fathers assembled at Nicaea with the Holy Spirit." The same penalties were foreseen for those who would be convinced of thinking or teaching "that which is contained in the exposition presented by the priest Charisios, that is to say, the tarnished and twisted dogmas of Nestorius."[32]

This second part of the decree, which manifestly concerns the dogmatic content of the pretended Nestorian confession, shows that the interdiction of "another faith" carried in the first part did not concern the very letter of the *Nicaenum*. The best proof of this is that the creed by which Charisios assured the council of his orthodoxy apparently raised no objection, although it was a hybrid Antiochian text that manifestly amounted to a personal confession.[33]

The affair introduced by the priest of Philadelphia does not reveal the real motivation behind the Ephesian decree on the sufficiency of the *Nicaenum*, however. It is possible that Cyril used the matter chiefly to aim a blow at the rival council of the Orientals, who had just deposed him. The Antiochians demanded the withdrawal of the twelve anathemas that Cyril had annexed to his third letter to Nestorius. They had refused from the beginning these "chapters" as Apollinarian and "super-added" to the faith of Nicaea, probably because they deemed them subject to the Nicene anathema of the mutability of the Son of God. The Oriental Council of Ephesus therefore asked Emperor Theodosius II to make all the bishops subscribe henceforth to the Creed of Nicaea, "without introducing anything foreign."[34]

At the beginning of August 431, the emperor deposed Nestorius and Cyril and, while soliciting the advice of the Fathers on the title of *Theotokos*, he ordered the two rival synods to reconcile themselves by following "the rule and the canon of Nicaea." The Antiochians hurried naturally to send to the court the pure text of the *Nicaenum*, properly signed, which they

32. CPG, n. 8721.3-4, Schwartz, pp. 95-106.
33. CPG, n. 8721.3, Schwartz, p. 97, 16-23.
34. CPG, n. 6325, Schwartz, pp. 129-31.

thought would automatically bring about the condemnation of the "heretical chapters recently proposed by Cyril of Alexandria."[35] This symbol, they wrote, "carries neither anything missing nor anything superfluous; it confesses concisely salvation because it includes in few words the sum of all that the holy Scriptures have given us of piety and because it banishes the opinions of those who wish to innovate with us while going astray." Consequently, they wrote, "we also, following the Fathers, neither add anything to nor take away anything from the faith and the expression of the confession, because the expression of the Fathers is sufficient for all."[36]

The Antiochian Fathers of Ephesus were in agreement therefore with the Cyrillians on the principle of the sufficiency of the *Nicaenum*. But they did not understand fidelity to "the faith of the 318 Fathers" as a narrow attachment to the letter. Nor did they hesitate to respond to the imperial demand concerning the mariological title with a new dogmatic declaration, a first rough sketch of what is called the Symbol of Union, which was to sanction, in 433, the agreement desired by Theodosius as the ecumenical conclusion of the Council of 431. In this symbol the Orientals declared their wish to speak "not by way of addition, but to give full assurance" according to "the holy Scriptures and the tradition of the holy Fathers, without adding anything at all to the faith defined by the holy Fathers at Nicaea."[37]

As for Cyril, who eventually accepted the formula of his adversaries, while commenting on it in his own way in his letter of Easter 433 to the archbishop John of Antioch, he said he also recognized this confession as expressing "a faith in agreement with the inspired Scriptures and the tradition of the holy Fathers," which amounted to admitting implicitly that it adds nothing to the faith of Nicaea. He was also able to write, in the same place, that "we do not support in any way that the faith or the symbol of the faith defined by our holy Fathers gathered in their time at Nicaea be shaken, and we do not permit either

35. CPG, n. 8742, Schwartz, p. 39, *1-11*, and *20-23*.
36. CPG, n. 6328, Schwartz, p. 69, *21-23*, and p. 70, *6-8*.
37. CPG, n. 6328, Schwartz, p. 70, *15-22*; CPG, n. 5339, Schwartz, p. 17, *2-5*.

ourselves or others to change one word of the text or to transform one syllable."[38] I must state here that the patristic affirmations that seem to demand the most literal fidelity to the *Nicaenum* in reality concern only its interpretation in the spirit of the traditional chain in which the symbol of 325 constituted the privileged link.

Since the two parties found themselves in unanimity on the principle of the sufficiency of "the faith of Nicaea," their reconciliation of 433 would normally have put an end to the controversy. But unfortunately the agreement rested on an ambiguous proposition of the "symbol" of 433: "For there has been [in Christ] a union of the two natures,"[39] a formula that the Antiochians and the radical Cyrillians continued to interpret according to their different christologies, each believing their view was the sole orthodoxy. After various discussions, the monophysite crisis soon exploded, for which the definition of Chalcedon sought a definitive settlement. The history of subsequent ecumenical councils and the persistence of the non-Chalcedonian churches prove it succeeded in this only imperfectly.

In 448, Eutyches, a venerable archimandrite of Constantinople, openly campaigned for the formula "one nature of God Word incarnate," in the spirit of the twelve Cyrillian "chapters." He was supported by the successor of Cyril, Archbishop Dioscorus of Alexandria. Denounced at the permanent synod of the capital, he was condemned there by his archbishop, Flavian of Constantinople. But he was sufficiently influential at the court of the old Theodosius to be able to obtain an appeal of his trial. First administrative, then properly ecclesiastical, this was concluded at the time of the council that the emperor assembled at Ephesus, in August 449. There its president Dioscorus had Flavian deposed in the same Church of St. Mary where Cyril had recently proclaimed the anathema of Nestorius.[40]

It is important to examine closely the justifying dogmatic

38. CPG, n. 5339, Schwartz, p. 17, 23-24, and p. 19, 20-23.

39. CPG, n. 5339, Schwartz, p. 17, 14.

40. See P.-Th. Camelot, *Ephèse et Chalcédoine*, Histoire des conciles oecuméniques, vol. 2 (Paris, 1962), pp. 79-114.

authorities that were invoked at the time of these inglorious events of the history of the ancient church. The two parties seemingly claimed for themselves the faith of Nicaea confirmed at Ephesus—without any allusion yet to the Second Ecumenical Council—but it was not the same content that each party intended in invoking the name of Ephesus.

For Archbishop Flavian, a moderate Cyrillian, the only canonical Ephesian texts were the second letter of Cyril to Nestorius, approved at the session of 22 June 431, and Cyril's letter of reconciliation to John of Antioch at Easter 433. The choice of these two texts probably rests on the affirmation in the first of the permanence of the difference of the two natures of Christ after their union (Eutyches held to one nature of God Word incarnate) and the recognition in the second of the double *homoousion* of Christ (it was repugnant to Eutyches to say the Savior was consubstantial to us according to his humanity). It was on the basis of these two authorities that the archimandrite was condemned by the permanent synod of 448.[41]

But for Eutyches and his protector Dioscorus, the ecumenical Council of Ephesus of 431 was not limited to the session of June 22; it also included the decree of July 22 on the sufficiency of the *Nicaenum*, which the Cyrillians had conceived and for which Cyril himself had personally interpolated the acts to defend his twelve "chapters" against the Antiochian attacks. It is therefore not surprising that Flavian of Constantinople and the Oriental adversaries of Cyril (Theodoret of Cyrrhus, Hiba of Edessa, and Archbishop Domnos of Antioch) were condemned by Dioscorus in 449 for having refused the Cyrillian anathemas.[42]

The Council of Chalcedon of 451, sought by the new emperor Marcion and his influential spouse, soon canceled that of 449, which Pope Leo had immediately stigmatized as the "Robber Synod" of Ephesus. This council produced a new condem-

41. CPG, n. 8904, Schwartz, pp. 104-6 nn. 239-40, 107-11 nn. 245-46, 139 n. 476.

42. CPG, n. 8937, Schwartz, pp. 82 n. 79, 189-90 nn. 905-43; CPG, n. 8938, Flemming, p. 146, 27-30, and p. 154, 10-14, 19-24.

nation of Eutyches and the deposition of Dioscorus of Alexandria as well as the posthumous rehabilitation of Flavian and the Orientals condemned two years previously.[43] As one might expect, the documents of the ecumenical Council of Ephesus that the Fathers of Chalcedon received as canonical were the two dogmatic authorities of the permanent synod of 448—that is, the second letter of Cyril to Nestorius and the letter to John of Antioch.[44]

But a new matter appeared to complicate the situation. By his letters and by the person of his legates to Chalcedon, Pope Leo insisted that the council receive the dogmatic "tome" that he addressed to Flavian to approve the condemnation of Eutyches but that Dioscorus had refused to have read at the "Robber Synod" of 449 and that certain Fathers of Chalcedon doubted was in complete conformity with the christology of Cyril. Moreover, the emperor wanted this reception to come in the form of a dogmatic definition. Such a procedure could seem to contradict the Ephesian decree, which forbade the composition of "another faith" than that of Nicaea, a decree that the Cyrillian majority at Chalcedon was able to prove actually figured in the acts of the Council of 431.[45]

The definition itself, finally imposed on the Chalcedonian Fathers in spite of their strong resistance, as well as the message of the Council to the emperor, which can be regarded as an authorized commentary to this *horos*, prove that the objection had actually been raised. The title of the message, which perfectly summarizes the content, affirms that the "tome" of Leo to Flavian does not constitute an innovation vis-à-vis the faith of Nicaea.[46] As to the definition, in the end it incorporates tacitly the text of the Ephesian decree of 22 July 431, as if to defend itself from the suspicion of having transgressed it.[47]

Such is without doubt the doctrinal motive of the first

43. See Camelot, *Ephèse et Chalcédoine,* pp. 115-37.
44. CPG, n. 9002, Schwartz, pp. 80-81.
45. CPG, n. 9000, Schwartz, p. 196, *4-6;* CPG, n. 9002, Schwartz, p. 78 nn. 3, 7.
46. CPG, n. 9021, Schwartz, p. 110, *11-15.*
47. CPG, n. 9005, Schwartz, p. 130, *5-11.*

appearance of the "symbol of the 150 Fathers of Constantinople" following that of the "318 Fathers of Nicaea" in the program and in the christological definition of Chalcedon.[48] Did the argument of the confirmation of the *Nicaenum* by the *Constantinopolitanum* not come at an opportune time to undo the criticisms that the Cyrillian majority had addressed to the principle itself of a new definition of the faith, criticisms based on a restrictive reading of the Ephesian decree on the sufficiency of the *Nicaenum*? In adding immediately the phrase "That is why we keep the decree of Ephesus,"[49] the *horos* of Chalcedon insinuated unequivocally that the Second Ecumenical Council had provided in advance, in some way, the authentic interpretation of the Ephesian canon as a legitimizer of subsequent dogmatic definitions.

The history of the reception of the *Nicaenum* through imperial edicts and subsequent ecumenical councils would certainly not be without interest, but it is not likely that it would alter substantially the traits of a development whose decisive stage took place at Chalcedon. We can therefore stop the patrological review with the Fourth Council and try to resolve in principle the choice that the search for a common confession of faith poses to the ecumenical movement today. According to the spirit of the Fathers, ought the churches to feel themselves still bound today by the letter of the ancient symbols, or would we rather be authorized, even encouraged, by the patristic tradition itself to reformulate the creed in such a manner as to better face the actual demands of church unity and witness?

At first reading, the axiom of the sufficiency of the faith of Nicaea often finds expression in the Fathers in terms that seem to exclude any variation in the text of the symbol: not a syllable may be modified affirms Cyril of Alexandria; nothing missing, nothing superfluous, affirm on their side his Antiochian adversaries.[50] This way of speaking seems to support conservative

48. CPG, n. 9005, Schwartz, pp. 127-28 nn. 32-33.
49. CPG, n. 9005, Schwartz, pp. 126, 22, to 127, 4.
50. See notes 36 and 38 above.

theologians who are content to explain to the faithful and to the non-Christian a formula irreformable in itself.

But it would be wrong to take such language at face value. The innovations that the Fathers rejected dealt exclusively with the dogmatic content of the Nicene faith, and the double form of the creed of Nicaea and Constantinople simply confirmed in their eyes their fundamental unity. Moreover, the definition of Chalcedon, after having recited each individually, referred to them in the singular and *per modum unius* as "the same," "this wise and salutary symbol of divine grace."[51] The numerous mutual contaminations of the two texts in the manuscript tradition concretely reflect this patristic conviction of their theological identity.[52]

In the East, at least until the epoch of Emperor Justinian, the ecumenical symbol, as the official norm of orthodoxy, did not at all exclude catechetical or liturgical use of the creeds proper to particular churches. These had been put into Nicene garb in diverse ways at the outcome of the Arian crisis, and it was these that the Greek Fathers of the fourth and fifth centuries quoted most frequently, for this reason, under the generic name of the "faith of the 318 Fathers of Nicaea."[53] For the baptismal rite of the *redditio symboli*, Rome and the West have even kept until the present day (in addition to the *Constantinopolitanum* introduced at the time of the Justinian reconquest of the sixth century) the old symbol of the apostles, which was never under the influence of Nicaea and did not experience until Charlemagne the unification of its different regional forms.[54]

Strangers to the sense of history that makes us value change, the Fathers were hardly sensitive to the development of dogma, and they found themselves inclined to justify by simple repetition of the ancient that which was in reality a new event. Persuaded that it was sufficient to transmit from one generation to

51. CPG, n. 9005, Schwartz, p. 128, 1, 15-16.

52. See G. L. Dossetti, *Il simbolo di Nicea e di Constantinopoli*. Edizione critica, Testi e ricerche di scienze religiose, 2 (Rome, 1967), pp. 255-84.

53. See note 18 above.

54. See J. N. D. Kelly, *Early Christian Creeds*, 3d ed. (New York: D. McKay, 1972), pp. 368-434.

another the truth already contained integrally in the original deposit, they could affirm undisturbed that everything was found already in the symbol of Nicaea, if not in formal terms at least according to the meaning, for the believer faithful to the spirit of the Tradition. Only an extrinsic circumstance—the germination of heresy that Satan does not cease to sow in the church—made it necessary, not to complete and still less to innovate the faith of the 318 Fathers, but rather to give it full assurance and confirmation.[55]

Nevertheless the Fathers unwittingly contradicted this historic conservatism when they regularly inserted the anathema of Arianism in the catholic Tradition, from the condemnation of the Gnostic speculations onward to that of the christological heresies of the fifth century.[56] Such a contextualization of the *Nicaenum* proves that while considering this as the privileged theological moment of the *paradosis*, patristic thought avoided isolating it and even more absolutizing it in the traditional chain of apostolic faith.

In extending this chain to the present day, one is tempted to hold that the example of the Fathers ought to encourage the churches to propose an ecumenical confession of faith. Without doubt the Fathers could not foresee that the Hellenic culture of the Roman empire, which they believed to be everlasting, would give way to the world that is ours. But if they could return among us, would they not find the challenges that the modern forms of unbelief address to the faith comparable to the heresies of their times? And would they not then define synodally with us a formulation of the ecumenical symbol that they would no longer fear to qualify as "new" in the modern sense of the word, provided it remained faithful to the spirit of the faith traditionally exemplified in the symbol of Constantinople?

One might perhaps object that since the reception of this symbol at Chalcedon no ecumenical council has published its definitions under the form of a creed. This undeniable fact, which no doubt reflects the tendency of all tradition to sacralize

55. See notes 22 and 37 above.
56. See note 17 above.

its earlier stages, manifests itself in the Chalcedonian *horos* itself, which wants to be simple instruction, conformed to the teaching of Jesus Christ and to the tradition of the symbol.[57] But let us not forget that the creed of Nicaea and of Constantinople was itself at the beginning only an "exposition of the faith" according to the current patristic expression that corresponded to what the actual ecumenical language calls a "common statement"—that is, to a theological declaration.

The "exposition of the faith of Nicaea" enjoyed an ecumenical character in the ancient sense of the term not only because it was valid for the church universal, in contrast to the local creeds and individual confessions, but above all because it was sanctioned by imperial law as the official norm of orthodoxy to regulate, among other things, the communion among the great sees and the reception of heretics. The *Nicaenum* and the *Constantinopolitanum* came from what the Fathers of the fourth and fifth centuries often called the *mathêma* of a particular church, which had probably in its turn followed what their predecessors of the second and third centuries called "the rule of faith."[58]

Maybe it would be convenient to distinguish better the local creeds—especially those destined for catechesis and instruction of the faithful as well as the ecumenical symbol derived from them—from the sacramental "symbol" properly so called, from whence all the others take their name—that is, the *stipulatio* of the baptismal faith consisting of questions and answers, themselves consecrated by the triple immersion.[59] It is only in the course of the sixth century that the *Constantinopolitanum* was progressively introduced in the baptismal ritual and in the eucharistic liturgy of all the churches, supplanting their particular confessions,[60] and it is thus only that the "exposition"

57. CPG, n. 9005, Schwartz, p. 128, 25, p. 129, 24, and p. 130, 2-3.

58. See H. Von Campenhausen, "Das Bekenntnis Eusebs von Caesarea (Nicea 325)," *Zeitschrift für die neutestamentliche Wissenschaft und die Kunde der älteren Kirche* 67 (1976): 129-38.

59. See H. J. Carpenter, "*Symbolum* as a Title of the Creed," *Journal of Theological Studies* 43 (1942): 1-11, and "Creed and Baptismal Rites in the First Four Centuries," *Journal of Theological Studies* 44 (1943): 1-11.

60. See Kelly, *Early Christian Creeds*, pp. 344-57.

transformed itself into a "confession" in the original existential sense of the *homologia*, or doxological proclamation of the faith.[61]

It is true that this liturgical sacralization has been acquired over more than thirteen centuries by the symbol of Constantinople, which also finds itself the most widely received by the great world Christian communions. A new ecumenical confession would no doubt age quickly, and in the present state of their separation, it is hard to see how the churches could agree to express their faith other than by a simple list of New Testament references. But these practical difficulties, humanly insurmountable, should not be hardened by theological objections, since the Fathers of Chalcedon who assured the reception of the ancient ecumenical symbol themselves established, following their predecessors, the principle and the path of all *aggiornamento* in affirming that it is in a return to the testimony of Scripture that the symbol of Constantinople had manifested the sense of the symbol of Nicaea.[62]

From the history of the ancient trinitarian and christological controversies one could be led to doubt the real utility of a common confession of faith. After all, the principle of the sufficiency of the *Nicaenum* was invoked by opposing parties to justify their respective theologies.[63] If it is true that, as already made clear by Athanasius and Basil, the faith of Nicaea is sufficient only for those who interpret the letter according to the spirit of the tradition,[64] would not an ecumenical formula recover only a purely illusory unanimity so long as it failed to consecrate a dogmatic communion already fundamentally existing?

It is well, however, to recall that the Fathers of Nicaea aspired less to comprehend the mystery of the divine unitrinity than to anathematize Arianism, as they suggested in their letter to the Church of Alexandria.[65] The dogmatic *horoi* of the ancient

61. See V. H. Neufeld, *The Earliest Christian Confessions,* New Testament Tools and Studies, vol. 5 (Grand Rapids: William B. Eerdmans, 1963), pp. 140-46.

62. CPG, n. 9005, Schwartz, p. 129, *6.*

63. See notes 23-24, 37-38, and 41 above.

64. See notes 16 and 20 above.

65. CPG, n. 8515, Opitz, pp. 47, *8,* to 48, *9.*

ecumenical councils marked frontiers that could not be trespassed without falling into heresy; they defined thus the fidelity to Tradition in a manner essentially negative, as the royal road preserving the footsteps from error, as a just midway between condemned extremes.

The Fathers of the fourth and fifth centuries untiringly opposed heretical "technology" with their conviction of the incomprehensible and ineffable mystery of the divine "essence" and thus of the properly analogical character of all theological language, and they knew how to manifest, when necessary, a remarkable tolerance vis-à-vis terminology in reproving the "fraternal battles" around "syllables," in which, they affirmed, "piety does not reside."[66] They recalled in this way that all rational conceptualization is inadequate to account for the faith transmitted in the creed.

Today as then, it is in the test of the *homologia* prayed and lived that the churches will know how to discern the spirits, and it is the Spirit of Christ who will inspire them, at the providential moment, with the historic responsibility of reactualizing the common confession of the apostolic faith. Only thus will the antagonisms of the exclusive confessional identities find themselves transfigured in the doxology of the unique ecclesial identity, in "reconciled diversity."[67]

66. See R. P. C. Hanson, "Dogma and Formula in the Fathers," in *Studia patristica,* vol. 13, ed. E. Livingstone, *Texte und Untersuchungen,* vol. 116 (Berlin: Akademie-Verlag, 1975), pp. 175-83.

67. See E. Lanne's account of the colloquium at Chevetogne, 22-26 August 1983, "Identité confessionelle et traditions ecclesiales," *Irénikon* 56 (1983): 412-21.

Toward a Common Historical Approach to the Affirmation of the Apostolic Faith in the Fourth Century: A Lutheran Perspective

WILLIAM G. RUSCH

FAITH TO CREED

For a number of years now there has been a consensus in patristic scholarship that Christianity arrived at an intellectually and theologically coherent doctrine of its God by means of a process. This procedure lasted several centuries and engaged some of the best minds available to the new faith. It centered in a period of controversy that lasted approximately sixty years, from A.D. 318 to 381, although one should not conclude from this fact that there was no Christian reflection about God prior or subsequent to these dates. Nevertheless, the Christian doctrine of God reached a formulation in A.D. 381 at the Council of Constantinople that remained by and large sacrosanct for centuries.

This process has always been of considerable interest to scholars and theologians of the church. The history of this scholarly and churchly study does not need to be reviewed here.

45

It stretches from some of the earliest historians of the church in the fourth and fifth centuries to some of the notable scholars of Christian thought of this and the preceding century.[1]

Different opinions have been given about this procedure. Interpretations have ranged from seeing this process as a betrayal of the original primitive and simple gospel of Jesus to understanding the unfolding process as making explicit in Christianity by use of intellectual and cultural tools what was implicit in the earliest gospel. In recent decades much scholarly judgment has moved away from positions holding that Christian thinkers succumbed to Hellenism, imperial pressures, or strong-willed individuals with the result that at least something of original Christian belief about God was compromised.

An accord by a number of contemporary patristic scholars has been attained that while the process certainly involved development of doctrine, it also included intentional faithfulness to the scriptural witness to the God and Father of Jesus Christ, who sent his Spirit to the church. While the debt to such scholars as Adolf von Harnack and H. M. Gwatkin is still acknowledged, research by such savants as Edward Schwartz, C. H. Turner, E. Boularand, J. N. D. Kelly, and Charles Kannengiesser, to mention only several of many, has led to what must be described as a new understanding of the formation of the Christian doctrine of God.[2]

Probably two quotations from the recent publication of R. P. C. Hanson express this scholarly opinion as well as any:

> The defenders of the creed of Nicaea were in fact fighting on behalf of tradition, not in the sense that they were defending what had been already determined to be the doctrine of the church, but in the sense that they were themselves engaged in forming dogma,

1. The process could be traced from Eusebius of Caesarea, Socrates, and Sozmenus to the recent work by R. P. C. Hanson, *The Search for the Christian Doctrine of God* (Edinburgh: T. & T. Clark, 1988). See Hanson, pp. 878-900, for a full bibliography.

2. For bibliography, see Hanson, *The Search for the Christian Doctrine of God*, pp. 888-96. See also *The Making of Orthodoxy*, ed. Rowan Williams (Cambridge: Cambridge University Press, 1989), and especially Williams's essay "Does It Make Sense to Speak of Pre-Nicene Authority?" therein, pp. 1-23.

in working out a form of one of the most capital and crucial doctrines not only of the Bible but of the very spirit and genius of Christianity itself. They only came gradually to realize this. It was in fact only the Cappadocian fathers who faced fully the fact that they were contributing to the formation of dogma, and they did so only reluctantly.[3]

But the pro-Nicene theologians were responding properly and honestly, as the circumstances of their age would allow, to a genuine compulsion. In spite of an inadequate equipment for understanding the Bible, in spite of much semantic confusion which required protracted and elaborate clearing up, in spite of being compelled to work with philosophical terms and concepts widely different from those of the Bible, they found a satisfactory answer to the great question which had fired the search for the Christian doctrine of God, and one which won not only imperial support but a wide consensus throughout the church. Development meant discovery.[4]

This scholarly and modern discussion, while always relevant for the faith and life of the church, was often conducted in isolation from the worshiping community of the church. In this regard it was distinct from the actual process of the formation of the Christian doctrine of God in the patristic church. This was achieved in the closest connection to the worshiping, believing, and confessing communities of the early church.

The erudite debate about the meaning of this series of developments, in fact, has been largely assumed by the vast majority of Christians without any special reflection. With a few periods (e.g., the Enlightenment) and with some churches that were anticredal providing about the only exceptions, most Christians at most times in Christian history would probably have been willing to assert that in publicly reciting the Nicene-Constantinopolitan Creed of A.D. 381 (1) they were declaring the faith of the Scriptures, (2) they were doing so using words different from those in the Bible, and (3) they were uncertain of the exact relationship of this creed to Scripture.

3. Hanson, *The Search for the Christian Doctrine of God*, p. 848.
4. Hanson, *The Search for the Christian Doctrine of God*, p. 875.

This situation has changed within the last twenty-five years as a direct result of the ecumenical movement. The patristic formulation of the doctrine of God and its interpretations by contemporary research have both been influenced by the quest of divided churches to find their visible unity. Themes of either assumed popular belief or pedantic erudition have taken on a new and almost startling relevance. Four ecumenical documents demonstrate this vividly.

Already at the Fourth World Conference of the Faith and Order Commission of the World Council of Churches in Montreal in 1963 the applicability of this patristic research to the quest for the visible unity of the churches was apparent. This can be observed particularly in the second section report, which carries the title "Scripture, Tradition and Traditions."[5] It is here that the significant distinction is made between Tradition with a capital *T*—the gospel itself, transmitted from generation to generation in and by the church, Christ himself present in the church—and tradition with a small *t* as the traditionary process. Part One of this section report on the relationship of Scripture, Tradition, and traditions still merits careful study.

Part Two of this same report, on the unity of Tradition and the diversity of traditions, speaks even more directly to our topic. This text states in part that

> many of our understandings and disagreements on this subject arise out of the fact of our long history of estrangement and division. During the centuries the different Christian communions have developed their own traditions of historical study and their particular ways of viewing the past. The rise of the idea of a strictly scientific study of history with its spirit of accuracy and objectivity, in some ways ameliorated this situation. . . . More recently, a study of history which is ecumenical in its scope and spirit has appeared. . . . We believe that if such a line of study is pursued, it can be of great relevance to the present life and problems of the Church. . . . We believe, too, that it would have great value in offering possibilities of a new understanding of some of the most

5. *The Fourth World Conference on Faith and Order: Montreal, 1963*, ed. P. C. Rodgers and L. Vischer (New York: Association Press, 1964), pp. 50-61.

contested areas of our common past. We therefore specifically recommend that Faith and Order should seek to promote such studies, ensuring the collaboration of scholars of different confessions in an attempt to gain a new view of crucial epochs and events in church history, especially those in which discontinuity is evident.[6]

This second portion of the Section II report concludes, "The past of which we speak is not only a subject which we study from afar. It is a past which has value for us, in so far as we make it our own in an act of personal decision. In the Church it becomes a past by which we live by sharing the one Tradition, for in it we are united with him who is the Lord of history, who was and is and is to come; and he is God not of the dead but of the living."[7]

These comments from Montreal had a continuing influence on the work of Faith and Order, as can be seen in the preface to *Baptism, Eucharist and Ministry,* published in 1982. This text observed that

as a result of biblical and patristic studies, together with the liturgical revival, and the need for common witness, an ecumenical fellowship has come into being which often cuts across confessional boundaries and within which former differences are now seen in a new light. . . . On the way towards their goal of visible unity, however, the churches will have to pass through various stages. They have been blessed anew through listening to each other and jointly returning to the primary sources, namely "the Tradition of the Gospel testified in Scripture, transmitted in and by the Church through the power of the Holy Spirit" (Faith and Order World Conference, 1963). . . . The resultant text aims to become part of a faithful and sufficient reflection of the common Christian Tradition on essential elements of Christian communion.[8]

The Faith and Order Commission addressed four questions to the churches that also serve to document the abiding influ-

6. *The Fourth World Conference on Faith and Order,* p. 55.
7. *The Fourth World Conference on Faith and Order,* p. 58.
8. *Baptism, Eucharist and Ministry,* Faith and Order Paper 111 (Geneva: WCC, 1982), p. ix.

ence of Montreal and the conclusions of patristic research on the ecumenical movement. In the first question the churches are asked if they can recognize in *Baptism, Eucharist and Ministry* the faith of the church through the ages. In the second question they are asked to explore the implications of this recognition with other churches that also see the text as an expression of the apostolic faith. In the final question the churches are invited to make suggestions about *Baptism, Eucharist and Ministry* as it relates to the ongoing work of Faith and Order on a common expression of the apostolic faith today.[9]

This continuing work of Faith and Order is reflected in several of its publications. Here mention will be made only of two. The first is the Faith and Order paper *The Roots of Our Common Faith* from 1984.[10] Both the individual essays and the group report it contains deserve attention. They reveal the growing importance of the Nicene-Constantinopolitan Creed for the unfolding work of the commission. The second is the Faith and Order paper *Towards a Common Confession of the Apostolic Faith.*[11] This text, published in 1987, is actually a commentary on the Nicene-Constantinopolitan Creed. It provides vivid proof of how the ecumenical movement is endeavoring to utilize the most commonly received credal text of the Christian Tradition as a resource for the churches today to confess together the apostolic faith. Even if it acknowledges that the Nicene-Constantinopolitan Creed is not the only means of confessing the apostolic faith today, the work of Faith and Order is assigning it a special place. This is clearly because of the wide reception of this creed in the church throughout time and space. But in giving the creed this special place, Faith and Order and the broader ecumenical movement are granting an authority to the interpretation in patristic scholarship alluded to above in the quotations from Prof. Hanson—namely, that the Nicene-Constan-

9. See *Baptism, Eucharist and Ministry,* p. x.

10. *The Roots of Our Common Faith,* ed. Hans-Georg Link, Faith and Order Paper No. 119 (Geneva: WCC, 1984).

11. *Confessing One Faith: Towards an Ecumenical Explication of the Apostolic Faith as Expressed in the Nicene-Constantinopolitan Creed (381),* Faith and Order Paper No. 140 (Geneva: WCC, 1987).

tinopolitan Creed formulation is a faithful articulation, and discovery, of the Christian doctrine of God witnessed to in the Scriptures.

It now seems that this conclusion of some patristic scholarship, being taken over by the ecumenical movement, is raising afresh questions both about the accuracy of the description of what occurred in the early church and about the validity of the Christian doctrine of God as expressed in a creed in A.D. 381. This may be noticed in the preparatory material of this study by the Faith and Order Commission of the National Council of the Churches of Christ in the U.S.A. The section of this prospectus entitled "Church Dividing Issues" speaks of several of these items:

> There have been very different points of view on the enculturation of the biblical faith in the Graeco-Roman culture and society in the 4th century. The most crucial issues were, from the second century, concerned with the "translation" of biblical words and concepts into non-semitic cultures. Some value Constantine as a saint and liberator of the church equal to the apostles. Others see this process of enculturation as the sort of apostolic fidelity required of the church in each era, paradigmatic for the churches of the Third World today, incarnating the Christian faith in a variety of non-Western cultures. Still others question the compromises they see the church inheriting from the "Constantinian era."[12]

Thus this study is raising anew questions about the possibility of an ecumenical convergence in patristic scholarship and the value of these expositions for divided churches seeking greater unity today. In view of the importance of these questions and their implications, these objections merit serious attention. This can perhaps be done best by exploring some of the key issues behind these suspicions.

For the entire Christian Tradition, Nicaea is a crucial point. All Christians must place themselves in some relation to the Nicene-Constantinopolitan formulation. This creed finally en-

---

12. "Faith to Creed: Prospectus," unpublished paper of the Faith and Order Commission of the National Council of the Churches of Christ in the U.S.A., 1989, pp. 1-2.

tered deeply into the traditions of various churches that claim to have received it and produced strong reactions on the part of some churches that did not accept it.

In the fourth century the council of Nicaea caused a number of strong objections. For a period of time it contributed to Christian divisions rather than unity. Concerns were expressed about a number of issues on which the churches in the fourth century were not in agreement. These include the vocabulary of the creed, the role of councils, and the reception or rejection of councils. While it is true that over the centuries a large Christian consensus arose on most of these items, questions surfaced again at the time of the Reformation, of the Enlightenment, and in the modern era.

Many of these matters are related to historical evidence and influence present ecumenical discussions. There is the challenge of the interpretation of the historical materials. The *acta* of Nicaea do not exist, although it must be granted that a great deal of source material is available both about the Council of Nicaea in A.D. 325 and the Council of Constantinople in A.D. 381. The role of Constantine encourages other questions. What was the primary concern of the emperor, and what was the degree of his intervention? How important was the rivalry of great sees and the fact that Arius came from the church of Alexandria? To what extent did cultural factors play a role and affect the debate of theological issues? What place should be given to soteriological and worship motives?

Other problems focus not so much on the historical evidence as on the reception of Nicaea and Constantinople. These concerns are both historical and contemporary. Many churches have formally, and in the past, received Nicaea and Constantinople. Are they willing to continue this process of reception and re-reception? What is the distinction between the content of a council and the proceedings of a council? Is it possible to speak about the reception of the content of a council without a reception of the council itself? What is the significance of the fact that a council itself is in the process of reception, and what is the relationship of a conciliar definition and its reception to the apostolic witness? Does a council develop, interpret, or simply point to the apostolic witness at a certain historical moment?

None of these complex concerns can be answered in detail in this brief presentation. But these various questions do have a common motivation. If clarity can be achieved on this point, then answers to the individual questions will be forthcoming. I would suggest that the common motivation of these questions can be stated in the form of two questions: What is the contribution of Nicaea-Constantinople to the understanding of the Christian faith? (This is a question of truth.) And what is the relationship of the acceptance of Nicaea-Constantinople to common membership in one church? (This is a question of unity.)

Thus the present ecumenical urgency forces us to examine once again the interpretations in patristic scholarship about the fourth-century resolution to the problem of the Christian doctrine of God. This cannot be accomplished here in any detailed manner. The topic is vast and complex and involves an examination of the intricate subject of the development of doctrine. But among the various points of view in patristic scholarship, is there one that is faithful to the historical evidence and provides some guidance to the two motivating questions indicated above?

It seems to me that the understanding expressed in the work of R. P. C. Hanson is exactly the point of view that is being sought. Indeed, Prof. Hanson's conclusions in this regard are enhanced in value because they are not unique to him.

J. N. D. Kelly in his work *Early Christian Creeds* puts forth a position very close to Hanson's. The Christian doctrine of God as expressed in the Nicene-Constantinopolitan Creed is the end product of a long process. In this procedure a number of political factors, both imperial and ecclesiastical, played a role. Development in doctrine, however this concept is finally defined, occurred. Orthodoxy, in contrast to heresy, evolved in the course of the process, especially in its controversial stage. In this entire process the motivation was to be true to the Scriptures, even if nonscriptural language had to be employed. One position prevailed finally because it excluded options seen to be contrary to the kerygma and because it was deemed by large numbers of the faithful to express the faith of the church reflected in Scripture, popular devotion, and the liturgy. Part of the newness of Nicaea and Constantinople was that a creed emerged which had the function of serving as a standard for correct belief regarding the Christian teaching about the Godhead. Now on this topic Christian thinking had certain confines that distinguished authentic Christian thought from false.[13]

Jaroslav Pelikan has adopted in the main the same interpretation as Hanson and Kelly. He traces a process of development from Scripture through the second and third centuries to the Nicene dogma of the Trinity. During the formulation and reformulation of the dogma, vigorous debate occurred. Church politics and conflicts of personality had their place. The intent and even the vocabulary of the Nicene doctrine was to safeguard the soteriological and liturgical concerns of the church, for which it was mandatory that Christ be divine. The dogma of the Trinity as given in the Nicene-Constantinopolitan Creed was enshrined in the liturgy and, if a person read them aright, was documented in the Scriptures. Pelikan sees the dogma of the Trinity as expressed in A.D. 381 in one sense as the end result of theology, for it brought together many of the themes of prior development. As regards trinitarian thinking, it determined the limits of Christian reflection for centuries and settled the extent of genuine Christian pluralism on this topic. In another sense Pelikan views A.D. 381 as the starting point for an ensuing christological debate.[14]

Thomas F. Torrance's views are also in harmony with those held by Hanson, Kelly, and Pelikan. According to Torrance, the Nicene-Constantinopolitan Creed represents the work of Greek Fathers reaching a careful expression of crucial points in the gospel that had been seriously misunderstood and distorted under the influence of dualist ways of thought. This dualism derived from Hellenism and Hellenized Judaism. The central place of Jesus Christ in the faith of the church called for a clear answer to the question of whether he was himself Lord and God or only a created intermediary between God and humankind.

13. See Kelly, *Early Christian Creeds*, 2d ed. (London: Longmans, Green, 1960), esp. pp. 23-29, 94-99, and 205-16.

14. See Pelikan, *The Christian Tradition: A History of the Development of Doctrine*, vol. 1: *The Emergence of the Catholic Tradition, 100-600* (Chicago: University of Chicago Press, 1971), pp. 203, 207-10, and 223-24.

The basic decision reached at Nicaea made it clear that the eternal relation between the Father and the Son in the Godhead was regarded in the church as the supreme truth upon which everything in the gospel depended. According to Torrance, it became indubitably clear to the church in the fourth century that it is only when the gospel is understood in this fully trinitarian way that both the New Testament teaching about Jesus Christ and the Holy Spirit and the essential nature of salvation, prayer, and worship can be appreciated. The church in the fourth century made a solemn corporate act of commitment to truth in affirming that in the divine revelation from the Father, through the Son, and in the Holy Spirit the very existence of the church and the validity of its evangelical message of salvation were at stake. The acceptance of this standard of orthodoxy of Nicaea, at Constantinople in A.D. 381, at Ephesus in A.D. 431, and finally at Chalcedon in A.D. 451 is of extreme significance. It set the boundaries for all subsequent discussion about the Trinity within the church.[15]

In terms of objective evaluation of current patristic research, it needs to be pointed out that the positions characteristic of the four scholars Hanson, Kelly, Pelikan, and Torrance are not shared by all working in this field. Some take a neutral stand about the legitimacy of the decisions of the early church. This is particularly true of such scholars as Alfred Adam, Adolf Martin Ritter, and Christopher Stead.[16] Others are in varying degrees negative about the process and the doctrinal formulation of the fourth-century church. Two examples in this latter category are Jürgen Moltmann and Maurice Wiles.[17]

It should be observed that if the positions held by Hanson,

15. See Torrance, *The Trinitarian Faith* (Edinburgh: T. & T. Clark, 1988), esp. pp. 2-4, 23, and 44-46.

16. See Adam, *Lehrbuch der Dogmengeschichte,* vol. 1, 2d ed. (Gütersloh: Gerd Mohn, 1970); Ritter, "Dogma und Lehre in der Alten Kirche," in *Handbuch der Dogmen- und Theologie-Geschichte,* vol. 1, ed. Carl Andresen (Göttingen: Vandenhoeck & Ruprecht, 1982), pp. 99-283 (esp. pp. 144-221); and Stead, *Divine Substance* (Oxford: Clarendon Press, 1977).

17. See Moltmann, *The Trinity and the Kingdom,* trans. Margaret Kolh (San Francisco: Harper & Row, 1981); and Wiles, *The Remaking of Christian Doctrine* (London: SCM Press, 1974) and *Working Papers in Doctrine* (London: SCM Press, 1976).

Kelly, Pelikan, Torrance, and others are accepted, then the title of this study has a certain potential problem. *Faith to Creed* suggests a certain movement or development. This should be applauded. But *Faith to Creed* can also imply a shift or a qualitative change. The scholarship of Hanson, Kelly, Pelikan, and Torrance, with which I wish to identify as an accurate reading of the patristic record, would reject the notion that between the apostolic kerygma witnessed to Scripture and the Nicene-Constantinopolitan Creed the message of the Christian faith has been altered or distorted. It is precisely this position that gives the creed of A.D. 381, with its unparalleled reception in the Christian Tradition, such ecumenical possibilities in assisting the divided churches to confess together their common apostolic faith.

A LUTHERAN PROSPECT

It is not strange for someone identified with the Lutheran tradition to support the view I have stated. Lutheran churches since the sixteenth century have formally and liturgically received the Nicene-Constantinopolitan Creed. This creed is given in full at the outset of the *Book of Concord* of 1530 with the Apostles' and Athanasian creeds. Together all three are described in the Latin text as "the three ecumenical symbols."[18] Thus the Creed of A.D. 381 is formally received in the confessions of Lutheran teaching. This is done to claim the identity of Lutheran teaching with the teaching of the early church, but also because the Lutheran tradition approved and accepted the doctrine of the Trinity taught in the creed. Throughout the *Book of Concord,* in each of the confessions one or more of these three ancient creeds is quoted.

The Nicene-Constantinopolitan Creed, usually described as the Nicene Creed in Lutheran liturgical books, is included and

18. The confessions of the Lutheran churches may be found in the original German or Latin in *Die Bekenntnisschriften der evangelisch-lutherischen Kirche* (Göttingen: Vandenhoeck & Ruprecht, 1959). The best English edition is *The Book of Concord,* trans. and ed. Theodore G. Tappert (Philadelphia: Fortress Press, 1959). See pp. 17-21 of the latter.

utilized in worship services. For example, the *Lutheran Book of Worship*, used by the majority of Lutherans in North America, states in its rubrics, "The CREED may be said. The Nicene Creed is said on all festivals and on Sundays in the season of Advent, Christmas, Lent, and Easter. The Apostles' Creed is said at other times. The Creed is omitted here if the service of Holy Baptism or another rite with a creed is used."[19]

In view of my stated acceptance of the interpretation of patristic research and the formal and liturgical reception of the Creed of A.D. 381 by Lutherans, what word of counsel can be offered at this time in the ecumenical movement by a Lutheran?

First it is necessary to stress that Lutheran churches need to continue their own process of re-receiving the Creed of A.D. 381.[20] They must be certain that such reception is not merely formal and liturgical but that the teaching of this creed informs their faith and life. Reception by any Christian community is never ended. Lutherans should make it clear to other Christians that they are receiving this creed because they see in it teaching that is in conformity with that of Christ and of the apostolic community, the gospel as witnessed to in Scripture. In this process Lutherans will be standing within their own confessional tradition, which has with very few exceptions accorded the Nicene-Constantinopolitan Creed such a status. Yet Lutherans will need to probe continually what this reception means not only for their understandings of the Trinity and Christ but for their discernment of the church and of the Christian life.

At this time in history Lutherans will have to reflect more carefully on the ecumenical implications of this process of re-reception of this creed. What implication for the unity of the church lie in the fact that Lutherans hold in common with other Christians from whom they are separated this widely received confession?

Common reception of the teaching of the Creed of A.D. 381

---

19. *Lutheran Book of Worship* (Minneapolis: Augsburg, 1978), p. 84.

20. Reception, and especially ecumenical reception, is a new and complex topic. See William G. Rusch, *Reception: An Ecumenical Opportunity* (Philadelphia: Fortress Press, 1988), esp. p. 31.

by divided churches—and this implies more than simply the acceptance of a text—should allow these churches to make progress in the procedure of mutual recognition. Indeed, ecumenical reception is a process that should make recognition possible. A basic issue in the ecumenical movement is how divided churches are to recognize one other in such a way as to allow for full communion among them. Clearly reception of the Creed of A.D. 381 would not in itself lead to such a recognition. Other issues would require resolution.

Even these brief comments hint at the significance of the ecumenical topic of recognition, which has received less study than the topic of reception. Recognition must be viewed as a graduated process, as the comments about reception and recognition of the Nicene-Constantinopolitan Creed make clear. Recognition of this creed in and of itself does not lead to full communion among the churches that receive it. But even if it only facilitates the recognition of *aspects* of a church at certain stages (e.g., the fact that churches teach this creed in common), it establishes a dynamic, initiates a process that leads in the direction of recognition of a church as fully church, and thus may eventually result in full communion.

Like reception, recognition is primarily a spiritual and theological judgment. This judgment has priority over legal church actions, although they also have their place. Recognition does involve legitimacy: one church recognizes another church in its uniqueness as legitimate and authentic. In this procedure recognition does not demand, but on the contrary excludes, the notion that all differences between churches must be overcome. Recognition of churches as fully churches makes possible both full communion and unity in legitimate diversity.

Second, Lutherans need to recall that mutual reception and recognition of the Creed of A.D. 381 as an ecumenical step will not be possible with all churches. Churches that have historically rejected creeds will find it extremely difficult to consider a common confession of the apostolic faith based on the Creed of A.D. 381. Other ways must be sought and found in such cases. The view of Scripture in Lutheran churches makes this challenging but not impossible. As Faith and Order pursues its work in this area, Lutherans can aid the commission to see the Creed of A.D. 381 as one way—even a primary way—toward a common confession of the apostolic faith, but never the only way.

The Lutheran tradition since the sixteenth century, as reflected in Luther and especially in the Lutheran confessions contained in the *Book of Concord,* has seen the Nicene-Constantinopolitan Creed as a way of confessing the apostolic faith.[21] This confessional reception has been reinforced in the liturgical life of Lutheran churches. Not only is the Creed of A.D. 381 employed in the liturgy, but the calendar for the church year commemorates such pro-Nicene theologians as Athanasius and the Cappadocians. The Creed of A.D. 381 could not easily be replaced or displaced in the Lutheran tradition. At the same time, the Lutheran tradition would not insist that the Nicene-Constantinopolitan Creed is the only or a complete confession of the apostolic faith. This tradition will always ask whether this creed, or any other, preserves and expresses the understanding of the gospel as God's justification to us by grace through faith.

The Lutheran tradition will always have an affinity with those other Christian traditions that believe, teach, and confess the three ecumenical symbols, and especially the Apostles' and Nicene Creeds. The statement on ecumenism of the Evangelical Lutheran Church in America, *Ecumenism: The Vision of the Evangelical Lutheran Church in America,* expresses this clearly.[22] Lutherans will probably anticipate forms of visible unity sooner with churches that share this credal disposition than with noncredal churches. Nevertheless, Lutheran commitments and goals regarding the unity of the church will never be limited to credal churches.[23]

---

21. See Luther, *The Three Symbols or Creeds of the Christian Faith,* vol. 34 of *Luther's Works,* ed. Lewis W. Spitz (Philadelphia: Muhlenberg Press, 1960), pp. 197-229; and *On the Councils and the Church,* vol. 41 of *Luther's Works,* ed. Eric W. Gritsch (Philadelphia: Fortress Press, 1966), pp. 9-178.

See also Marc Lienhard, *L'Evangile et L'Eglise chez Luther* (Paris: Les Éditions du Cerf, 1989), pp. 131-48.

22. *Ecumenism: The Vision of the Evangelical Lutheran Church in America* (Chicago: Office for Ecumenical Affairs, Evangelical Lutheran Church in America, 1989), p. 5.

23. *Ecumenism: The Vision of the Evangelical Lutheran Church in America,* p. 11.

The Fourth-Century Church: The Monastic Contribution

ROBERTA C. BONDI

It is my impression that beginning church history students in our seminaries are rarely exposed to the kind of study of church history that encourages an ecumenical understanding of either the ancient or the modern church. These students are trained to believe that the main business of the patristic church was the hammering out of doctrine. Consequently, they graduate believing that the only significant contribution of the age of the ecumenical councils to the modern church was to provide the later church with a kind of universal theological touchstone of truth. In the context of the development of doctrine, new students of church history meet bishops and archbishops almost exclusively. Thus, they quickly perceive the nature of the patristic church to be clerical, hierarchical, authoritarian, and thoroughly tied in to imperial politics. The complexity of ancient Christians' positions toward life in the world, their nuanced answers to the heart- and life-wrenching questions about what it means to be a Christian living in a fallen world, their views on what salvation means and how Christians appropriate it—all issues that stood at the center of Christian understanding in the fourth and fifth centuries—appear to today's students only marginal to what is

really significant about the early church: its doctrinal formulations and definitions.

This false perception of the early church and its concerns
works against ecumenism. Rather than leading the church to a
deeper understanding of our common heritage that helps us
grow together in the knowledge and love of God, it encourages
us all to think that the early church belongs in a special way to
those communions that seem to stress correctness of doctrine.
At the same time, it excludes those communions whose major
stress is on the importance of Christian life and witness over
against the larger culture. As a result, an ecumenical project such
as the explication of the Nicene Creed can founder because
many Christian groups simply find it irrelevant to them.

I believe we can make one truly significant adjustment to
broaden this disastrously narrow and misleading focus and to
allow many more Christian communions to find their own
history in that of the early church: we must give appropriate
weight to the meaning of the rise of monasticism and the ascetic
tradition in the early church. Before we are able to see this
tradition for what it is, however, we must make some general-
izations about the way in which doctrine related to the Christian
life in the early church.

DOCTRINE AND THE CHRISTIAN LIFE
IN THE EARLY CHURCH

Since the eighteenth-century Enlightenment, the modern
world has done its best to separate reason on the one hand from
emotion and its commitments on the other. This is because we
believe that it is only reason, untainted by emotion or passionate commitment, that allows us to find the truth about
reality. Science and the so-called scientific worldview osten-
sibly depend on such a separation of reason and emotion. In a
similar fashion, much of the theology and church history written during the last two centuries has sought a foundation in a
rational theology free from the errors and privatization of
subjectivism. As a result, theology and the study of doctrine are

commonly cut off from questions having to do with the Christian life and worship, which are relegated to the sphere of personal piety, private religious experience, and subjectivity. Though church histories as well as the various liberation theologies have challenged this separation of theology from practice, it is still a dominant conviction in the teaching of theology in many liberal Protestant seminary classes that "piety" and a serious study of doctrine and theology are to be kept separate from each other.[1]

To the patristic church such a separation would simply have been unthinkable. For them, the world in general and human beings in particular are made according to the pattern of the very Logos, the Word of God. Through the Word, God has provided all that has been created with structure and order and meaning. This being so, as Athanasius says in "On the Incarnation of God the Word," if Adam and Eve had not had their vision obscured by sin, they would have been able to see God everywhere in the natural world.[2] But who is this Logos they would have seen? Not the "God of the philosophers" whose basic relationship with the world is distant, impersonal, and essentially unseeing. While it is true that Greek-speaking writers of the early church speak of God's immutability, impassibility, and incorruptibility, these writers do not forget easily that their God is the God of Scripture, who is passionately involved with the lives and well-being of God's people. The most fundamental governing principle of the universe is not reason or even justice but rather love that is concerned with each person.[3]

1. For one assessment of the complexity of the elements going into the development of doctrine in the early church, see Jaroslav Pelikan's *Development of Christian Doctrine: Some Historical Prolegomena* (New Haven: Yale University Press, 1969). See also Andrew Louth's little essay "Theology and Spirituality" (Oxford: Fairacres Publications, 1978), in which he argues not so much from the perspective of the historian of doctrine as from that of the historian of the spiritual life for the need to understand the interconnectedness of theology and the Christian life.

2. Athanasius, "On the Incarnation of God the Word," in *Christology of the Later Fathers*, ed. and trans. E. R. Hardy (Philadelphia: Westminster Press, 1954), p. 65.

3. Gregory of Nyssa speaks for the tradition of the early church in his

For Christians of the early church, God's love was not, however, simply an interesting fact that only made sense within the sphere of personal piety and had nothing to do with the kind of knowledge of God expressed in doctrine. Christians of the patristic church were absolutely convinced that any real knowledge can only be based on an affinity between the knower and the thing known.[4] Trustworthy knowledge of God, therefore, depended upon a sustained living out of a Christian life deeply rooted in private and public prayer with the ongoing community on the one hand and Christian ethical practice on the other. It was inconceivable to early Christians that one could understand the meaning of doctrine without being fully grounded in the kind of prayer and practice that involved continual growth in intimate knowledge of and likeness with the God of Scripture who is witnessed to by the life of the church. Knowing God was grounded more in the formation of a certain kind of character than in the possession of a certain kind of knowledge.

On the other hand, the capacity to be formed in that character also depended on a faithful and real understanding of doctrine. In his Great Catechetical Oration, Gregory of Nyssa speaks of the need of the one being baptized to understand the affirmations he or she makes about the Trinity:

> What happens in the sacrament of baptism depends upon the disposition of the heart of him [or her] who approaches it. If [one] confesses that the holy Trinity is uncreated he [or she] enters on the life which is unchanging. But if, on a false supposition, [one] sees a created nature in the Trinity and then is baptized into *that*, he [or

---

"Address on Religious Instruction," in *Christology of the Later Fathers*, p. 290. Andrew Louth has some important clarifying remarks on the relation between non-Christian Platonism and the Christian Platonists in the *Origins of the Mystical Tradition* (Oxford: Clarendon Press, 1981); on Origen, for example, see pp. 52-53.

4. Gregory of Nyssa says, for example, "If then, [humanity] came into being for these reasons, viz., to participate in the divine goodness, [it] had to be fashioned in such a way as to fit [it] to share in this goodness. For just as the eye shares in the light through having by nature inherent brightness in it, and by this innate power attracts what is akin to itself, so something akin to the divine had to be mingled with it. In this way its desire could correspond to something native to it" ("Address on Religious Instruction," p. 276).

she] is born once more into a life which is subject to change. For offspring and parents necessarily share the same nature.[5]

Doctrine, Christian life, and the sacraments were absolutely inseparable.

All this being so, we can draw two conclusions. First, practically speaking, modern readers must be extremely careful about how we read ancient "doctrinal" texts coming out of the controversies of the ancient church. Though reading many of the documents of the theological controversies of the period would not necessarily reveal it, worship, practical action, and theological reflection were continuous with each other. If we wish to understand texts relating to the Arian controversy, for example, including the Nicene-Constantinopolitan Creed, then we must look for the meaning of their terminology not only in doctrinal texts of the period. We must also try to see the whole context of the Christian life and worship into which the controversy fits in the early church.[6] Second, we have to remind ourselves that doctrine was never the main business of the patristic church anyway. The principle concern was for Christian living and Christian worship; sustained reflection on Christian living was chiefly the product of monastic ascetic theology. This second conclusion is of the utmost importance to the ecumenical historian in search of our common history.

THE CENTRALITY OF MONASTICISM IN THE FOURTH-CENTURY CHURCH

However significant the virtue of humility was in early monastic theology and spirituality, the founders of monasticism did not

5. Gregory, "Address on Religious Instruction," p. 322. Needless to say, Gregory is not speaking in any magical sense when he warns the baptismal candidate against an Arian understanding of the Trinity. The key is to be found in the connection between doctrine and the Christian life. For an excellent exposition of exactly how this dynamic works, see Robert Gregg and Dennis Groh, *Early Arianism: A View of Salvation* (Philadelphia: Fortress Press, 1981).

6. For an attempt to relate the *Life of St. Anthony* to the Arian controversy, see Gregg and Groh, *Early Arianism*, pp. 131-59.

have a modest vision of what the movement that they led was about. They understood themselves to be the heirs of the martyrs, who were, for their part, the heirs of God's promises to the Old Testament patriarchs and prophets to bring the whole world into the family of God.[7]

Monasticism and the ascetic movement at the time of the ecumenical councils belonged to the very heart of the early church. There were thousands upon thousands of men and women who deliberately took up its lifestyle,[8] but the self-understanding of the monastics, their theology, and their way of life had an enormous influence on the rest of the church, lay and clerical, as well. The holy men and holy women of antiquity stood at the center of their own culture.[9] They exercised great political power on behalf of the lay people among whom they lived, and they taught a radical spirituality that was seriously at odds with the values of a secular world. More than that, a huge number of the bishops and archbishops who participated in the Arian and christological controversies and the councils that "resolved" them had either been drawn from the monastic ranks or, like Athanasius of Alexandria, maintained extremely close ties with the monks. In fact, no true picture of the history of the

7. They were the "athletes" of Christ in ascetic discipline and in the imagination of the church as they embodied and modeled Christian ideals. Occasionally, even in Egypt, which was noted for ascetic moderation, asceticism could lead to death, which was equated with martyrdom. For the story of two teenaged brothers who died this way, see *Sayings of the Desert Fathers*, trans. Benedicta Ward (London: Mowbray, 1981), p. 134.

8. In Egypt alone, Athanasius tells us, Anthony was so well emulated that "the desert was made a city by monks, who left their own people and registered themselves for the citizenship of the heavens" (*Athanasius: The Life of St. Anthony and the Letter to Marcellinus*, trans. Robert Gregg [New York: Paulist Press, 1980], pp. 42-43).

9. See especially Peter Brown, "The Saint as Exemplar in Late Antiquity," in *Saints and Virtues*, ed. John Stratton Hawley (Berkeley and Los Angeles: University of California Press, 1987), pp. 3-14. In this essay Brown comments on his own deepening understanding of the way the holy men (and, presumably, women) in Christian antiquity embodied Christian values for that culture. Brown's article "The Rise and Function of the Holy Men in Late Antiquity," *Journal of Roman Studies* 61 (1971): 80-101, has been truly ground-breaking in patristic studies.

period portrays monasticism and the understanding of the gospel that undergirded it as being of only secondary significance to what was really going on in the church.

Theologically, monasticism belongs at the center of the patristic church. Its original impulse is to be found in Jesus' call to his followers to leave behind them the values and social relations of the ordinary world in which they lived in exchange for the kingdom of God. The postbiblical theology that prepared for and fed monasticism was written by the great mainline teachers of the early church from the second century onward: Irenaeus, Clement of Alexandria, Origen, Athanasius, the Cappadocian Fathers, John Chrysostom, Cyprian, and Augustine, to name only a few.

Contrary to much popular belief, monasticism in all its varieties did not consist of a small number of eccentric self- and world-hating men and women all sharing a similar lifestyle. Its adherents were enormous numbers of men and women of every kind of temperament from every social class and every part of the Roman Empire. The monastic movement of the fourth and fifth centuries embraced tightly structured large communities such as the Pachomian houses in Egypt and the imposing monastery of the Sleepless Ones in Constantinople. It included Augustine's early community of friends at Cassiciacum and informal communities in Egypt organized around an "Abba" or teacher. Loosely organized small communities of men in Palestine who came together only to share in weekend worship were a part of it, as were ascetics living as solitaries in the Egyptian desert and in the hills around Edessa.

Monasticism was everywhere, and it incorporated all kinds of people from every social class. Anthony, its legendary founder, had been a wealthy Egyptian peasant.[10] Arsenius, who took up monastic life in Egypt at the end of the fourth century, had been a fabulously wealthy Roman nobleman and the tutor to two sons of emperor Theodosius I.[11] The aristocratic Macrina,

10. Athanasius's biography of Anthony had a galvanizing effect on the ancient world. Even Augustine's conversion to Christianity was influenced by hearing Anthony's story (*Confessions*, 8.8.15).

11. Derwas Chitty, *The Desert a City* (Oxford: Basil Blackwell, 1966), p. 63 n. 55.

the sister of Basil the Great and Gregory of Nyssa, founded and headed a convent in Cappadocia.[12] The Roman Melania the Elder, who established a monastery in Jerusalem with Rufinus and was in contact with important monastic figures all over the Empire, is another aristocratic example.[13] Monasticism drew heavily from the very poor and uneducated as well. We see many illustrations of this in the monastic literature of the time. In Sayings of the Desert Fathers, for example, we read of the Roman Arsenius's ability to learn from his illiterate Coptic-speaking peasant monk neighbors and also of a Coptic-speaking monk's complaints about the relative luxury in which Arsenius lived, suggesting that at least some of the monastics were formerly poor enough to have improved their physical lot by taking up a monastic life.[14]

Originally, male monasticism was deliberately a lay movement. Offering a way to live out the commands and promises of the gospel in freedom from the power games of everyday life in society, the monastic life for men represented a kind of reversal of all ordinary social values. Egyptian monasticism's male founders believed that there was no way to exercise the authority of a priest at the same time one was trying to become free

12. Her brother Gregory of Nyssa wrote her biography; for an English translation of "The Life of Macrina," see St. Gregory of Nyssa: Ascetical Works, trans. Virginia Woods Callahan (Washington: Catholic University of America Press, 1967), pp. 163-91. Macrina also figures as the main character in a dialogue modeled on those of Socrates entitled "On the Soul and Resurrection" (Saint Gregory of Nyssa: Ascetical Works, pp. 198-272).

13. Melania made a significant contribution to both monastic practice and theology when she sent the brilliant Evagrius Pontus to a community of Origenistic monks in Egypt after having diagnosed and dealt with his serious illness. See Palladius, The Lausiac History, trans. Robert Meyer (New York: Newman Press, 1964), pp. 112-13.

The ambiguity of the relationships of several aristocratic women with such male church leaders and supporters of monasticism as Jerome and John Chrysostom is particularly helpfully discussed by Elizabeth Clark in "Ascetic Renunciation and Feminine Advancement: A Paradox of Late Ancient Christianity" and "Authority and Humility: A Conflict of Values in Fourth Century Female Monasticism," in Ascetic Piety and Women's Faith: Essays in Late Ancient Christianity (Lewiston, N.Y.: Edwin Mellen Press, 1986), pp. 175-228.

14. Sayings of the Desert Fathers, pp. 10, 16-17.

from the need to dominate and judge others. The first Egyptian monastics, therefore, received the eucharist at their local village churches from their parish priests. It was not too far into the fourth century, however, before it was deemed necessary for monastic communities to have their own priests. Within a short time bishops and archbishops were increasingly appointed from monastic ranks. Nevertheless, ambiguity about exercising ecclesiastical power over others remained at least vestigially within the spirituality of early monasticism.

Women participated in monastic life as well, and it is significant that it did not, as we should expect, have precisely the same meaning for women as for many men.[15] During this period most women did not really have much control over their own lives and destinies. Outside of monasticism, Christian women were always in significant ways at the disposal of husbands, fathers, or brothers, to whom they owed obedience. Women were expected to marry, and it is important to remember that for women a large portion of marriage was a matter of pregnancy, childbirth, and child rearing. As the beginning of Gregory of Nyssa's treatise "On Virginity" makes poignantly clear, these were all physically very dangerous, and women bore the brunt of that danger.[16] The step of taking up the monastic life during this period could have very different meanings for men, depending on their wealth and status in their former life—some were wealthy and powerful, like the senator Arsenius, whereas others

15. For a particularly helpful collection of much of the material discussing this point, see *Maenads, Martyr, Matrons, Monastics: A Sourcebook on Women's Religions in the Greco-Roman World*, ed. Ross S. Kraemer (Philadelphia: Fortress Press, 1988). This book includes more non-Christian material from the ancient world than Christian. See also Elizabeth Clark, *Women in the Early Church* (Wilmington, Del.: Michael Glazier, 1983), which includes helpful commentary on these selections. *Holy Women of the Syrian Orient*, trans. Sabastian Brock and Susan Harvey (Berkeley and Los Angeles: University of California Press, 1987), is particularly valuable in that it includes translations of Syriac texts that are otherwise extremely hard to obtain and that give a very different view of women monastics than most Greek and Latin material, which seems to be principally interested in aristocratic women on the one hand and converted prostitutes on the other.

16. "On Virginity," in *Saint Gregory of Nyssa: Ascetical Works*, pp. 13-20.

were dirt-poor peasants used to sleeping on the ground. For a woman, however, it was at the most basic level to step into a realm of freedom from slavery to her body and freedom from the control of male relatives. At another level, as a monastic, she was regarded as having put off "feminine weakness" and was allowed to mingle with and be taken seriously by her male colleagues in ways that were not possible for nonmonastic women. For a woman, to embrace the monastic life meant to claim emphatically Jesus' vision of a world in which a person's true identity came not from fulfilling society's role expectations but from living in the kingdom.[17]

Female asceticism was extremely varied in its expression. Pachomius, the founder of cenobitic monasticism in Upper Egypt, started a monastery for women across the Nile at the same time he founded two monasteries for men.[18] Many women lived as consecrated virgins within their own family homes, while others lived together informally, relatively speaking, in Christian households in which they put into practice monastic ideals.[19] Still other wealthy and aristocratic women chose to leave their family responsibilities, using their wealth and influence to found monasteries of their own for themselves and other women, to travel freely, and to find a place in the larger monastic world they shared with men.

It is true that these monastic women as a group were being assimilated into a lifestyle that was still largely controlled and

17. This is not to say that monastic women were truly seen as the equals of their male counterparts: we do not see any but wealthy and aristocratic women moving around with the kind of freedom monastic men had, as Elizabeth Clark makes clear. Women were not ordained to the priesthood, and monastic women rarely held public roles of leadership outside their own communities. The fact that literature pertaining to women's monasticism hardly even survives from the early church is perhaps the most telling indication of how women were valued.

18. Arman Veilleux has published a three-volume translation of and introduction to the major documents relating to Pachomius and Pachomian monasticism. See "First Greek Life of Pachomius," in *Pachomian Koinonia*, vol. 1 (Kalamazoo: Cistercian Publications, 1980), pp. 318-19.

19. See particularly, Peter Brown's discussion of these women in " 'Daughters of Jerusalem': The Ascetic Life of Women in the Fourth Century," in *The Body and Society: Men, Women, and Sexual Renunciation in Early Christianity* (New York: Columbia University Press, 1988), pp. 256-84.

directed by men. But we must also remember that the new "life of virginity" gave individual women a freedom from male control and biological destiny and that the monastic virtues shaping this new life were often in serious opposition to the dominant values with respect to women of the time.

SOME BASIC EARLY MONASTIC CONVICTIONS

Who were the monastics in terms of their own self-identities? How did they understand themselves? If we only look at them on the surface, we can perhaps find no single answer. At a deeper level, however, they shared some important convictions which begin to appear when we examine the lives and calls of two legendary founders of Egyptian monasticism, Anthony and Pachomius.[20]

According to tradition, the first pioneer of monasticism was Anthony. He was born around the year 251 to wealthy Christian peasant farmers in a little town on the Nile and left orphaned as a late adolescent. His call to a new life came soon after his parents' death when he heard the story of the Rich Young Ruler read in church. Jesus seemed to Anthony to be telling him personally that *if he would be perfect* he would sell all he had and give to the poor to follow Jesus. By 285 Anthony had sold his family property, put his younger sister in the care of a household of Christian female virgins, taken instruction from solitaries who lived around his little town, and begun his new and very

20. At least in popular imagination, Egypt was the original home of monasticism; certainly its monastic heroes and their teachings were well known throughout the Empire. Ascetic forms of Christianity go back to Christianity's beginnings. Monasticism would appear to have had a good start among Syriac-speaking Christians very early, with celibate groups of men and women, the "sons of the covenant" and "daughters of the covenant," living together in loose communities of Christian discipline and prayer. For a brief introduction, see Roberta C. Bondi, "The Spirituality of Syriac-Speaking Christians," in *Christian Spirituality: Origins to the Twelfth Century,* ed. Barnard McGinn and John Meyendorff (New York: Crossroads, 1985), pp. 152-61. The major source for the first true Syrian fathers of monasticism is Theodoret of Cyrrhus's *History of the Monks of Syria,* trans. R. M. Price (Kalamazoo: Cistercian Publications, 1985).

long life as a solitary—but one whose solitariness did not exclude his travel to Alexandria to publicly encourage the martyrs, nor his spending a large portion of his life surrounded by disciples and visited by other monastics, soldiers, government officials, pagan priests and philosophers, local landowners, and peasants, all of whom came to him for advice concerning the affairs of the secular world as well as of the spiritual.

Pachomius, the founder of cenobitic monasticism in Egypt, received his call in a different way. He had grown up a pagan. According to his first Greek biography, his initial encounter with Christians came after he had been conscripted into the army. As a cold, hungry, miserable young soldier he was locked up with fellow conscripts in the city of Thebes. While he was there, some Christians came to bring them food and drink and other necessities as an act of charity, and Pachomius was overwhelmed by this. When he asked who they were, he was told that Christians are people "who bear the name of Christ, the only Son of God, and they do all manner of good things for everyone, putting their hope on him who made the heaven and the earth and us [human beings]."[21] Pachomius was so struck by this that he promised God that if he were allowed to escape alive, he would also become a Christian. Later, after his release, and seeking the will of God for himself, he heard his own call to the desert via the voice of an angel telling him three times that "the Lord's will is to minister to the race of [human beings] in order to reconcile them to himself."[22] After an abortive attempt to found a monastic community in which he taught and exercised authority only by setting an example with his own behavior, he went on to establish the first real highly organized monastic communities. At the time of his death, the combined population of Pachomian monasteries in Egypt was enormous.

What common convictions did Anthony and Pachomius and their followers in Egypt share? Most fundamental of all their convictions, each understood his or her call—to perfection, to serve all people and reconcile them to God—to be a radical

21. "First Greek Life of Pachomius," p. 300.
22. "First Greek Life of Pachomius," pp. 311-12.

living out of the gospel command to "love the Lord your God with all your heart, and all your strength and all your mind, and your neighbor as yourself." Love was the heart of the gospel. Dorotheos of Gaza, a particularly winsome sixth-century interpreter of Egyptian monasticism, illustrates this helpfully:

> Suppose we were to take a compass and insert the point and draw the outline of a circle. The center point is the same distance from any point on the circumference. . . . Let us suppose that this circle is the world and that God [Godself] is at the center; the straight lines drawn from the circumference to the center are the lives of human beings. . . . Let us assume for the sake of the analogy that to move toward God, then, human beings move from the circumference along the various radii of the circle to its center. But at the same time, the closer they are to God, the closer they are to one another; and the closer they are to one another, the closer they become to God.[23]

The goal of the originators of monasticism was love, perfect love of God and of humanity.

Undergirding their striving for this goal lay solid patristic theology. They believed that human beings are created in the image of God. This meant to them that human beings are created with free will and reason so that they can solve moral problems. It also meant, however, that we are created having as part of our very definition and nature, as our goal in life as God meant life to be, the love of God and the love of God's image, other people. It is true they believed that in our fallen state we do not love as we are intended to love, but they also believed that Christ had come to overcome death and restore our capabilities for love, showing us the way back to the original image of God. Thus we may now, with God's help, be able to love fully as God intended, not just in heaven, but in this life. This basic understanding of the significance of love of God and neighbor and their relationship to each other stood at the heart of early monasticism.[24]

23. "On Refusal to Judge Our Neighbor," in *Dorotheos of Gaza: Discourses and Sayings*, trans. Eric P. Wheeler (Kalamazoo: Cistercian Publications, 1977), pp. 138-39.
24. For a discussion of the centrality and characteristics of love in the

It is important to note here that, while the individual monastic had to "grow into" an ability to love, this love emphatically
belonged in a social context. The early monastics understood
themselves to be heirs to the martyrs, and as the introduction to
"The First Greek Life of Pachomius" makes quite clear, the
business of the martyrs that the monastics inherited was ultimately the transformation of the whole human world into a new
society in which all God's promises to the Old Testament patriarchs would be fulfilled.[25] We can glimpse something of how
Athanasius saw this already happening in the monastics who
settled around Anthony's fortress:

> [The monks'] cells in the hills were like tents filled with divine
> choirs—people chanting, studying, fasting, praying, rejoicing in
> the hope of future boons, working for the distribution of alms, and
> maintaining both love and harmony among themselves. It was as
> if one truly looked on a land all its own—a land of devotion and
> righteousness. For neither perpetrator nor victim of injustice was
> there, nor complaint of a tax collector.[26]

The early monastic did not view any of this human love of
others coming from the self: it was always viewed as a response
to God's own love of human beings, which precedes anything
human beings can do. The intimate and touching quality of this
love, as the monastics saw it, is illuminated by this image drawn
from one of the Macarian Homilies:

> A baby, even though it is powerless to accomplish anything or with
> its own feet to go to its mother, still it rolls and makes noises and
> cries as it seeks its mother. . . . And she picks it up and fondles it
> and feeds it with great love. This is also what God, the Lover [of
> mankind], does to the person that comes to [God] and ardently
> desires [God.][27]

---

spirituality of Egyptian monasticism, see Roberta C. Bondi, *To Love as God Loves:
Conversations with the Early Church* (Philadelphia: Fortress Press, 1987), pp. 20-40.

25. See "First Greek Life of Pachomius," pp. 297-99.

26. *Athanasius: The Life of St. Anthony and the Letter to Marcellinus,* p. 64.

27. Homily 46, in *Intoxicated with God,* trans. George Maloney (Denville,
N.J.: Dimension Books, 1978), pp. 212-13.

The monastics never forgot that it is this divine love that is the source of creation, the incarnation, God's church (which is the body of Christ), and all human salvation.

Four further convictions of relevance to our ecumenical project flowed from this fundamental conviction about the centrality of love. The first, which Anthony and Pachomius shared with the other monastics of their time, was, paradoxically, that the radical nature of Jesus' command to love made it impossible for them to live out that love in ordinary life as they knew it. This did not mean that they believed one had to be a monastic to be a Christian; they did not. They hated neither the world nor their own bodies, nor did they believe that marriage was somehow un-Christian.[28] They did not view ordinary life as evil, but they did see a long way into the ambiguities, compromises, self-serving-ness, and desire for mastery over other people that are an every-day part of earning a living, owning property, pleasing family, and striving for success. It was only by giving up that life that they felt they would able to live out God's promise of the New Creation and witness to its reality to the nonmonastic world.

A second shared early monastic conviction has to do with respecting the real variety of ways it is possible to live out the Christian life according to an individual's or, presumably, a Christian community's own temperament. The *Sayings of the Desert Fathers* provide one ancient conversation on the topic.

> A brother questioned an old man saying, "What good work should I do so that I may live?" The old man said, "God knows what is good. I have heard it said that one of the Fathers asked Abba Nisterius the Great, the friend of Abba Anthony, and said to him, 'What good work is there that I could do?' He said to him, 'Are not all actions equal? Scripture says that Abraham was hospitable and God was with him. David was humble and God was with him. Elias loved interior peace and God was with him. So, do whatever you see your soul desires according to God and guard your heart.' "[29]

28. For a full discussion of Egyptian monastic views of sexuality in the context of the development of attitudes toward sexuality and marriage in the early church, see Brown, *The Body and Society*, pp. 213-340.

29. *Sayings of the Desert Fathers*, p. 154.

Monastic respect for variety was based in a theological principle that went back to Origen: the Christian life is grounded in God's revelation, and God reveals God's self to each person according to that person's need.[30]

It is important to note here, however, that the belief of the monastics in the need to respect the varieties of ways people are called to live out their faith was not completely open-ended. In general they took the importance of correct doctrine quite seriously.[31] Athanasius reports that Anthony participated in the Arian controversy, and monks participated, sometimes discreditably, at all levels in various other doctrinal controversies, sometimes in roles of theological leadership, sometimes as mobs.[32]

A third common conviction of the early monastics was that judgmentalism in all its forms is the enemy of love. To act judgmentally toward another was to risk driving that other away from God. At one end of the scale was a form of judgmentalism that consisted of a continual critical and complaining attitude toward others in small but wearing ways. At the other end of the scale was a judgmentalism that manifested itself in deciding who could and could not belong within the monastic community and ultimately the kingdom of God itself. One of the most frightening stories to come out of the Egyptian desert illustrates this point:

> Abba Isaac of the Thebaid came to a community and saw one of the brothers to be blameworthy, and sentenced him. But when he had gone out to the desert, the angel of the Lord came and stood in front of the door to his cell, and said, "I will not let you go in." He asked, "Why not?" And the angel of the Lord answered, "God sent me to say this to you: 'Where do you command me to send that blameworthy brother whom you sentenced?'" And at once

30. The understanding that God reveals God's self according to the need of the individual is common in Jewish as well as Christian sources from the period. See *Gregory of Nyssa: The Life of Moses*, trans. Abraham Malherbe and Everett Ferguson (New York: Paulist Press, 1978), p. 174 n. 163.

31. The debates in the desert over Origenism, for example, were fierce. For the main players, see Chitty, *The Desert a City*, pp. 46-60.

32. See Chitty, *The Desert a City*, pp. 101-22.

> Abba Isaac did penance, saying, "I have sinned; forgive me." And the angel said, "Arise, God forgives you. But in the future take care you judge no person before God has judged that person."[33]

Monastics were to give up judging the people around themselves, for to judge another was to break the fundamental law of Christ. As Abba Theodore said, "Do not judge the fornicator, for you yourself would then transgress the law just as much yourself. He who said 'do not fornicate' also said, 'do not Judge.'"[34]

The fourth conviction was that the single most important virtue a monastic must cultivate to make love possible was humility.

> When Abba Macarius was returning from the marsh to his cell one day carrying some palm-leaves, he met the devil on the road with a scythe. The [devil] struck at him as much as he pleased, but in vain, and said to him, "What is your power, Macarius, that makes me powerless against you? All that you do, I do, too; you fast, so do I; you keep vigil, and I do not sleep at all; in one thing only do you beat me." Abba Macarius asked what that was. He said, "Your humility. Because of that I can do nothing against you."[35]

The monastics did not equate humility with a kind of groveling self-hatred or a refusal to recognize anything right about oneself. It meant the acceptance of oneself and all the other people in the world as both infinitely beloved of God and at the same time subject to weakness. It meant giving up heroic expectations of oneself and of others. It meant not being surprised or made cynical by finding sin in oneself or in others. It meant accepting that whatever any Christian does right is due only in small part to his or her own effort; mostly it is a result of the gift of God's grace and love. Finally, it meant being able to learn from very different kinds of people without being judgmental or secretly

33. *Western Asceticism*, trans. Owen Chadwick (Philadelphia: Westminster Press, 1958), p. 102.

34. *Sayings of the Desert Fathers*, p. 60.

35. *Sayings of the Desert Fathers*, pp. 129-30. For a further discussion of the character of humility according to the Egyptian monastic tradition see Bondi, *To Love as God Loves*, pp. 41-56.

convinced of one's own superiority or the superiority of the group to which one belongs.

Again, human humility for the early monastics was only an imitation of the humility of God displayed in Jesus:

> Just as neither the ages above nor the ages below can grasp the greatness of God and [God's] incomprehensibility, so also neither the worlds above nor the worlds on earth can understand the humility of God and how [God] renders [God's] self little to the humble and small.[36]

In the view of our monastic ancestors, as human love is grounded in God's love for us, so human humility is grounded in the very humility of God.

HEARING THE CREED THROUGH EARLY MONASTIC EARS

How does the early ascetic tradition broaden and deepen our understanding of the basic affirmations of the church of the time of the councils of Nicaea and I Constantinople? It will be helpful to listen to the Nicene Creed briefly through the theological ears of the early monastics to hear a little of what they surely heard affirmed in it, in addition to what a study of the creed from the perspective of the development of doctrine in the context of the history of the councils has already taught us.

Please keep in mind three things while reading the following paragraphs:

1. They are not meant to highlight *all* the most important points the early monastics would have heard affirmed in the creed. I have selected only a very few points, and these often to the exclusion of what they would have regarded as crucial. I say nothing, for example, about demons and the pagan gods, about baptism, or about the resurrection. Furthermore, I am aware that what I say is so brief that it is

36. *Intoxicated with God*, p. 180.

sometimes almost in shorthand. It should be taken as an experiment in hearing the creed with ears trained in the monastic life I have been describing above.

2. These paragraphs are meant to *supplement* our understanding of the bishops' work in the ecumenical councils. I do not mean to suggest that the bishops heard the creed in one way while the monastics heard it in another.

3. These paragraphs are also meant to point to potentially profitable areas for future work on illuminating the meaning of the Nicene Creed in a modern ecumenical context.

That God is "Almighty Father, maker of heaven and earth" told the early monastics that God has power over everything God has made. God loves us and wishes us life. God has the power and uses it to see that whatever befalls us, if we love God, it becomes life-giving for us. We are therefore able to be fearless in the world we live in, and because we are fearless, we are able to give up a need to dominate others, hoard our property while withholding from others what they need, and so forth.

That God is "Almighty Father" and that Jesus Christ is "One Being with the Father" (that is, *homoousias* with the Father) means that God chooses to exhibit God's power precisely in God's gift to us of freedom. God's almightiness is especially revealed in God's refusal to dominate us, crush us, or subdue us. We know this because that is the way Jesus Christ related and relates to us, and we know that parents and children share the same nature. This is one of the most important points we have to affirm over against Arianism, which says that Jesus Christ and the Father do not share the same nature.

That the One Lord Jesus Christ is "one in being with the Father" and that "for us and for our salvation he came down from heaven" also tells us that it is God's own self who saved us. Whatever we do, God goes before us extending to us the grace we need. Our salvation is not simply the product of our own hard work, as Arian spirituality might suggest.

That the One Lord Jesus Christ was "incarnate of the Holy Spirit and the Virgin Mary" reminded them that God values and blesses the physical processes of pregnancy and birth, over against a tendency of late Roman culture to believe that women's biological functioning makes them more "animal-like" and less capable of holiness than men.

Just as significantly, "incarnate . . . of the Virgin Mary" told them that the life of virginity, whether for men or women, was a higher calling than that of marriage. Most modern Christians might disagree with this, but it is important to remember what the life of virginity meant in their context. For women, the fact that Mary was a virgin affirmed that whatever expectation society put on women to fulfill their social destinies, to become wives and mothers and submit to male authority, women had a freedom in God that allowed them to refuse to be defined and limited by their biology and social roles. The Holy Spirit did not reside in Mary because she was a good wife.

According to the creed, in Christ God "became truly human." To be truly human in fourth- and fifth-century theology meant to be functioning fully as the image of God, to be what God intends us to be. In Anthony's terms, God's intention is that we be fully loving of God and neighbor, as God is loving. Jesus Christ shows us what God's infinite love looks like when it is translated into human behavior. Because God in Christ is indeed human, in him we can see what we both need to be and can be. This vision of what human beings can be was individual, but it was also social.

Starting with the assumption that Jesus is in this sense a role model, "For our sake he was crucified . . . he suffered death" told the early monastics that, as he carried his love and his witness to God to the point of suffering for it, so should they expect to suffer daily. That he died a humiliating death modeled a Christian's willingness not to hold on to his or her dignity or need to be above reproach in seeking the well-being of the people to whom the Christian ministers. The affirmation carried both an element of constraint ("expect to be crucified") and an element of freedom ("you do not need to worry about your pride, your dignity, or your appearance of goodness").

"He will come to judge . . ." said to the monastics that because Christ is Judge, we must not assume this role ourselves.

God's judgments are always made on the basis of what people are actually capable of, given their life experiences and who they are, and we do not have access to the sort of knowledge necessary for such determinations. God can be counted upon to judge more gently and mercifully than human beings ever will.

To affirm the "Holy Spirit, the Lord, the giver of life" reminded the monastic that God is ever present with both the individual and God's people to encourage, to heal, and to enlighten the heart.

That the Holy Spirit "has spoken through the prophets" emphasized that the promises the monk lived out in the fourth century had their basis in God's ongoing and consistent revelation of God's self to God's people all the way back to Old Testament times, a revelation proclaimed in the Old Testament as well as the New. To confess "one holy catholic and apostolic church" was to acknowledge that God through the church was bringing and would continue to bring about the transformation of the whole world in order to fulfill the promise to Abraham that his descendants would be more numerous than the sands on the shore of the sea.

On the other hand, the confession that the church was both "one" and "catholic" probably did not suggest to early monastics that it should be uniform in its practice, and perhaps not even in the expression of its faith. Early monastics in Egypt and Syria assumed that it was the task of the individual to find a Christian way of life suited to his or her temperament. It did suggest to them, however, that the church should be "one" in an even more significant sense: in its confession, in its witness to and care for the world, and in its care and concern for all its parts. They understood this unity to be the result of Christians' faithful transmission of the teaching and witness of the apostles up until their own time.

SOME FURTHER MODERN ECUMENICAL CONCLUSIONS

I hope the preceding paragraphs suggest the lively interchange of doctrine and the Christian life in the early church, at least as it relates to the Nicene Creed. But in addition to the help it offers in the understanding of the Nicene Creed, I believe that the serious study of early monastic spirituality has much to contribute to modern ecumenism. Broadly speaking, for those communions that have understood the history of the fourth-century church as at least gravely compromised by its intertwining with the political world, a glimpse into early monasticism should encourage them to look again to see whether they do not after all find some ancestors there. In the same way, those communions that stress the centrality of love in the Christian life over against doctrinal purity might find themselves much more present in the fourth-century church than they could have suspected.

Conversely, those communions that in ecumenical dialogue feel the need to emphasize the preservation of pure doctrine inherited from the early church can remind themselves of the importance of the larger context in which doctrine developed. Further, those groups that stress the importance of the clerical, hierarchical structure of the church as guarantor of truth and therefore have difficulty understanding communions that are suspicious of such structures can also study with profit the meaning of early monasticism as a lay movement.

Knowing something of the convictions of fourth-century monastic spirituality can help the historian of the ancient church enormously in understanding the meaning of early Christian doctrine. These same convictions shared in the context of our ecumenical work together can also further our work together. Love, both of God and of each other, after all, is at the center of what we are about. In the context of that love, we too must remember that God does "come to each of us according to our need." Many of our differences and the things that alienate our communions need to be understood and overcome, but many need to be understood and respected as part of the mystery of the work of the Holy Spirit. Like the early monastics, we too must remember that it is a risky business for us to believe that we, either individually or as representatives of our communions, are in a position to decide for the whole church who does or does not belong fully to the people of God. Judgmentalism in all its force drives us away from each other, sometimes even out of the body of Christ. All of us together need to share in a common pursuit of a humility that enables us to remember that whatever good we have or do, whatever common life we share, it is possible only because God has given it to us.

The Fourth-Century
Cappadocian Witness

ROSEMARY JERMANN

Although they were more successful than anyone before them in working out a trinitarian vocabulary, the Cappadocians were neither

> wedded to a formula nor determined to impose a set form of words which should subsequently be a compulsory text for deciding what was and what was not orthodoxy. There never has been a single formula adopted by the majority of Christians designed to express the doctrine of the Trinity, and the Cappadocians never imagined that there could be one.[1]

This is an initially surprising statement given that communion with Gregory of Nyssa became a touchstone of orthodoxy.

When we refer to the Cappadocian contribution in church history, we invariably think of the trinitarian theology of Basil the Great (330-379), his brother Gregory of Nyssa (ca. 331–ca. 394), their friend Gregory of Nazianzus (ca. 329-390), and their influence at the Council of Constantinople. I do not question that

---

1. R. P. C. Hanson, *The Search for the Christian Doctrine of God* (Edinburgh: T. & T. Clark, 1988), p. 677.

contribution, but I believe it important to consider their contribution to the context in which the creed of Nicaea-Constantinople was articulated.

The Cappadocians did think they had reached an accurate expression of the scriptural witness within their culture,[2] but they were involved in Christian witness in other ways, and in their spirituality they were open to much variety. How do their spirituality and their Christian reaction to social conditions of the time influence our view of Christian history in the fourth century? In today's ecumenical context, can those traditions that do not accept the creed appropriate other elements from the Christian tradition in the fourth century? Can those traditions that do accept the creed see it as one of many elements that express the apostolic faith?

We shall focus on the period from 379 to 395, the reign of Theodosius. During this time the seat of both political and religious power moved definitively to Constantinople. True, Constantine had made Constantinople the capital, but emperors after him had taken up residence in other cities (Julian and Valens at Antioch), so that Constantinople had played only a secondary role. Before 379 the Cappadocians had been more oriented to Antioch. When Theodosius entered Constantinople, they naturally turned their attention to that city.

We shall look at social conditions in the Empire, specifically in Cappadocia and Constantinople, the reaction to these of church writers in that area at the time, and the basis of that reaction. Second, we shall consider the spirituality of the Cappadocians, indicate some connections with their theology, and suggest that attitudes in their spirituality can be helpful ecumenically.

SOCIAL LIFE

Two significant factors in social life of the era were the development of a state bureaucracy (which changed the ancient munic-

2. See Hanson, *The Search for the Christian Doctrine of God*, p. 731.

ipal organization) and the disappearance of the middle classes, with a consequent contrast between the luxury of the wealthy and the misery of the poor.[3] State bureaucracy here refers especially to administration of the provinces. The Empire was divided into dioceses, themselves composed of provinces.

To this point, the middle class, the bourgeoisie, had filled curial positions in the cities. In each city they levied taxes and administered various functions—public services, the baths, and the games. The games were a prominent part of city life. Held in amphitheaters, they included fights with animals, gymnastic games, and chariot races. There was much enthusiasm for the chariot races at Constantinople. Since the games required a great deal of attention and planning, it was a problem when so many of those who had been in charge left for provincial offices.

The bourgeoisie were attracted to these official provincial positions under Theodosius both because their duties in the cities had become burdensome and because as government centralized it offered more opportunities to advance their careers. They could raise themselves socially by becoming notaries or secretaries. Under Constantine, access to these official posts had been through stenography; under Julian it had been through general cultural education; now under Theodosius it was Latin and law that gave access to officialdom.

Who were the bourgeoisie? They were defined by birth, fortune, and classical culture.

Fortune, or property, usually meant land. In Antioch the bourgeoisie hardly ever lived in the country. It was the opposite in Gaul, where wealthy rural classes lived on their estates. It was apparently the same in Cappadocia. Gregory of Nyssa's family was typical. They owned property in Pontus so spread out, says Gregory, that they were subject to three prefects (*Life of Macrina*, *PL*, 46.965A). Yet this provincial bourgeoisie became poorer under Theodosius, while a class of nouveau riche was formed among the high officials who were favored with imperial benefits.

Classical culture—*paideia*—characterized the bourgeois

3. Unless otherwise indicated, the bulk of this section follows Jean Daniélou, *Le IVᵉ Siècle. Grégoire de Nysse et son milieu* (Paris, 1967), pp. 11-21.

milieu. The pagan Libanius attached even more importance to it than to religion, linking it to the ancient city. As Christians gained access to *paideia,* they were incorporated into the ancient city. It was in the era of Theodosius, with the Cappadocians and Ambrose, that Christianity replaced paganism as the transmitter of *paideia. Paideia* remained a mark of the ruling class in the Byzantine Empire. Other languages (Coptic, Syriac, Cappadocian, Armenian, Celtic, Germanic, and Punic) subsisted, but Greek in the East and Latin in the West remained a condition of access to the ruling class for a long time. And, of course, Latin and Greek were also the languages of official theology and of the councils.

We also have some knowledge of the rest of the population: artisans, peasants, workers, tradesmen, and slaves. Gregory of Nyssa negotiated with artisans to build a martyrium. He thought those of Cappadocia charged too much, and so he tried to get his friend Amphilocus to put him in touch with artisans in Iconium. He refers to the tradesmen in his complaint that when one went to the money changer, one received a speech on whether the Son was begotten or unbegotten; when one asked the price of bread, one heard that the Father was greater than the Son; at the bath, one was told the Son came from nonbeing (*Oration on the Deity of the Son and the Holy Spirit, PL,* 46.554-76).

We note that Gregory speaks of the opinions of these tradesmen. Elsewhere he stresses that Arian doctrines came from humble origins. Aetius was a blacksmith, Eunomius the son of a peasant. What credit could one give to opinions of such people (*PL,* 45.260D, 264B)?

Peasants could be small property owners (gradually being wiped out by taxes), farmers, slaves, or agricultural workers. Hunters and fishermen were important in Cappadocia. Gregory's own family was involved in hunting.

Elements common throughout the Roman Empire were also found in Cappadocian society—an attraction to Constantinople and a centralized administration. Cappadocia supplied many officials for the government—which weakened provincial life. Socially, the gap grew between property owners and the lower classes. The latter, pressured by taxes, were often reduced to lives of desperation. A contrast between rich and poor is notable in the sermons of Basil, John Chrysostom, and Gregory of Nyssa. Basil preached several sermons against the rich when an earthquake destroyed Nicaea in 368. He began the tradition of bishops taking on the role of helping the poor and downtrodden.[4]

The gap between rich and poor was exacerbated by several factors. The lower classes bore the brunt of the tax burden, landowners exerted terrible pressure on those who worked the land (Chrysostom says landowners were more cruel than the barbarians), and usurers continued to lend money to the poor who were already overwhelmed with debt.

On the other hand, luxury was evident in the homes and country villas. Gregory describes dwellings with wonderful gardens and table settings (PL, 44.653, 1238A; 1172D; 46.468B). He criticizes lavish after-dinner drinking sessions replete with singing, mime, and concerts. During the dancing and celebrations in houses of the wealthy, he wrote, the cries of the blind and lame were drowned out by the singing and laughter within: "Christ's friends are chased away, and within, . . . some vomit . . . and others fall asleep" (PL, 46.468C-D).

Such luxury was not possible without an accumulation of wealth by some and an impoverishment of others. Gregory was one of many who denounced the usury that fueled this situation (PL, 46.433-452). When it was time to pay a debt, a creditor had no pity and would insist on sale of the debtor's house (PL, 46.445D). Lending at interest is simply theft, said Gregory (PL, 46.672B-C). Money, like brass, is a sterile thing, and we cannot expect it to be fruitful, he insisted (PL, 46.441D). Finally, there was a scriptural basis for his objection: "If you lend money to your brother, you shall not oppress him" (Exod. 22:25), and "Lend, expecting nothing in return" (Luke 6:35).

Besides the poor, there was another sorry group—those who suffered long-term illness. Their lot was a miserable one in the pagan world. The lepers especially were rejected. Gregory

4. See Charles Kannengiesser, "The Spiritual Message of the Great Fathers," in *Christian Spirituality: Origins to the Twelfth Century,* ed. Bernard McGinn, John Meyendorff, and Jean Leclercq (New York: Crossroad, 1986), p. 68.

vividly describes them dressed in rags, walking on all fours, gripping a piece of wood in an amputated stump (*PL*, 46.477A-B), banned from public assemblies, condemned to exile (*PL*, 46.477B-D). Basil seems to have been the first to found an institution for lepers at Caesarea. There were hospices for the poor in some villages, and Julian set up others to compete with those of the Christians. But Basil's had wider scope, being open to all those who were unfortunate.

By contrast Libanius, who knew lepers at Antioch, had nothing but scorn for them. He was a conservative, aligned with institutions, concerned to maintain the ruling class. The lower classes in society represented for him a refusal to accept the existing order. He believed the poor to be lazy and viewed Christian charitable institutions as a means of maintaining abuses.

The Christian writers, coming from the perspective of the human being as image of God, expressed principles by which society was to be judged. Gregory categorically condemned slavery as against the law of nature, asserting that human beings are free and autonomous by nature. Human freedom is one way of imaging God. The value of a human being cannot be paid for at any price: "How many little mites will you pay out for the image of God?" (*PL*, 46.664C). How many images on coins will be exchanged for the image of God?

On the principle of sharing wealth, Gregory believed such words as *mine* and *yours* to be fatal. As sun, air, and God's grace are common to all, so should other goods be at the disposal of all (*PL*, 46.463B). In his spirituality, Gregory viewed social ills as limitations in the human condition.

The scriptural vision of the human image of God evident in the Cappadocians' preaching led them to an active involvement in attempts to better society. The fact that we find nothing in the creed regarding this commitment suggests that we should view the Cappadocian contribution to the creed in the context of that community's commitment to the apostolic faith—which included commitment to Christian principles they thought should govern society. It also suggests the importance of looking beyond the confines of the creed itself to take account of other ways that

Christianity was being expressed in the fourth century. A cursory examination of the forms of spirituality in Cappadocia will show consistency with Cappadocian theology and with the credal profession. It was a spirituality with room for much variety.

SPIRITUALITY

The era under Theodosius was a time not only of dogmatic discussion but also of intense spirituality—in figures such as Gregory of Nazianzus, John Chrysostom, Gregory of Nyssa, Ambrose, Augustine, and Martin—which was evidenced especially in monasticism. There were centers of spirituality in Syria, Egypt, Palestine, and Gaul. This spirituality was expressed in many different forms—by hermits, clusters of hermits, cells with two or three living together, and whole communities. It was also the era of the bishop-monk—Augustine at Tagaste, Basil and Gregory of Nyssa in Cappadocia.

Eustathius, Bishop of Sebaste, had carried asceticism to an excess. He influenced Basil's interest in monasticism, though Basil parted ways with him theologically because of Eustathius's stand against the divinity of the Holy Spirit.

Macrina, Basil's sister, was instrumental in making their property on the Iris River in Pontus into a monastic site for women. Basil was impressed with the group and himself founded a group for men in Annesi.[5] First he visited monastic sites in Egypt, Palestine, and Syria. Then he embraced the monastic life upon his return, praying that he might imitate the monks he had visited. He did not originally intend to start a religious community, since he saw the life of perfection as a living out of the gospel and as intended for all, lay and monk alike.

Basil wrote a rule by gathering texts from the New Testament summarizing what Christian life should be. He strove to channel the zeal for ascetic practice into gospel virtues. Later his brother Gregory of Nyssa would write the theology of the spiritual life, supplying a theological foundation for the tradition from Antony

5. Kannengiesser, "The Spiritual Message of the Great Fathers," p. 68.

and Pachomius. Basil is often called the administrator, the organizer, but we glimpse his spiritual depth when he speaks of God's "unstinting goodness" and "deeply desired beauty."[6]

Longing always for the contemplative life, Gregory of Nazianzus nevertheless accepted active duties so he could be both "useful to myself as are the contemplatives and useful to others as are those who embrace active life" (PL, 27.1049-1050). But he always mourned his loss of privacy. His way was more heremetical than cenobitic. He praised community life but added, "If one wishes to live alone with Christ alone, that also is good" (PL, 27.643A). His own life alternated between periods of solitude and activity.

Gregory's spirituality of solitude was essentially contemplative, a mental activity. Theology was contemplation; contemplation was theology. The object of contemplation was the Trinity. His writing witnesses to this again and again. He is a mystic of the divine *ousia*, says Daniélou.[7] In contrast to Gregory of Nyssa, his was a mysticism of light.

Gregory believed the bishops and priests had a role in maintaining orthodoxy, but only if they were contemplative and philosophically trained. He found much to criticize in the clergy of his day and was especially insistent on their need for training in Scripture.[8]

Gregory of Nyssa's spiritual teaching is worth considering in greater detail because he summarizes much in the other two Cappadocians and adds his own stamp of originality. Four aspects are considered here.[9]

6. Hex I, 2, cited by Hanson in *The Search for the Christian Doctrine of God*, p. 687.

7. Daniélou, *Grégoire de Nysse et son milieu*, p. 67.

8. "My inclination is to avoid all assemblies of bishops, because I have never seen any council come to a good end, nor . . . be a solution of evils. On the contrary, it usually increases them. You always find there love of contention and love of power" (Let 130, cited by J. Stevenson in *Creeds, Councils and Controversies* [London: SPCK, 1978], p. 150). On his assertion of their need for training in Scripture, see Kannengiesser, "The Spiritual Message of the Great Fathers," p. 70.

9. This follows Jean Daniélou's interpretation. See *Platonisme et Théologie mystique: Essai sur la doctrine spirituelle de St. Grégoire de Nysse* (Paris, 1944). A succinct version can be found in Daniélou, *Grégoire de Nysse et son milieu*, pp. 184-87.

1. *Human freedom* is important in Gregory. It is a way human beings image God. It is so important that in a sense we are our own parents, "giving birth to ourselves by our own free choice" (*Life of Moses*, II, 3). We "make ourselves" into the kind of persons we become. This emphasis on human effort is always in the context of the incarnation. Only because human nature has been grasped and graced by the Word is one able to move toward God.

2. The *action of the Holy Spirit* is even more important. What Gregory professes in the creed is part of his spirituality. The Spirit is divine, and it is the wings of the dove that lift us into knowledge and experience of God. The Spirit is the dove who sets one's

> soul on fire after the manner of a bird who broods upon her eggs to hatch them . . . then gives birth to many excellent offsprings. These children are good actions, holy words, faith, piety, righteousness, temperance, chastity and purity. These are the children of the Spirit. (*PL*, 46.421B)[10]

In baptism "we bow before the Holy Spirit that we may be made what he is in fact and in name."[11] Later "The Word . . . bids the bride . . . to become beautiful by being changed . . . into the form of the Dove" (*Commentary on Canticles*, 5).[12]

3. *Movement from light to darkness.* One first moves from the darkness of sin to the light of the supernatural, where there is purification and restoration of the image of God. A growing resemblance to God makes possible a knowledge of God in the mirror of the soul. But this is not a knowledge of God's essence, for the divine essence *(ousia)* is incomprehensible.

The basis of the experience of God is the indwelling of the Trinity by grace, divinization of the soul. God is known by action

10. James J. Collins, "The Holy Spirit's Transforming Activity in Gregory of Nyssa's Sacramental Theology," *Diakonia* 12 (1977): 238. Author's translation from Migne.

11. Collins, "The Holy Spirit's Transforming Activity in Gregory of Nyssa's Sacramental Theology," p. 239. Author's translation from text in W. Jaeger, *Opera Gregorii Nysenni* (Leiden: Brill, 1952-), vol. 9, p. 229.

12. *From Glory to Glory: Texts from Gregory of Nyssa's Mystical Writings*, trans. and ed. Herbert Musurillo (Crestwood, N.Y.: St. Vladimir's Seminary Press, 1979), p. 118.

in the soul. The experience of God fills one, but in its advance the soul learns that true knowledge of God is to know he is unknowable (*PL*, 44.377A). One thus enters into darkness before the incomprehensibility of God: "our goal transcends all knowledge and is everywhere cut off from us by the darkness of incomprehensibility" (*Life of Moses*, 377A).[13] While we don't know God's essence or see him directly, we can experience God's presence: "He gives the soul some sense of his presence, even while he eludes her clear apprehension, concealed as he is by the invisibility of his nature" (*Commentary on Canticles*, 11).[14] The experience of God fills one, but in its advance the soul discovers that "to find God is to seek God ceaselessly" (*PL*, 46.97A).

4. *Perpetual progress*. The most basic characteristic of the human being for Gregory is its *movement* from nonbeing to being. The move from nonexistence to existence so radically imprints human nature that we never get away from it. We never stop moving. But movement is not necessarily progress. In climbing a sand dune, says Gregory, there can be much movement but no progress. Progress comes only when one's foot is firmly fixed on the rock of Christ. One begins to realize that progress itself is perfection. In other words, one never "reaches" perfection. One never absorbs all there is to know of God. It is like watching a spring bubbling up: "no matter how long you might stay at the spring, you would always be beginning to see the water. . . . [So is God's beauty] constantly being discovered anew" (*Commentary on Canticles*, 11).[15] This notion is expressed scripturally in Paul's "Forgetting what lies behind and *straining* (ἐπεκτεινόμονος) forward to what lies ahead" (Phil 3:13).

This character of *epektasis* is a human ratification of the human condition, a recognition of one's inability ever to possess God. The human condition of being finite is permanent, as is God's "condition" of being infinite. The distinction between Creator and creature will persist in eternity, and so will the constant growth in knowing God. At every point we will be

---

13. *From Glory to Glory*, p. 118.
14. *From Glory to Glory*, p. 248.
15. *From Glory to Glory*, p. 246.

filled to capacity, but each fresh experience of God will increase the capacity to know God: "As often as [the Word] says Arise, and Come, he gives us the power to rise and make progress" (*Commentary on Canticles,* 5).[16] And "Those who share in the divine Goodness . . . will always enjoy a greater and greater participation in grace throughout all eternity" (*Commentary on Canticles,* 3).[17]

For Gregory, then, knowledge of God is not a possession but a dispossession. "In place of relating God to the soul, he relates the soul to God. He thus passes from an intellectualist spirituality to the ecstatic spirituality of love."[18]

What does this spirituality context of the creed suggest for understanding the creed?

1. Gregory of Nyssa's teaching that our advance into God is an advance into darkness recalls the limits of the human mind in any attempt to express what we know of God, whether credally or otherwise. The Cappadocians did not imagine that they had articulated a definitive expression of God or of their faith. Nor do those traditions who continue to use the creed think that it exhausts the expression of their belief. Gregory's teaching on perpetual progress is consonant with the belief that there is no "rest" in the search for God or in attempts to formulate an adequate expression of faith.

2. The Cappadocian conviction that God is unknowable in his essence but that we can know his character by his action was expressed both in the creed and in Cappadocian spirituality. Acknowledging limits in speaking of what God is, they did not try to apply *homoousios* to the Spirit but indicated different activities of the Spirit.

The Holy Spirit that proceeds from the Father within the Trinity is also active in human hearts and is known there by divine activity. One way to *profess* God is in the creed; God can be *known* in relationship, through spirituality, through liturgy, through reading of Scripture, in community, and in solitude. In

16. *From Glory to Glory,* p. 191.
17. *From Glory to Glory,* p. 212.
18. Daniélou, *Grégoire de Nysse et son milieu,* p. 187.

our different traditions can we identify with any of the Spirit activity in the fourth century? With the activity of the Spirit in other ecclesial bodies today?

3. The variety of spiritualities in the fourth century can open us up to variety in the Spirit's action today. There was a difference in Cappadocia between Basil's stress on community living and Gregory of Nazianzus's fierce defense of his solitude.

Each tradition can ask what part of it is touched by what touched those in the fourth century. What insight into their spirituality helps us realize we are partaking of the same life-giving breath of God?[19] If we can touch base here, can we realize that what we express in the creed and in our spiritualities are not at variance with each other?

19. Lauree Hersch Meyer, Apostolic Faith study group, unpublished comments, March 1988.

Reflections on a *Kainotic* History: Basil of Caesarea as a Paradigm for Ecumenical Dialogue

PAULO D. SIEPIERSKI

The French historiographic school initiated by Marc Bloch and Lucian Fébvre in their review *Annales d'histoire économique et sociale* in 1929 has been called *New History*.[1] Its major contribution was opening the discipline of history to the contributions of other social sciences and acknowledging that no topic can be understood except in relation to other periods and topics. Insisting that in order to understand any event, history must be total—material civilization and culture must interpenetrate one another within a social analysis—New History focused on the average person, whose presence and action in history were not recorded. This *nouvelle Clio* is concerned with people in all dimensions of their activity and, unlike the English narrative tradition, does not rest on a linear conception of time.

Jean Delumeau, among others, has applied the *Annales* frame of mind to the history of Christianity, adding quantitative

1. For a description of that school's method, see Jacques Le Goff, *La Nouvelle Histoire* (Paris, 1978), and T. Stoianovich, *French Historical Method: The Annals Paradigm* (Ithaca: Cornell University Press, 1976).

history—statistical details—as the backbone of religious history. In his works Delumeau has sought to achieve rigor and imagination, keeping a balance between facts (New History ·impatience with factual history is well known) and mentalities. In *Catholicism between Luther and Voltaire: A New View of the Counter-Reformation*, his concern for attitudes and behaviors is quite clear. More recently he supervised the group who produced *Histoire vécue du peuple chrétien* (History as Lived by the Christian People).

His methodology is known in ecumenical circles.[2] *History as Lived by the Christian People* pays less attention to important figures, dogmas, and institutions of the church than to those who consumed—and to a certain extent asked for—the religious services and products of the church. Delumeau and his team attempted to draw conclusions from the sources they had (they were quite conscious of who had the monopoly of the word in Christianity's history) as to how common Christians might have lived their faith.

Enrique Dussel has also profited from New History's approach. He earned his doctorate in history at the Sorbonne in 1967, writing about the Hispanic-American bishops' defense of the Amerindians during the first two centuries of Iberian colonization in America. While Delumeau introduced quantitative history to religious studies, Dussel has emphasized the ultimate meaning of history—namely, liberation—and how one should understand history in the light of faith. Dussel advocates a history that goes beyond New History. The past is no longer, as Bloch had said, the historian's tyrant; on the contrary, the past has the potential to become *meaningful* in the present "so that it can provide eschatological thrust towards the future."[3] Dussel's

2. See Francesco Chiovaro, "History as Lived by the Christian People: Hypotheses for a New Methodic Approach to Christian History," in *Church History in an Ecumenical Perspective: Papers and Reports of an International Ecumenical Consultation Held in Basle, October 12-17, 1981*, ed. Lukas Vischer (Bern: Evangelische Arbeitsstelle Oekumene Schweiz, 1982).

3. Dussel, *History and the Theology of Liberation: A Latin American Perspective*, trans. John Drury (Maryknoll, N.Y.: Orbis Books, 1976), p. 28.

history is not merely a new history. Because of its liberating quality, it deserves to be called *kainotic*.[4]

THE POOR GIVE MEANING TO HISTORY

Historicity is a relational quality. A historical event is not historical in and of itself. It is historical because it was related to people's presence and activity in history. It is people who *historify* an event. Therefore, the subject of history is primarily people and their action in time and space. *Kainotic* history concentrates on a particular kind of people—the poor—because they reveal *kainotic* history's strictly Christian character.

In the process of selecting the most significant data for consideration from an infinity of events, the guiding element must be the presence of the oppressed. God's epiphany takes place more fully in the poor, thus giving historical significance to them.[5] To track the history of the poor is to verify the presence of God in human history; it is to access God from the *other* history, from the world of the oppressed. Accordingly, ecumenical scholars from around the world have concluded that

> The history of the Church is the Gospel actually experienced. The experience of the poor and oppressed people is especially important. Since it was to them that Jesus himself turned especially, we

4. It is *kainotic* because it is not only new in time *(neos)* but also new in nature, superior in value, and leads to the apocalyptic promise of a new *(kainos)* creation.

5. In Matthew 25 Jesus identified himself with the poor; the poor are the *personae* of Jesus. Thus one's relationship with God is expressed in his or her relationship with the poor. Acknowledging that fact, Dussel said that "in reference to the revealed criteria of historical interpretation there is one absolutely essential principle, and for history it can transform itself into a revealer of its strictly Christian character. . . . He who sees Jesus in the poor and serves him is the only one who can be saved. It appears that this should be the essential *criterion* of our history. It would be a history that raises questions regarding whatever problem and whatever description, questions such as: What relation does this have with the poor?" (*A History of the Church in Latin America: Colonialism to Liberation, 1492-1979,* trans. Alan Neely [Grand Rapids: William B. Eerdmans, 1981], pp. 304-5).

have here in a real sense the key to the correct interpretation of church history. The task of the historian is to trace out the history of the Gospel in relation to the poor and the oppressed.[6]

In order to relate meaningfully to the real world, church history has to address two worlds simultaneously, the past and the present. Because two-thirds of humanity live in a state of domination and dependence in which millions of people die young because of unjust social structures, it is natural that any meaningful church history must deal with the issue of liberation. The form in which Christians in the past struggled against exploitation must be rescued and presented in a way that enriches the agenda of the contemporary church in its mission for liberation.

Since the way the poor perceive their past is extremely important in shaping the way they see reality and understand reality, the task of church history becomes extremely important in the process of liberation.[7] And in such a task there is no neutrality. Church history has to choose between maintaining a situation of oppression and participating in the liberation of the oppressed.

THE CONSCIOUS PARTIALITY OF THE METHOD

Since an event does not exhaust itself in its occurrence or in the documents that record its occurrence, the interpreter must identify the event's effect in his or her own historical experience.[8]

6. *Church History in an Ecumenical Perspective*, p. 107.

7. Dussel has insisted that "liberation does not arise out of a vacuum but out of the negation of the liberation values of the past" (Roberto S. Goizueta, *Liberation, Method and Dialogue: Enrique Dussel and North American Theological Discourse* [Atlanta: Scholars Press, 1988], p. 163).

8. "True historical thinking must take account of its own historicality," writes Hans-Georg Gadamer. "Only then will it not chase the phantom of an historical object which is the object of progressive research, but learn to see in the object the counterpart of itself and hence understand both" (*Truth and Method*, trans. Garrett Barden and John Cumming [New York: Seabury Press, 1975], p. 267).

This means that a past event has the ability to cause other events in the present and the future. The interpreter can direct the effective power of a past event toward the liberation of the oppressed.

In the procedure to describe—that is, to recover the meaning—of an event, the interpreter is required to attend, to understand, to judge, and to act. In all these steps the interpreter is conditioned by the horizon of comprehension in which he or she is located. These limitations, if one applies Stassen's social ethics theory model to history, may be classified in three main dimensions: ground of meaning or theology, center of value or loyalties, and empirical definition of situation.[9]

The first dimension reveals the existential assumptions that condition the interpretation of an event. In an explicitly Christian framework, these assumptions are related to the existence of God and God's action in history; therefore, the concepts of the creation and of the mission of the church are essential in order to understand the limitations in this dimension. The second dimension reveals the loyalties of the interpreter, who always will be captive to one or more groups. It is impossible to interpret an event without allowing the values of a group to interfere or assist in the interpretation. These groups may be characterized by language, race, social class, confession of faith, and so on. The last dimension reveals how the interpreter perceives not only his or her situation but also the situation of the event. The rules of selection, synthesis, and interpretation of reality "are mostly unconscious, habitual, instantaneous and uncritical."[10] Therefore, the power those rules have in shaping perception constitutes a tremendous limitation to the interpreter's task. Yet without such rules, interpreters would hardly see. They would be like babies who have not yet learned rules of selection, synthesis, and interpretation of reality and hence do not comprehend what they see—do not, in fact, even *see* what adults see.

These limitations imposed by the interpreter's horizon of

9. See Glen Stassen, "A Social Theory Model for Religious Social Ethics," *Journal of Religious Ethics* 6 (1977): 9-37.
10. Stassen, "A Social Theory Model for Religious Social Ethics," p. 16.

comprehension imply that it is impossible to achieve total objectivity, since the same event can be interpreted from various perspectives and thereby suggest diverse meanings. Thus, total objectivity must be replaced by contextual objectivity. Moreover, the limitations also imply that it is impossible to achieve full nonsubjectivity, since any interpretation is affected by subjective historical, sociological, and economic conditionings.[11]

A critical interpretation presupposes taking into consideration those conditionings and choosing perspectives. A historical methodology that intends to cooperate in the liberation of the oppressed will be committed to the point of view of the poor. The task of rescuing the meaning of an event—curing the memory—is undertaken with the objective of providing a usable past promoting the emancipation of the marginalized.

Indeed, because historians no longer ignore the powerful role of historical interpretation, they face a paramount question in their task: For whom, for whose benefit, do they work? Dussel and Hoonaert have argued that the only possible answer is the formulation of a history from the viewpoint of the marginalized with the clear objective of contributing to their liberation. Such an approach requires a method quite different from the kind of history that aims at preserving rather than transforming institutions, which in Christian circles may be called Eusebian history.[12]

In order to preserve church institutions, church historians have produced historical interpretations oriented to intellectual history. In doing so they have revealed the historicity of individuals, but to a large extent they have dehistoricized the social structures in which they lived. Therefore, the major challenge for a non-Eusebian approach is not only to discover new facts but also and mainly to offer new interpretations of them. Eusebian history has made valuable contributions, and without its investigations it would be much more difficult to offer new

---

11. Dussel, *A History of the Church in Latin America*, pp. 300-301.
12. See Eduardo Hoornaert, *The Memory of the Christian People*, trans. Robert R. Barr (Maryknoll, N.Y.: Orbis Books, 1988), pp. 16-22.

interpretations of the old; nevertheless, the Eusebian preference for official theology, hierarchy, and accepted structures must be complemented and sometimes challenged by an "interpretation designed to empower communities and individuals to gain a sense of their identity in their pilgrimage for the future."[13]

New interpretations are possible not only because a shift in the present perspective—Eusebian to non-Eusebian—unveils different aspects of the event but also because the event itself has a reservoir of meaning that allows it to speak differently in new situations. In the case of early Christianity, it is dialectic social analysis that provides the best tools for discovering that surplus of meaning.

Dussel has explained that anadialectical method is dialectic in the positive sense. Beyond *(ano-)* the horizon of totality is produced the unfolding *(dia-)* of the comprehension of a new horizon *(logos)*.[14] Since totality is equated with the status quo, going beyond it entails identifying with the other whose exteriority is objectified by the totality.[15] Such identification brings a new perspective for a new interpretation of the event. Thus the point of departure of the anadialectical method is an ethical decision, an option on behalf of the poor.

Dialectical social analysis, which emphasizes the conflicts and contradictions of a system rather than its harmony and equilibrium (as functionalist social analysis does), eliminates the dangerous tendency of a historical interpretation to become excessively speculative, focusing only on theological categories. In order to become meaningful, an event must be placed within the social context of its time. The event gains meaning only when related to the other components of its system.

13. See "Teaching Church History from an Ecumenical Perspective," in *The Teachings of Ecumenics,* ed. Samuel Amirtham and Cyris H. S. Moon (Geneva, 1987), p. 115. On the need for new ways of thinking about the past, see T. V. Philip's essay "Church History in Ecumenical Perspective," in the same book, pp. 42-53.

14. Dussel, *Philosophy of Liberation,* trans. Aquilina Martinez and Christine Morkovsky (Maryknoll, N.Y.: Orbis Books, 1985), pp. 158-70.

15. See Goizueta, *Liberation, Method and Dialogue,* pp. 55-86.

THE PROBLEM OF COLLECTING EVIDENCE

Since history is traced mainly through documented sources, it always seems to be the history of the powerful. Only the powerful (at least until the rise of modern democracies) have had their history recorded; and what is more important, only the powerful have had the ability to preserve records for posterity.[16] So the history of the powerful became *the* history.[17] However, the perception of history is more than a mechanical consultation of sources. Historiography entails the interpretation of documents, and that requires a commitment to a certain point of view. Any discourse on a past event is made with a commitment to a present situation. Obviously there are different levels of commitment, but the interpreter, aware or not, will always be committed to a certain perspective.

So although the oppressed may lack *Historie* ("historical narrative"), they still can have *Geschichte* ("history"). Even if the oppressed lack evidence of their existence as an entity in the

16. This is especially true regarding early Christianity. Peter Brown has observed that contemporary authors "have made plain the mechanisms by which the aristocracies of the Hellenistic and Roman worlds had concentrated to themselves not only an almost total monopoly of real power, but also the ability to explain and record the political process. The 'grass roots' politics of lesser men, in their towns, in their *quartiers* and in their associations, survives only as so many vivid but tantalizing fragments. All that we can say is that it happened and happened vigorously. As a result, attempts to judge the role of the Christian church in Roman society from the first century onwards have been largely frustrated, not because the Christian evidence is slender, but because evidence of a similar quality for the non-aristocratic majority of the Roman world is, by comparison, almost nonexistent" (*The Role of the Christian Bishop in Ancient Society*, ed. Edward C. Hobbs and Wilhelm Wuellner [Berkeley: The Center, 1980], pp. 16-17).

17. Jaroslav Pelikan has observed that "to the victor, it has been said, belong the spoils. It is likewise to the victor that there usually belongs the privilege of providing both the definitive historical narrative of how the triumph was achieved and the official explanation of why it came out as it did. . . . And when a later historian . . . undertakes to recast the narrative . . . from the perspective of the conquered rather than of the victor . . . such a historical reconstruction is still largely dependent on what has survived, or more precisely, on what the victors have permitted to survive and what their successors have gone on to edit and collect" (*The Excellent Empire: The Fall of Rome and the Triumph of the Church* [San Francisco: Harper & Row, 1987], pp. 15-16).

past—they are invisible in history—they still can rescue their past, since the oppressed actually participated in events. Because of the actual existence of oppression, interpreters committed to the liberation of the oppressed can identify in past events the presence of the oppressed and give voice to their *Geschichtlichkeit* ("historical significance"), aiming at their liberation. Again, existential historicity is essential for liberation. When interpreters make the oppressed aware of their historicity, therefore revealing the historicity of oppressive social structures, both become participants in the *Freiheitsgeschichte* ("history of the freeing of humanity"). When the link between the oppressed in the present and in the past is restored, the oppressed are enabled to find identity and strength from the past that help guide them in their struggle for liberation.

A *KAINONIC* READING OF NICAEA

Anadialectical history "is not concerned primarily with the sequential, 'objective' account of historical events as such (though these, of course, are important) but with the attempt to derive meaning from those events *in the light of* present experience of a people." Thus, historical analyses cannot be undertaken "in isolation from theological, epistemological, etc. . . . considerations, but inform and are informed by those considerations."[18]

What considerations must be taken in using the Nicene Creed as a central element for expressing the apostolic faith today? From the point of view of the poor, a few important considerations should shape the search for a meaningful account of the Nicene event.

First of all, the creed was drafted by bishops for bishops. Earlier creeds, baptismal in character, were designed for all Christians. The Nicene Creed, on the other hand, was designed for the leadership.

Second, the council was convened under the auspices of the

18. Goizueta, *Liberation, Method and Dialogue*, p. 55.

imperial power: an oppressive regime not only sponsored the gathering but influenced its outcome. The divisiveness of the council, clearly manifested in the following years, was partially consolidated by the presence of the imperial power.

Third, the council's formulations were too restrictive. Naturally, the council was a product of the tensions of that time and dealt with issues related to the divinity of the Son. The council did not deal with Jesus' humanity, his sojourn among people, which is of extreme importance for a liberating christology.

These are just a few considerations. Many others must be acknowledged. What was the people's participation in the council? How did the council's formulations affect the way people expressed their faith? How did the council legitimize the political power? What were the social implications of an official episcopacy? How did that affect the life of the marginalized (those who live at the margins of the official space)?

Many other questions could be asked about the ecumenical importance of the Nicene event. In asking such questions, one does not neutralize the event but in fact rescues its meaning. Indeed, a *kainonic* approach will point out aspects of the event that have been overshadowed by other perspectives and then *discover* its meaning for the great majority of contemporary Christians.

THE MEANING OF BASIL OF CAESAREA'S MINISTRY

Among the many events that took place in the fourth century, the ministry of Basil of Caesarea imposes itself as a paradigm for ecumenical dialogue. The fourth century was not characterized solely by doctrinal disputes. An unjust social order posed a special challenge to Christianity. Deep social inequalities were being aggravated by natural cataclysms, and for the first time Christianity was in position to promote social justice and relief for the poor. Before Constantine, Christianity had exercised basically curative efforts, working almost solely on the consequences of social injustice. But with the ascension of Christianity to the highest sphere of political power, Christianity saw itself in position to exercise preventive activity as well and thus to change the causes of social inequalities. Unfortunately, if as a whole Christianity met the challenges posed by paganism in areas like theology and spirituality, it failed to impose a social order based on Christian values. Basil is one of the few exceptions of his time. The bishop of Caesarea added orthopraxy to his orthodoxy; he lived out the consequences of the double nature of Christ and the full divinity of the Holy Spirit. His commitment to the Christian faith led him to experience a liberation from the things of this world, reflected in his change of social place, and to become a liberator of the oppressed, reflected in his pastoral activity.

This aspect of Basil's *leitourgia* has not been fully appreciated because past studies have lacked a perspective of commitment to the oppressed. The two major works on Basil's social teachings, by Yves Courtonne and Stanislas Giet, appeared in France some fifty years ago as a reaction to socialist influence and thus presented a conservative view of Basil's social involvement.[19] Barnim Treucker explored further Basil's social activity but restricted his study to Basil's correspondence.[20] Recently Jean Gribomont showed that Giet was wrong in suggesting that Basil considered the sharing of properties a counsel rather than a precept,[21] and he began to develop a liberating reading of Basil.[22] Paul J. Fedwick has also criticized Giet's unsuccessful attempt to disclaim Basil's "communism."[23] However, no one has approached Basil's social involvement exclusively from the perspective of the oppressed. The anadialectical method helps to fill that gap. A reading of Basil from the point of view of the

19. The volumes were *Saint Basile. Homélies sur la richesse*, ed. and trans. Yves Courtonne (Paris, 1935), and Stanislas Giet's *Les idées et l'action sociales de S. Basile* (Paris, 1941).

20. Treucker, *Politische und sozialgeschichtliche Studien zu den Basilius-Briefen* (Bonn, 1961).

21. Gribomont, "Un aristocrate révolutionnaire, évêque et moine: S. Basile," *Augustinianum* 17 (1977): 179-91.

22. See the volume edited by Gribomont, "Commandments du Seigneur et libération évangélique," *Studia Anselmiana* 70 (1977).

23. Fedwick, *The Church and the Charisma of Leadership in Basil of Caesarea* (Toronto: Pontifical Institute of Mediaeval Studies, 1978), p. 96 n. 128.

oppressed will point out his experience of liberation and his praxis on behalf of the oppressed.

Indeed, such a reading will show that Basil lived out his liberation through a *leitourgia* directed to the liberation of the poor. In his monastic community, Basil revived the old Christian ideal of *koinōnia* lived out by the first Christians in Jerusalem. In making the sharing of possessions a central commandment in the community, Basil gave evidence of his option for the poor. Although the Basilian communities do not present all characteristics of a modern perception of liberation (since the objective conditions for the development of such characteristics were lacking), one nevertheless senses in the Basilian project practices of resistance against theocratic power. Indeed, the Basilian communities constituted a vehicle for the defense of the marginalized and the formulation of an alternative for the established society.

Basil's *kērygma*, which came out of his community, evidenced his genuine engagement in the liberation of the oppressed. Like the organic intellectual Antonio Gramsci, Basil rejected the interests of his class and denounced the unjust structures that dehumanized the poor. He articulated a discourse to confront the powerful and comfort the marginalized. Even his apologetic proclamation, which may at a first glance seem abstract, intellectualized, and distant from the people, since fourth-century heresies had no connection with the faith of ordinary people,[24] actually carried a liberating objective. In affirming Jesus' double nature, very God become very human, Basil automatically confirmed the sacredness of human life. Similarly, in affirming the equality of the Spirit within the Trinity, Basil set the ground for construction of a nonhierarchical doctrine of God the liberating components of which have only recently been grasped.[25]

24. See J. Lebreton, "Le désaccord de la foi populaire et de la théologie savante dans l'Église chrétienne du 3ième siècle," *Revue d'histoire ecclésiastique* 19 (1924): 481-506; 20 (1925): 5-37.

25. See Leonardo Boff, *Trinity and Society*, trans. Paul Burns (Maryknoll, N.Y.: Orbis Books, 1988), and Jürgen Moltmann, *The Trinity and the Kingdom: The Doctrine of God*, trans. Margaret Kohl (New York: Harper & Row, 1981).

The former aristocrat assumed the life of a servant in his community. Basil demonstrated his liberation in changing social place and living with the marginalized. Basil's *diakonia* sealed his engagement on behalf of the poor with action and deeds. In providing food for the hungry, shelter for the homeless, relief for the lepers, clothes for the naked, and comfort for the prisoners, Basil recognized the person of the Lord in the destitute.

In seeking a common expression of the apostolic faith, the ecumenical dialogue is surely opening channels for actualizing Christian unity. However, apostolic faith cannot be restricted to council formulations. On the contrary, the meaning of the apostolic faith for contemporary Christianity must be found in the daily life of those who embraced the apostolic faith. The way people lived out their faith is more meaningful than the abstract formulations of the councils. Those have importance only when they reflect a popular concern.

The Nicene Creed and the Unity of Christians

EDUARDO HOORNAERT

1. The first impression we get from a reading of the "Symbol of the Faith" drawn up by the Fathers of Nicaea (325) and completed by those of Constantinople (381) is that of a text affirmative in the extreme. The formulation is lapidary, incisive, insistent: "God from God, Light from Light, true God from true God." One suspects a clear and resolute position taken against the tendencies of the Alexandrian priest Arius and those who followed him in relativizing the relationship between Jesus and God. The Fathers wanted none of this relativization. For them, Jesus was "Son of God, alone begotten of the Father, that is to say, of the substance of the Father, not created but begotten, of the same substance as the Father" *(homoousios, consubstantialis)*. They affirmed with insistence the unique character of the Jesus event, his absolute uniqueness in history, his absolutely unique relation to God and consequently to all of us: "Who sees me, sees the Father" (John 14:9). They affirmed with one stroke the importance of Jesus in the history of humanity. He comes to reveal to us the Father, to communicate his way of thinking and feeling, of reacting to things.

The Council of Nicaea did not mainly take a position on the

doctrine of the Trinity in itself, without relation to us; they signified above all an interpretation of society, a peculiar way of perceiving human society.[1] The council was not a closed discussion among specialists in theology but an interpretation of the history of humanity. "He came down for us and for our salvation." It is quite clear that if the One who descended is the Son of God himself, his coming among us takes on an importance beyond comparison. That is what Nicaea and Constantinople affirm in the face of Arianism, which seemed to hesitate on this central point. Jesus is unique. Only he can show definitively the meaning of things. There is no one after him to perfect or clarify his message.

Right away the gospel of Jesus becomes a universal message of critical importance for all humanity, be it Christian or not. Hence, Nicaea acquires a central importance in the history of Christianity for having made things so clear: Jesus is unique for all, for all ages of history and all regions of the world. This is what the Council of Ephesus (431) wished to say when it affirmed that the text of Nicaea, later enriched by the "addenda" of Constantinople, was henceforth unchangeable and meant to be proclaimed by all Christians as "Symbol of the Faith." The struggle of the Fathers of Nicaea against Arianism was a struggle of the absolute affirmation of Jesus and the unique value of his gospel against those who in one way or another would open the door to relativization.

2. This being firmly established, one nevertheless cannot avoid a certain frustration in reading the symbol of Nicaea. While the text affirms categorically the absolute uniqueness of Jesus in the history of humanity, it does not state the exact purpose for which Jesus and his Father are One in thought, feeling, and way of being. The text affirms that Jesus is the Unique One but does not make clear *why*, given the drama of humanity. If in fact Jesus is "descended for us and for our salvation," it is quite clear that there is a drama, a great question to resolve. But of this the text says nothing further; it does not explain the function of this very special and even unique way

---

1. See Leonardo Boff, *A Trindade, A Sociedade e A Libertação* (Petropolis: Vozes, 1986).

of being of Jesus. Son of God, certainly, but for what reason? To save us? Save us from what? Or simply to prove to us that God is Love? The text limits itself to saying that Jesus "descended from heaven for us and for our salvation"—a vague expression that could be explained in diverse ways, as indeed it has been in the course of history. Some catechisms say that he came to deliver us from "our sins," thus giving a penitential tone to Christianity. Having been reticent on this point concerning the concrete interpretation of the life, passion, and death of Jesus, Nicaea opened the door to the most diverse interpretations, and above all to an ahistorical reading of the Christian event.

The addenda of Constantinople remedied to a certain extent this lack of historicity by giving three precious indications that lead us to a historical reading of the Christian event: "also crucified for us under Pontius Pilate" (Staurōthenta te hyper hēmōn epi Pontiou Pilatou—Crucifixus etiam pro nobis sub Pontio Pilato). Staurōtheis especially is a precious indication, because we know the cross was an instrument of torture used in the Roman Empire. Jesus was tortured. Why? What was the historical reason for this torture? The hyper hēmōn indicates an alliance with groups of people in society. With what kinds of people was Jesus concretely allied? And what groups were against him? In the third place, the epi Pontiou Pilatou contains both historiographic and sociological indications, since the people of Palestine lived under the domination of the Roman Empire, and Jesus was delivered to death by the representative of Roman power through a process built up against him.

One may thus ask why the text of Nicaea does not make clear the causes of the torture, the condemnation, and the putting to death of Jesus. I think the reason must be sought in the concrete circumstances of the development of the document.

3. A reading of chapters 2 and 3 of the Life of Constantine by Eusebius of Caesarea may throw light on this point. The council of Nicaea was made possible by the active collaboration of Emperor Constantine, who sent the invitations, facilitated the means of transportation (the imperial post), offered the place of reunion (the imperial palace at Nicaea), participated actively in the discussions, and (according to Eusebius) drew up the final

text of the resolutions of the council. On reading the letter of convocation as it has been given us by Eusebius, one understands that Constantine concerned himself only in a very limited way with the so-called theological aspects of the Arian dispute, and in fact minimized and even ridiculed them:

> Such research, which is prescribed by no law, but suggested by idleness, mother of vain disputes, may well serve as an exercise of the spirit, but should be kept among ourselves and not launched lightly into public assemblies or confided inconsiderately to the ears of the people.[2]

It was only episcopal pressure that induced Constantine to accept the theological dimension of the debate with Arianism; his principle concern was with the political dimension of the matter. He viewed the conflict with Arianism as above all inopportune and calling for a quick resolution. It was a needless dispute among brothers, and it should not be handled in public.[3] It is quite true that Eusebius does not represent well the posture of all the bishops of Nicaea and that therefore his information should be read critically, but what he says about the role of Constantine at the council of Nicaea is confirmed by other ancient historians such as Socrates and Sozomenos and is today accepted unanimously by historians of Christianity.[4] One may say that the emperor had quite simply taken the council in hand and brought it where he wanted it:

> He listened to all with a great patience. He followed with attention the discussion of problems. He took over the assertions made by correcting them or by softening them, in such a way as to prevent the discussion from degenerating into dispute. . . . Those whom he could not convince, he made blush. When someone spoke judiciously, he eulogized him. He preached concord to all. He arrived at his goals and put everyone in agreement on the point at issue.[5]

2. *Vita Constantini* (VC), 2.69.
3. VC, 2.71.
4. On the subject of the ideological positions of Eusebius of Caesarea, see my book *The Memory of the Christian People* (Maryknoll, N.Y.: Orbis Books, 1988), pp. 11-22.
5. VC, 3.13.

It was the intervention of the power of the Constantinian state that conferred on the text of Nicaea its character, at once theological and political.

It is perhaps the relatively nonmilitant character of the symbol of Nicaea that has made of it over the course of centuries a doxological text, in praise of the holy Trinity, rather than a text that involves the Christian and responds to questions the Christian community faces. The symbol has long been a text used in the liturgy, symbolizing the union of Christians who recite together the same words of praise, thanksgiving, and proclamation, rather than a text that calls them to action.

One must therefore see the council of Nicaea and this formulation of its credo as part of a process of change in the Christian ecclesial model. Nicaea is situated in a movement that has substituted for the pluriform, communitarian, and largely democratic model of the origins of Christianity a uniform and "catholic," hierarchical and clerical model. The historian Sozomenos, who wrote one hundred years after the death of Constantine, summed up the transformation well:

> Under earlier emperors those who worshipped Christ, though they differed in their opinions, were considered the same by Hellenizers and were similarly badly treated. They could not interfere with each other because of their common sufferings, and for this reason each group used to assemble without difficulty and form a church. . . . But after this law [the Constantinian antiheresy law] they could neither assemble publicly, because they were prevented, nor in secret, because the bishops and clergy kept them under observation.[6]

The imperial church, represented by the emperor and his bishops, took the offensive against "heresies," which were often attempts by churches to conserve in a radical form certain traits of the origins of Christianity, such as Montanism and Marcionism. It is difficult today to offer an impartial judgment on these discordant ecclesial models, because many texts have been

6. Sozomenos, *Ecclesiastical History*, 2.32.3, cited by W. J. Sheils and D. Wood in *Voluntary Religion* (London: Basil Blackwell, 1986), p. 1.

burned, as historians Socrates and Eusebius note in different places.[7] The writings of Arius were burned on the recommendation of the council of Nicaea, as were those of the majority of "heretics." A veritable *damnatio memoriae* took place to create the new memory of the Christian people, a post-Constantinian memory: one church, one empire, one faith, one truth.[8] The unity and even uniformity of the faith proclaimed symbolizes, and in a very concrete way realizes, the unity of the empire. Constantine foresaw this, with perspicacity.

4. The history of the production of the text of Nicaea-Constantinople enters into contradiction with that which it affirms. While it affirms that Jesus was "crucified for us under Pontius Pilate" and that he was put to death by the power of the Roman state (at least with the favor of this power), it was elaborated under the presidency of the one who represented in that epoch the power of the state. This is contradictory and obliges us to make a distinction between the theological content, properly speaking, of the text and the reticences or even camouflages that were imposed upon it in the process of its elaboration. It is necessary therefore to try to determine what was camouflaged at Nicaea, and the best way for us to do that is the historical way. In going back to the history before Nicaea, one is able to verify how the Christians of the first generations understood their adhesion to Christianity. One very beautiful example can be found in the baptismal symbols, the texts pronounced on the occasion of baptism, but also in other texts that circulated among the communities.[9]

A general impression emerges: to become Christian in that epoch signified making a choice—a choice between life and death, good and evil, light and darkness. The words vary, but the fundamental idea that emerges is well defined in the theme of the "two ways" that runs like a golden thread through the texts of primitive Christianity. Let us quickly look at some expressions of this theme from the time of oral tradition, trans-

---

7. Socrates, *Ecclesiastical History,* 1.9, 7.7.1; Eusebius, VC, 3.65.3.
8. See *The Memory of the Christian People,* pp. 151-64.
9. See *The Memory of the Christian People,* pp. 151-64.

mitted from mouth to mouth, in the form of counsels relating to daily life.

- The *Gospels* witness to the theme in Matthew 6:24: "One cannot serve two masters. For one will reject the one and love the other, be faithful to one and reject the other. You cannot serve God and Mammon."
- The *Didachē*, a Syrian or Palestinian text from about the year 120, proclaims in chapter 5 that the "Path of Death" is represented by different sins, among which one finds the following: "Not pitying a poor man; not laboring for the afflicted; not knowing him that made them; murderers of children; destroyers of the handwork of God; turning away from him that is in want; afflicting him that is distressed; advocates of the rich; lawless judges of the poor; utter sinners [*panthamartētoi*]."
- Chapters 18 to 20 of the *Epistle of Barnabas* explain the "Way of Darkness" as follows: "Those who attend not with just judgment to the widow and orphan; persons who pity not the needy, who labor not in aid of him who is overcome with toil; who are murderers of children, destroyers of the workmanship of God; who turn away him that is in want; who oppress the afflicted; who are advocates of the rich; who are unjust judges of the poor; who are in every respect transgressors [*panthamartētoi*]."
- In the second "Mandate" (nos. 4 to 6) of the *Shepherd of Hermas*, one finds the same indications under the heading of "good actions": "The good deeds are helping widows, looking after orphans and the needy, rescuing the servants of God from necessities, being hospitable, never opposing anyone, reverencing the aged, watching the brotherhood, not oppressing debtors and the needy."
- The *Apostolic Constitutions*, the largest juridical and liturgical collection of early Christianity, drawn up in Constantinople or Syria around 380, containing many texts that circulated among the Christian communities, repeat the theme of the "two ways" in Book 7, section 1: "Be not a lover of money, lest you serve Mammon instead of God. . . . Thou

shalt not grudge to give to the poor; thou shalt not turn away from him that is needy; thou shalt communicate in all things to thy brother, and shalt not say 'thy goods' are thine own; for the common participation of the necessaries of life is appointed to all men by God."[10]

One may say that the symbol of Nicaea constitutes the first summary of the Christian faith that makes no allusion to the ethical imperative so characteristic of early Christianity, which one may, in concert with the Third Episcopal Conference of Latin America at Puebla (Mexico) at the end of January 1979, characterize as the "option for the poor." The failure of the symbol of Nicaea to speak of "the option for the poor" distanced it from early Christian tradition and served to inaugurate a new Christian tradition that no longer demanded of Christians a firm and public stand toward the poor and their poverty.

5. The indefiniteness on the subject of a universal proclamation of Christian faith in ethical terms continues in our day, and it is exactly on this point that we today are most distant from the Christianity of early times, which was founded on a theology of the divine election of the marginalized of society and a communitarian ethic of alliance with the struggle of the poor for their liberation.[11]

To give only one example: recently (in 1987) the Belgian episcopate, moved by the dynamic of a "new evangelization," produced a very beautiful volume entitled *The Book of the Faith*, which is in general a commentary on the Symbol of Nicaea-Constantinople. In commenting on the passion and death of Jesus, this book does not even mention the addenda of Constantinople—*staurōthenta hyper hēmōn epi Pontiou Pilatou*. It merely says that "the Cross appeared only as a revelation of the love of God for us," a commentary on John 3:11. No reference is made to the concrete action of Jesus for the rejected of this world, the marginalized of Palestinian society with whom he stood in

---

10. Citations are taken from *The Ante-Nicene Fathers*, 10 vols. (Grand Rapids: William B. Eerdmans, 1950-1951), 7.379; 1.137-49; 2.25; 7.465ff.

11. See *The Memory of the Christian People*, pp. 41-70.

solidarity in such a moving manner, nor to the relation between this involvement and the passion and death. What can one expect of a Christian who does not see this point clearly, above all in our capitalist society?

On the other hand, there are some signs of the times that raise hope. The Seventh Interchurch Encounter of Base Communities of Brazil, celebrated at Duque de Caxias, Rio de Janeiro, 10-14 July 1990, which reunited 120 Protestant representatives (five bishops) with 1,680 Catholic representatives (85 bishops), adopted as its basic text Luke 4:18-19: "The Spirit of God is upon me: he has sent me to bring Good News to the poor, to announce liberty to captives." At Duque de Caxias the symbol of the faith according to Nicaea was proclaimed at different times, and with enthusiasm, but always in the light of the proclamation of Jesus himself in the synagogue at Nazareth. I do not think one can bring Christians together without reminding them of the evangelical imperative: Liberate the poor!

The Nicene Creed Viewed from the Standpoint of the Evangelization of the Roman Empire

E. GLENN HINSON

Given their serious traditional reservations about creeds, Baptists will not be likely to look kindly on the effort to confess one faith, especially through the Nicene-Constantinopolitan Creed, unless they can visualize its role in ways other than that which they experienced in the seventeenth century. What they experienced there, of course, was an effort to impose uniformity in thought and worship in the form of the Book of Common Prayer (in England and Virginia) or of the whole Puritan ethos (in New England). From their predominantly Calvinist theology they drew a theological principle that they made the axle around which their well-known concern for religious liberty turned. "God alone is Lord of the conscience," they insisted. "Therefore, to be authentic and responsible, faith must be free. If it is imposed, it is not faith." This voluntary principle stands behind Baptist rejection of infant baptism, for, in their view, infants could not voluntarily yield their wills to God.

As you might expect, Christians of the free-church tradition, which includes Baptists, have not looked kindly on the fourth

117

century. To many it was the century in which the church "fell" as a consequence of its alliance with the state or, perhaps more accurately, the state's embracing of Christianity as its official religion.[1] What happened at Nicaea more or less epitomized the "fall," for Nicaea, convened by the emperor and deeply influenced if not dominated by his presence, set the stage for centuries of religious persecution.

I speak here, of course, with awareness that one can seriously question whether Southern Baptists any longer belong to the free-church or Baptist tradition. Numerically dominant in virtually every county east of Texas and south of the Mason-Dixon line, they should appreciate Constantine and the fourth century as their forebears never could. Today, as a matter of fact, many of them not only question whether separation of church and state belongs to their tradition but even denounce it as a "heresy." Although an inborn prejudice against the fourth century and the churches that obtained their chief features there prevents them from giving attention to the Nicene Creed, they have a near obsession with "orthodoxy" defined in terms of biblical inerrancy. As I have argued elsewhere, it would be far healthier if they returned to the fourth century and sought to recover a more holistic and wholesome view of Christian faith.[2]

Their walk through history, however, has turned most Baptists into poor ecumenists. In their entire history they have seldom united even with other Baptists and not at all with non-Baptists. Where they have manifested any serious interest in Christian unity, they have operated on what I would call a principle of "ecumenical pragmatism" which has virtually precluded visible, structured unity.[3] Once again, Baptist corporate memory of jails and fines and gallows stirs up no small measure

1. For bibliography representing this historical perspective, see W. Morgan Patterson, *Baptist Successionism: A Critical View* (Valley Forge, Pa.: Judson Press, 1960).

2. E. Glenn Hinson, "Creeds and Christian Unity," *Journal of Ecumenical Studies* 23 (Winter 1986): 25-36.

3. See E. Glenn Hinson, "William Carey and Ecumenical Pragmatism," *Journal of Ecumenical Studies* 17 (Spring 1980): 75-83; and *Baptists and Ecumenism,* ed. Glenn Igleheart and William Jerry Boney (Philadelphia: Judson Press, 1980).

of fear of the sort of binding commitments that could result in a recurrence of such things. They will cooperate and fellowship and worship with others, but they will falter when it comes to joining structurally.

What all of this means is that the fourth century and particularly the Nicene Creed require a lot of recontextualization before Baptists can look at them with different eyes. Southern Baptists, of course, will have a decided advantage by virtue of the close analogies between their situation in the southeastern portion of the United States and that of the church in the Roman Empire in the fourth century, for Southern Baptists have become as it were the Catholic Church of the South. This means that they appreciate in ways minority groups cannot the idea of a Christian state favoring the majority, and many of them actively strive toward that end today along lines envisioned by the Puritans in New England three centuries ago. I say they "ought to," but the fact is, comparable situation notwithstanding, they do not, because long-standing conventional thinking prevents them from seeing the analogies. So their biases against the fourth century remain strong, and we must not raise our hopes high that they will be drawn into the present dialogue about confessing one faith.

A POSSIBLE ENTRYWAY

There may be several ways to soften Baptist antipathy to the fourth century in general and to the Nicene Creed in particular, but I have believed for a number of years that Southern Baptists, and possibly others as well, will be more likely to undertake a sympathetic and objective reappraisal if they can look at the fourth century in light of an understanding of the church as mission. Southern Baptists have a mania for fulfilling the Great Commission (Matt. 28:19). When they hear the Johannine version of that in Jesus' "high priestly" prayer (John 17:21), their thoughts glide right past the petition "that all may be one" in order to get to the purpose clause "that the world may believe."

How does the creed look when viewed from the vantage

point of the evangelization of the Roman Empire? Obviously what happened in the fourth century has a quite different look than what happened prior to that time as Christianity found itself in a radically different situation vis-à-vis the state. State support for the churches' evangelistic efforts and enforcement of decisions of synods and councils created a Christian ethos unlike what a persecuted minority could ever have envisioned. This radical change of status, however, did not effect a complete loss of identity, as the concept of a "fall" of the church suggests. Quite the contrary, the creed itself, or "confession of faith" if we use the designation preferred by Baptists, helped Christianity to conserve its identity as the covenant people of God, Israel under a new covenant, despite the intervention of the state.

This, I think, is the best way to view confessions or creeds in the life of the church. Christianity, like its parent religion, is a covenant faith. In baptism believers enter into a covenant relationship with the God who, out of *hesed* ("covenant love"), has sought them out. The confession recited in baptism is, as it were, the covenant *in nucleo*. In corporate worship the faithful assemble to hear God's word of demand and promise and to reiterate their covenant vows made in baptism, especially in the eucharist. But, once again, the creed verbalizes what both baptism and eucharist symbolize in a kind of acted parable. Discipline seeks to restore the "fallen" to the covenant faithfulness of baptism through the withholding and restoring of eucharistic communion.

The more historians can turn attention away from the dogmatic character of creeds and their utility in drawing lines setting the parameters of faith for theologians and redirect attention toward their covenant character and utility in the very basic task of establishing Christian identity, the more readily will persons in the free-church tradition be open to a reconsideration of them. Considering them in relation to covenant highlights their personal and relational character rather than the dogmatic character that has dominated historical accounts in the past. Stated another way, it helps us to look at confessions from the perspective of the little people whom historians often neglect rather than the giants whom they talk about too much simply because records concerning them are more readily available.

The Baptismal Confessions

In the first several centuries of Christian history, confessions or creeds were employed in a variety of ways to establish or confirm Christian covenant identity with respect to baptism and catechumenate, liturgy and preaching, exorcism, persecution, and polemic against heretics.[4] The principal usage, however, was in instruction of converts and baptism. From the early second century on, local confessions underwent alterations in response to various crises, usually of heresy or schism. With the passing of the Gnostic crisis, the New Testament gradually became the pivotal doctrinal norm, and even the rule of faith had to be substantiated by it. The fourth- and fifth-century doctrinal controversies refined and made more precise the local baptismal confessions, but they did not change their basic character.

In a paper entitled "The Apostolic Faith as Expressed in the Writings of the Apostolic and Church Fathers" prepared for the Rome Consultation of Faith and Order of the World Council of Churches, I pointed to an evolution from "a more fluid and less precisely defined state in which 'spiritual intuition' of tradition played a fairly significant role, toward a more fixed and exactly defined state in which certain formulas became near-absolute norms which could be imposed, if necessary, from without."[5] The stage of "credally informed expressions" of the apostolic

4. Concerning baptism and catechumenate, see Acts 8:36-38; 1 Pet. 3:18-22; Peh. 4:5; Ign. *Smyrn.* 1; Justin, 1 *Apol.* 61; Iren. *Adv. haer.* 1.9.4; Tert. *De spec.* 4; *De cor.* 3.

Concerning liturgy and preaching, see Phil. 2:6-11; 1 Cor. 15:3-7. See also C. H. Dodd, *The Apostolic Preaching and Its Developments* (London: Hodder & Stoughton, Ltd., 1936), pp. 9ff.; A. M. Hunter, *Paul and His Predecessors,* rev. ed. (London: SCM Press, 1961), pp. 15ff.

Concerning exorcism, see Acts 3:6; Mk. 1:24; 3:11; 5:7; Justin *Dial.* 30.3; 76:6; 85.1.

Concerning persecution, see 1 Tim. 6:12-16; *Mar. Pol.* 8.2; 9.3.

Concerning polemic against heretics, see 1 John 4:2; Ign. *Trall.* 9; *Smyrn.* 1; *Magn.* 11; *Eph.* 18.2.

5. *The Roots of Our Common Faith,* ed. Hans Georg Link, Faith and Order Paper No. 119 (Geneva: WCC, 1984), p. 115.

faith was not reached until the late fourth century, and then somewhat reluctantly. Athanasius, whose name has become almost synonymous with the Nicene Creed, did not emphasize it as the more or less definitive standard precluding a need for further statements until 350 or 351, after the Western synod at Ariminum and the Arian-dominated synod at Seleucia. Indeed, as J. N. D. Kelly has concluded, before that time, he "was still at an Origenist phase of this theological development, attached to the doctrine of three hypostases and highly suspicious of the emperor's chosen term."[6] The churches obviously did not place great emphasis on the Nicene Creed either, for they continued to use their own baptismal confessions throughout the century. As a matter of fact, the council Fathers at Constantinople in 381 had to draw on a local baptismal statement because the Nicene Creed had gotten lost somewhere as a result of nonuse.

None of this is to be construed as a repudiation of the creed. My intention, rather, is to point up the flexible practice that characterized the churches' use of it even during the fourth century, a fact that makes it far less threatening. To be sure, I will always want to keep up some defenses against an alliance of state with church that may lead to the use of state force to compel adherence to particular religious doctrines or modes of behavior. What has been happening in the United States in the past decade should sandpaper the sensitivities of all persons to the very real danger posed by the idea of a "Christian America."

Use of confessions in instruction and baptism or, as happened later, in corporate worship is not threatening. The churches cannot "make disciples" without confessions, for persons cannot become Christians without some kind of expression of their faith, their covenant commitment. We must always recognize that no statement can encompass all that apostolic faith is. Human beings simply cannot formulate confessions that will do justice to the mystery of God. The baptismal confessions that laid the foundation for the fourth-century creeds, however, conserved what is essential in this covenant-making process. In their very formulation they made clear that faith is, above all, faith in the living God, Father, Son, and Holy Spirit, and not faith in a set of propositions. The introductory formula (Greek *pisteuein eis*), derived, I am convinced, from the Gospel of John, emphasizes commitment. "I commit myself to One God . . . Jesus Christ . . . the Holy Spirit." It is personal and relational and not propositional. Western rationalism has turned the creed into something it was never intended to be and, I would perceive, is not in the liturgies of Orthodox churches.

SCRIPTURES AND CREED

Most Protestants, especially those of the free-church tradition, will be constantly vigilant about displacement of the authority of Scripture by the authority of creeds. It is important, therefore, to look at the relationship between the two.

In relationship to baptism and catechism and other activities, these formulas of faith, in their varying degrees of precision, made their principal contribution as summaries of the essential apostolic faith that could guide the faithful in their interpretation of the Scriptures. Various formulas, of course, preceded the Scriptures of the New Testament. But once the canon had taken recognizable form, it supplied the main pole of a tripolar base—of canon, creed, and episcopate—for regulating the faith and practice of the churches. The teacher (eventually the bishop) interpreted and applied the teachings of Scriptures in accordance with the "rule of faith."

This tripolar conception of authority can be seen developing at an early date in connection with newly founded churches. Paul enforced adherence to a "type of teaching" or "traditions" that he delivered (Rom. 6:17; 16:17; 1 Cor. 11:2; 2 Thess. 2:5; 3:6). This traditional teaching was, by his own admission, "according to the Scriptures"—that is, in agreement with the Old Testament (1 Cor. 15:3-4; Rom. 15:4; 16:26; Acts 17:2, 11; 18:24, 28). The Pastoral epistles urge the selection of persons suitably qualified to hand on the "deposit" of teaching faithfully (Tit. 1:9) and at the same time stress the full inspiration of the Old Testament (1 Tim. 3:16). Clement believed the apostles had appointed bish-

ops and deacons city by city to continue their ministry of preaching and the like in accordance with the Old Testament Scriptures
(1 Clem. 42:44). Ignatius posited the solution to the Judaistic-
Gnostic crisis in the churches of Asia Minor in the submission
of all to episcopal authority. As a bishop, he put his faith in the
traditional summary of faith he had received as fulfilling the Old
Testament.[7]

In response to the Gnostic, Marcionite, and Montanist crises,
Irenaeus and his successors stated the tripolar formula in its
classical form. The question they first had to answer was *What
are the Scriptures?* Since the Gnostics and Montanists had a
wide-open canon and the Marcionites a narrowly circumscribed
one, the Fathers had to invoke some norm for testing. The
second question was *How do you interpret those Scriptures considered authoritative?* By allegorical exegesis the Gnostics could
make Scriptures say what they pleased. Though Irenaeus or
Tertullian could criticize their opponents' hermeneutic for dis-
regarding context and interpreting clear passages by obscure
ones, they could not make the accusations stick so long as they
too used the allegorical method. As the *Clementine Homilies*
pointed out, one could assemble proof texts for any doctrine.[8]

The answer to both questions, of course, was to invoke the
"rule of truth" received in baptism. Irenaeus claimed for the
church "dispersed throughout the whole world" a fairly precise
trinitarian formula "received from the apostles and their disciples" that the (orthodox) teacher dared not violate. "For since
the faith is one and the same, the person who could expound at
length about it did not add to it, nor the one who could say little
subtract from it."[9] To this point, the argument held. But the
Gnostics also claimed a secret tradition or rule of faith "not
delivered by means of written documents, but *viva voce*,"[10]

7. Ignatius, *Phila.* 8.2; *Smyrn.* 1.1-2; 7.2.
8. Clement, *Hom.* 3.9.
9. Irenaeus, *Adv. haer.* 1.10.2; Harvey, I, 94. Cf. 1.22.1; 2.9.1, 28.1, 30.9;
Tertullian, *De praescr.* 3, 9, 12, 13.
10. Irenaeus, *Adv. haer.* 3.2.1; Tertullian, *De praescr.* 22-25. Note that Clement,
Strom. 6.7.15, and Origen, *C. Cels.* 2.13, both held the same doctrine. See Hanson,
Origen's Doctrine of Tradition, pp. 53-90.

which allowed them to sustain their own wild speculations by both Scriptures and Tradition. Irenaeus's answer to this was to limit Tradition to "that tradition, which is from the apostles, which is preserved by the successions of presbyters and churches" of apostolic foundation.[11] When confronted by this tripolar combination of Scriptures interpreted according to the Tradition handed on by a succession of teachers in apostolic churches, the Gnostics had no other recourse but to reject both Scriptures and Tradition and to claim a higher revelation.

Among orthodox writers, of course, there was diversity of opinion about the creeds, which meant that Scriptures were interpreted in varied ways. For instance, as Hanson has demonstrated, Clement and Origen held a looser conception of the rule of faith than Irenaeus. Clement identified the rule with the secret tradition. Origen, however, distinguished them. The rule of faith, he believed, was the guide for "the majority of the church,"[12] apparently "simply the way the Church always had interpreted Scripture, as far as he knew."[13] Both Clement and Origen professed to approach Scriptures by the rule of faith. Origen himself expressed the necessity in terms of the diversity of opinions, not only about trivial but also about important matters, among professed Christians.[14] He was quick to note, however, matters on which the church had no clear tradition,[15] and he was capable of setting aside the church's rule of faith if he thought Scriptures allowed it.[16] His thorough commitment to the allegorical method thus paved the way for free-ranging interpretations such as the Gnostics alone could rival. In his mind authentic interpretation rested in the hands of those who possessed "the methods of interpretation that appear right to us, who keep the rule of the *heavenly* church of Jesus Christ through the succession

11. Irenaeus, *Adv. haer.* 3.2.2; cf. Tertullian, *De praescr.* 20-21, 32.
12. Origen, *Comm. in Joann.* 13.16.
13. Hanson, *Origen's Doctrine of Tradition*, p. 95.
14. Origen, *De princ. praef.* 1; cf. *In Num. Hom.* 9.1; *Comm. in Joann.* 10.13.
15. Origen, *De princ. praef.* 4-10.
16. See Origen, *Comm. in Ps.* 119.85; PG, XII, col. 1601; *C. Cels.* 5.18, 19; *Comm. in Matt.* 11.15; 17.29; *Comm. in Joann.* 13.16; Hanson, *Origen's Doctrine of Tradition*, pp. 106ff.

from the apostles."[17] It would appear, then, that both Clement and Origen set two "rules"—one for the simple, one for the Gnostic. The very complexity of the hermeneutical task gave them immense latitude in their adherence to one or the other.

In the final analysis, the solution to the hermeneutical problem lay in the magisterial authority of the churches. Athanasius, after stressing the complete adequacy of the Scriptures, proceeded to emphasize the need for sound teachers to expound them, and he accused the Arians of shipwrecking the faith by failing to keep their bearings through sighting "the ecclesiastical mark (σκοπός)."[18] Hilary maintained that those who did not accept the church's teaching could not comprehend the Bible.[19] Augustine counseled the explanation of doubtful or ambiguous passages by the rule of faith[20] and contended that the church's authority also guaranteed their veracity.[21]

In the early fifth century, Vincent of Lerins brought to a head the lengthy process of reflections. He had learned from others, he explained, a twofold plan for exposing heresy and remaining sound in faith: (1) by the authority of the divine law and (2) by the Tradition of the catholic church. Scriptures alone do not suffice because of diverse interpretations. Distortions must be averted, therefore, by following "the norm of the ecclesiastical and cátholic meaning." What is "catholic"? "What has been believed everywhere, always, by all." Vincent elaborated upon this principle in its three major points: (1) *universality*—to "acknowledge only this one faith to be true which the whole church confesses throughout the lands"; (2) *antiquity*—to deviate in no way "from those interpretations [*sensibus*] which the greater saints and our Fathers proclaimed"; and (3) *agreement*—to follow the definitions and statements of all or at least almost all of the bishops [*sacerdotium*] and teachers.[22]

17. Origen, *De princ.* 4.2.2; Butterworth, p. 272.
18. Athanasius, *C. gent.* 1.
19. Hilary, *In Matt.* 5.1.
20. Augustine, *De doctr. chr.* 3.2.
21. Augustine, *C. ep. Manich.* 6; *De doctr. chr.* 2.12; *C. Faust.* 22.79; *C. ep. Fund.* 5.6.
22. Vincent, *Common.* 2.1-3; Moxon, pp. 10-11.

CONCLUSION

In retrospect, I am not at all sure Baptists will or should ever feel comfortable with the fourth century, particularly with the creed. If they are going to gain greater objectivity about the period and the creed, they will have to view them in a different light than they have for several centuries. The light they've had up to now has been overshadowed by fear of church-state alliances and persecution. I have tried to ameliorate attitudes on the subject by looking at the development of confessions in the context of early Christianity's evangelization efforts, underscoring their essentially catechetical and baptismal character rather than their use in differentiating orthodoxy from heresy, which appears to me a minor role, divergent from their main purpose. As regards catechesis and baptism, I believe we can legitimately call attention to the relational rather than propositional nature of faith called for in the creeds, including the Nicene-Constantinopolitan.

While recontextualizing early confessions from the standpoint of evangelization, I have found a somewhat different angle from which to address the all-important issue of Scriptures and Tradition. Far from detracting from the role of Scriptures for determining faith and practice, confessions served as summaries of the essentials of apostolic faith that could guide the faithful in their interpretation of the Scriptures. Yet neither Scriptures nor Tradition stood in isolation from the whole problem of legitimate and authoritative interpretation. In early Christianity there developed what I have called a "tripolar formula" of canon, creed, and authoritative teaching which could assure that the churches, while incorporating a highly diverse and syncretistic constituency from the Greco-Roman world, would retain their identity as a covenant people.

The creed is, of course, only one of the institutions of early Christianity that will have to be recontextualized if Baptists are to look at the fourth century without thinking "Fall of the Church." The system of penance, the eucharist, church hierarchy, and the relationship of church to state all raise Baptist hackles. The challenge is to get Baptists, as much as other

Christians, to embrace the fourth century as *their* history. More broadly, we must all come to the point where we embrace all of church history as the history of us all. It will be all right then if we feel uncomfortable with the fourth and a lot of other centuries. We should, because they are ours, and we will always feel more vexed by what is ours than by what is theirs.

Trinitarian Orthodoxy, Constantinianism, and Theology from a Radical Protestant Perspective

A. JAMES REIMER

INTRODUCTION

I have been asked to reflect on fourth-century theological developments from a Mennonite theological perspective. It is well known that the so-called "Believers' Church" tradition (a rather presumptuous title for those Christian groups, like the Mennonites, who adhere to a "visible church" ecclesiology that marks them off from other mainline Christian groups)[1] has historically seen the fourth century as the sign of widespread Christian apostasy, the "fall of the church." This negative evaluation of the Constantinian period, which gave the Christian church privileged status within Roman imperial society, has commonly

---

1. The "visible church" ecclesiology is premised on the notion that the church is a visible social entity constituted only of individuals who have expressed their personal faith by means of adult baptism and committed themselves to a life of discipleship and nonconformity to the world. I much prefer the designation of "radical Protestantism" for those groups who have their historical and spiritual origins in the left-wing groups of the Reformation.

spilled over into a suspicion of the historical ecumenical creeds, seen as intrinsically linked to and legitimating a growing ecclesiastical hierarchy and political power rather than faithfully expressing biblical truth.

In this essay I will first outline what I consider to be the representative position for a significant number of contemporary Mennonite thinkers. I will not survey all the contemporary literature, nor look at Anabaptist sources, but will focus on the thought of one of our foremost contemporary theologians and ethicists, John Howard Yoder. After having outlined Yoder's views and that of a younger interpreter of Yoder, J. Denny Weaver, I will make my own proposal. I will argue that theological orthodoxy and Constantinianism are not intrinsically linked, as is so often assumed, but are in fact in tension with each other. I will propose that classical orthodoxy needs to be retrieved in contemporary Christian theology after having eroded in the eighteenth and nineteenth centuries, so that it can serve as a basis for taking a stand against various forms of twentieth-century Constantinianism. Nicene orthodoxy needs to be retrieved by the Christian church in general and by the Mennonite church in particular as a way of remaining faithful to the Bible, as a way of preserving the essential tenets of the Christian faith within a postbiblical context, and as a theological framework for contemporary ethics.

In emphasizing so strongly the relevance of Nicaea and Constantinople for contemporary Christian theology, I am admittedly departing from much recent Mennonite thinking, but not from what I consider to be the central conviction of our historical Anabaptist beginnings—a trinitarian orthodoxy with a heightened ethical consciousness. In other words, I do not see moral and ethical fidelity to the Jesus narrative as offering an alternative to Nicaea, Constantinople, and Chalcedon but as a position that needs to be incorporated into the framework of classical theological orthodoxy. In this process of retrieval, I believe we need to enter vigorously into conversation with other theological traditions such as Eastern Orthodoxy, which can teach us much in this regard. These other traditions, however, may themselves also be able to learn something from the radical Protestant emphasis on personal and social ethics based on a

particular reading of the Gospels—especially political nonconformity and a view of the church as a visible, prophetic minority
within society.

THE "CONSTANTINIAN SHIFT"

As an ethicist and historical theologian (rather than as a systematic theologian), John Howard Yoder has in the last three decades
become the leading interpreter of Anabaptist-Mennonite theology both for the Mennonite communion itself and for the larger
ecumenical Christian community. He has in his writings, more
than any other person except perhaps Harold S. Bender (who
was largely responsible for the twentieth-century renaissance of
Mennonite interest in its Anabaptist sources), shaped Mennonite
self-understanding in the second half of this century.[2] His primary preoccupation has been with the social and political rele-
vancy of the biblical Jesus (a position he calls "biblical realism")
for our age and the concomitant understanding of the church's
relation to the world. He has been outspoken in his prophetic
assertion that the churches have taken the wrong direction ever
since the time of Constantine. Many of his writings deal either
explicitly or implicitly with the ethical implications of what he
calls the "Constantinian shift," represented by the imperial decree of toleration toward Christianity in 311, the "conversion"
and later baptism of Constantine, and the crucial role he played
in the formulation of theological orthodoxy, especially at Nicaea
in 325, as the great negative watershed in Christian history.
While, according to Yoder, the shift occurred gradually,[3] Con-

2. Of Yoder's many books, including *Nevertheless* (1971), *The Original Revolution* (1972), *The Politics of Jesus* (1972), *What Would You Do?* (1983), and *When
War Is Unjust* (1984), his *Christian Witness to the State* (1964) is in my opinion still
one of the best. A whole generation of young educated Mennonites who have
been interested in their Anabaptist heritage have read Yoder's books and taken
him as the definitive interpreter of what it means to be an Anabaptist in the
contemporary situation.

3. Dennis D. Martin wrongly charges Yoder with portraying the "Constantinian reversal as an overnight occurrence" ("Nothing New under the Sun?
Mennonites and History," *The Conrad Grebel Review* 5 [Winter 1987]: 8 n. 21).

stantine's person and period symbolize a "great reversal" in the relation of the church to the larger society that can only be considered an apostasy. No longer is the church a critical, prophetic, and suffering minority within a hostile pagan world; it has taken on a privileged role as legitimator of power, wealth, and hierarchy. In a series of three essays, "Radical Reformation Ethics in Ecumenical Perspective," "Anabaptism and History," and "The Constantinian Sources of Western Social Ethics," Yoder has consistently articulated his position.

In the first of these, "Radical Reformation Ethics in Ecumenical Perspective," first published in 1978, Yoder presents what for him is the heart of the matter—a doctrine of the church. What happened in the Constantinian era was a reversal of the New Testament doctrine of the church. The three criteria for a sound doctrine of the church are (1) disestablishment (i.e., a church neither governed nor supported by civil government), (2) voluntary adult membership (church membership based not on infant baptism but on an adult confession of faith), and (3) renunciation of all violence, wealth, and imperial office. These characteristics of the true church were assumed by the New Testament Christian community, the early church before the fourth century, sixteenth-century Swiss Anabaptists, and seventeenth-century Quakers. The mainline churches, however, fell from faithfulness when they changed from a critical prophetic minority into a privileged minority and gradually into a majority from the fourth century onward. With the medieval synthesis of church and state, clergy and sword, ecclesiastical hierarchy and wealth, Christianity came to be identified with "violence, money, and social stratification." Jesus as revelatory norm for social ethics was gradually overshadowed by common sense, natural reason, and a sense of responsibility for society and history as sources for ethics. Yoder in this essay does not address the theological agenda as such, although he suggests that "A different ethic obviously involves the possibility of a different doctrine of humanity or Christology, or of nature, of sin or grace or law."[4] He also states that for the radical Reformers

4. Yoder, "Radical Reformation Ethics in Ecumenical Perspective," in *The*

"the humanity of Jesus of Nazareth" and "human obedience" were the primary grounds for Christian ethical decision making. His primary concern, however, is not with a systematic treatment of Christian doctrine but an analysis of Christian social ethics.

In the second essay, "Anabaptism and History," Yoder outlines the three basic characteristics of the "restitutionist" pattern of historical thinking as espoused by Anabaptism: a past normative state of the church, a radical fall of the church, and a radical renewal. The *normative state* is the incarnation as related in the canon—more specifically "a very particular story of the New Testament," the story and claims of Christ. This is a historical norm with "historical objectivity and distance," equally accessible to all. The *fall* occurred in the Constantinian era with the strategic church-state alliance, the development of the just-war approach to violence, and the repression of dissent. For the Anabaptists the fourth century was wrong in the light of the New Testament not "because it was older than the New Testament, but because wrong fourth-century options were chosen rather than right fourth-century options."[5] According to Yoder, Anabaptists viewed the pre-Constantinian Fathers and "over two centuries of fallible, divided, confused church life" favorably because the official teaching remained basically sound. He adds, "If twentieth-century restitutionism needs correction or refinement at this point, it would be to look for still earlier or deeper pre-dispositions toward the Constantinian shift (anti-Judaism? Neoplatonism? creeping empire loyalism despite the commitment to pacifism?)."[6] Radical *renewal* requires offering a social alternative to fallen Christendom, finding a normative stance within Scripture, and locating the authoritative interpretation of Scripture outside the establishment—as in the congregation or with the prophet.

In the third essay, "The Constantinian Sources of Western

Priestly Kingdom: Social Ethics as Gospel (Notre Dame, Ind.: University of Notre Dame Press, 1984), p. 108.

5. Yoder, "Anabaptism and History," in *The Priestly Kingdom*, p. 129.

6. Yoder, "Anabaptism and History," p. 208 n. 25.

Ethics," Yoder spells out the conceptual and ethical implications of the "Constantinian shift" especially in regard to the church's attitude toward war and peace. Before Constantine, violence was considered to be morally wrong; after Constantine, there was a growing acceptance of imperial violence as a Christian duty. What is presupposed is a new ecclesiology, a new eschatology, and a new metaphysics, among other things. The *new ecclesiology* is reflected in the shift from the church as a persecuted minority to the church as everybody, with paganism now becoming the minority and heresies now being officially repressed. The *new eschatology* has to do with a new view of providence and history. God's way with the world and history as a whole had previously been ambiguous and a matter of faith; only the present status of the church was clear. After Constantine this was reversed. The true church came to be viewed as invisible, and God's working within history and through the empire came to be considered beyond dispute. Imperial values and culture, legal tradition, and social structures were identified with Christianity. One's duties of station, office, and vocation within the civil government replaced Jesus and his teachings as the ethical standard. With the "Constantinian wedding of piety with power," efficacy and utility replaced the principles of revelation, nature, and "received" standards as sources for ethical principles.[7] At the bottom of this was a *new metaphysics,* a neo-Platonic dualism between invisible spirituality and visible worldliness. Christianity became interiorized and individualized, and the distance between Jesus and worldly authorities grew. This perceived gap between ourselves and the Bible, in which the New Testament is perceived to be irrelevant to the pressing duties of the historical moment, constitutes apostasy. What is called for is radical "disestablishment" and "de-Constantinianization." Yoder puts it unequivocally: "What the churches accepted in the Constantinian shift is what Jesus had rejected, seizing godlikeness, moving *in hoc signo* from Golgatha to the battlefield. If this diagnosis is correct, then the cure is not to update the fourth-century mistake by adding

---

7. Yoder, "The Constantinian Sources of Western Social Ethics," in *The Priestly Kingdom,* p. 140.

another 'neo-' [as in neo-Constantinianism] but to repent of the whole 'where it's at' style and to begin again with kenosis."[8]

Yoder's position as articulated in these essays is the product of years of writing and teaching on Christian pacifism. His lecture notes on the subject have been collected and informally published under the title *Christian Attitudes to War, Peace, and Revolution.* In the first few chapters of this volume Yoder traces the gradual shift that occurred within the early church from an initial total rejection of soldiering to a slow acculturation by the church to the Greco-Roman world and an accommodation to the military requirements of the Empire with the church becoming less and less rigorous in its ethical requirements. There came to be two levels of Christians, with different ethical obligations: the religious monastics, for whom the high moral claims of Jesus especially in regard to nonviolence continued to apply, and average Christians, for whom a lower commonsense approach to life sufficed. Constantine represented this basic reorientation and the lowering of standards for ordinary believers. The concept of the "just war" as articulated by Ambrose and Augustine, a moral theory not based on Jesus' teachings but dependent on an extrabiblical commonsense epistemology, is an ethical outworking of this reorientation. Yoder suggests but does not demonstrate in detail that this shift was theologically legitimated by the council of Nicaea and its theological formulation of trinitarian orthodoxy. Constantine, intent on unifying the church as a means of uniting the Empire, played a decisive role at Nicaea, calling the council, chairing it, and providing the crucial terminology. As the theological formulation of trinitarian orthodoxy was completed only by 381, so the political and legal consequences of the shift gradually but ineluctably became visible: by 390-392 pagan temples were closed, by 420 dissenting Christians were officially repressed and persecuted, and by 436 non-Christians were not allowed to be in the army.[9] This is a long way from New Testament Christianity.

---

8. Yoder, "The Constantinian Sources of Western Social Ethics," p. 145.
9. Yoder, *Christian Attitudes to War, Peace, and Revolution: A Companion to Bainton* (Elkhart, Ind.: Co-op Bookstore, 1983), pp. 23-66.

TRINITARIAN ORTHODOXY

It is not entirely clear whether Yoder considers the Constantinian shift and trinitarian orthodoxy as defined at Nicaea and Constantinople to be part of the same movement, to be intrinsically linked. There are times when he seems to suggest that the two are thus connected—that is, that theological orthodoxy, as assisted (if not dictated) in its official definition by Constantine, is little more than a theological reflection and legitimation of Constantinianism (and therefore also a sign of apostasy). On other occasions, though, he offers a more sympathetic reading of the theological development of doctrine that these councils and resulting creeds represent. His most significant work in this regard is *Preface to Theology: Christology and Theological Method.*[10] I will summarize briefly his analysis of the development of doctrine in the postbiblical period as reflected in the Apostles' Creed and the Nicene Creed.

The Apostles' Creed, which was basically in place by the third and fourth centuries according to Yoder, retains the christological emphasis of the the first New Testament confessions— "Jesus Christ is Lord." The second article is the longest, and is in narrative form like the New Testament kerygma, with the first article a kind of prologue and the third an epilogue. Nevertheless, there is already a deviation from the biblical narrative. There is no reference to the Old Testament narrative, nor is there any allusion to the life or teachings of Jesus. What we have in the second article is a leap from birth to crucifixion. More noteworthy than this is the lack of any sense of urgency concerning repentance. As Yoder puts it, "By this time we have had Constantine. The pagan world is moving under the control of the church. So the concept of the minority church calling people to listen, to repent, to believe, to receive forgiveness, does not quite fit."[11] Instead there is reflected in the creed the beginnings

10. Yoder, *Preface to Theology: Christology and Theological Method* (Elkhart, Ind.: Co-op Bookstore, early 1980s). Like *Christian Attitudes to War, Peace, and Revolution,* this volume is a collection of Yoder's lecture and seminar notes gathered over a twenty-year period (from the early 1960s to 1981).

11. Yoder, *Preface to Theology,* p. 104.

of the sacramentalism and metaphysical speculation so prevalent in the medieval church with the Catholic Church itself
becoming an object of belief.

The fourth-century debates on the question of the Trinity are
a further expansion of the tendency already present in the Apostles' Creed. What we see in effect is the triumph of Alexandrian
intellectual, philosophical, and systematic thinking over the
simple, exegetical, historical, narrative, and more unphilosophi-
cal Hebraic approach of Antioch. Yoder concedes the partial
similarity between the wisdom *(sophia)* tradition of the Scriptures
and Greek notions of cosmic rationality *(logos)*. He is, consequently, sympathetic to what the theologians in the patristic
period were trying to do with the concept of Jesus as Logos being
both equal to and distinct from God.[12] He appears also to support
the attempt by the church to define an orthodox position over
against the various heresies, particularly Arianism—that is, with
the desire to maintain both the diversity and unity of God. But it
is clear that Yoder understands the fourth-century debates primarily within a sociopolitical framework (both ecclesiastical and
imperial), and this makes him suspicious of them. This is the age
of accommodation to Greco-Roman culture. A radical conversion
is no longer required. Neither is there a strong sense of sin. The
pressure to stress the uniqueness and deity of Jesus as a necessary
means of God's breaking in to save the world from sin is weaker,
replaced by a preoccupation with the dignity and transcendence
of God. The growing strength of Arianism mirrors this kind of
accommodation to a Hellenistic and imperialistic culture and
theological deviation from the New Testament.[13]

Yoder's treatment of the political context and implications
of the Arian–Alexander/Athanasius debates behind the Nicene
formulation is particularly noteworthy. He admits that Arius's
theology fit imperial aims better than Athanasius's theology: "If
you lower the concept of who Christ was, then you raise your
vision of the emperor, because the logos was in both Jesus and
the empire. . . . If Jesus is a little smaller, the king will be a little

12. Yoder, *Preface to Theology,* pp. 123-26.
13. Yoder, *Preface to Theology,* p. 133.

higher, and that is just what Constantine and his advisors wanted."[14] This is why Arius had more friends in the imperial court. In contrast, Athanasius had more popular support. The Athanasian-orthodox position did in fact safeguard the christological content of the New Testament ("that Jesus, the Word in Jesus, is genuinely of the character of deity and genuinely human, and that his work is the work of God and yet the work of a man")[15] relatively well even though it employed nonbiblical concepts and language. Nevertheless, there is a serious change of mood and style, a deviation from the biblical center.

What for Yoder is this biblical center that was departed from at Nicaea? It is the "gospel story." And what is the "gospel story"? This is how he puts it: "The form of the confession is still used but it has been so padded out with statements about the essence of Christ that you don't recognize any narrative to it anymore. One is not driven to think of the movement of time, of God doing something among men in a given time and place, as being very important."[16] Yoder concedes that one finds in the Bible references to the existence of God the Father, the Son, and the Spirit and the assumption that they are the same. This is not, however, given in the Bible as revealed information. The doctrine of the Trinity as later formulated does not appear in the Bible but is rather "the solution of an intellectual difficulty which arises if we accept the statement of the Bible."[17] The doctrine itself is not revealed. What is revealed is the revelation in Jesus and ongoing revelation in the Holy Spirit. "The doctrine of the Trinity is a test of whether your commitment to Jesus and to God are biblical enough that you have the problem which the doctrine of the Trinity solves."[18] In other words, the trinitarian formulation is itself secondary in importance; it tries to solve an intellectual problem that follows logically from asserting both Jewish monotheism on the one hand and God's revelation in Christ and the Holy Spirit on the other. Other words and solu-

14. Yoder, *Preface to Theology*, p. 136.
15. Yoder, *Preface to Theology*, p. 138.
16. Yoder, *Preface to Theology*, p. 139.
17. Yoder, *Preface to Theology*, p. 140.
18. Yoder, *Preface to Theology*, p. 140.

tions, possibly better ones, could potentially be found. What is important is the commitment "to the man Jesus, and . . . to the unique God" manifested in Jesus behind the trinitarian struggle of the fourth century. If we do not possess the same commitment as the early Church Fathers who debated the trinitarian question, we have departed from the Christian family. Yoder is, in short, distinguishing between (1) revelation (and commitment to that revelation) and (2) intellectual reflection upon that revelation (Nicaea-Constantinople).

Yoder is struck by the fact that many Christians who reject the teaching of "anything above the Bible or beyond the Bible" continue to give equal authoritative status to the Nicene Creed and the doctrine of the Trinity. Despite his positive and empathetic portrayal of the patristic controversies of the first four centuries, in the end Yoder is highly dubious about the political motivations behind the final statement:

> If we look back at the politics that were played between 325 and 381, the methods these men used, some of their motives, at the personal quality of Constantine, or if we ask in what sense he was a Christian when he dictated this dogma, then we have to be pretty dubious about giving to this movement any authority. If we call into question the acceptance of *Hellenistic* thought forms which are foreign to the way the Bible thinks, which don't fit with the *Hebrew* mind, or with the *modern* mind either for that matter, then again we have to challenge whether it does us much good.[19]

Yoder can understand why the high church tradition would give the Nicene Creed and the later creeds a certain kind of hermeneutic authority that in practice stands above the Bible even if it does not do so theoretically. After all, orthodoxy becomes the official kingly position. For the "believers' church" tradition (and the modern reader), however, the only authority is the

19. Yoder, *Preface to Theology*, p. 140; italics mine. Yoder here manifests the kind of suspicion of Hellenistic influences on Christian sources that is so prevalent in modern theology, and he implicitly suggests a connection between the biblical, Hebraic, and modern mind. The reference to the "modern reader" not being able to accept the Nicene wording is noteworthy. It implies that Yoder sees the Anabaptist-Mennonite reading of the Bible (biblical realism) as more palatable to the modern mind than the classical orthodox reading.

claims of Jesus, creating the intellectual problem to which the Nicene statement tries to find an answer. "The doctrine is not supernatural truth, supernaturally communicated for its information value. It is not learning which the Holy Spirit gave to the Council Fathers of Nicea because these were bishops assembled from the whole world at the invitation from the Roman Emperor. It is valid because it reflects the serious struggle of men, within their language and their culture, with their commitment to an absolute God and to a normative Jesus."[20]

J. Denny Weaver, a younger Mennonite theologian, is heavily indebted to Yoder's general theological orientation and follows Yoder's critique of the Constantinian shift almost word for word, drawing even more radical conclusions than does Yoder (i.e., he is less sympathetic to trinitarian orthodoxy) in his critique of the theological developments that occurred between the Gospels and the fourth and fifth centuries. This is especially evident in his recently published essay "Christology in Historical Perspective," in which he argues that Mennonites as "charter members" of the Believers' Church tradition—that is, as descendants of the radical wing of the Reformation who are "neither Catholic nor Protestant"—have a unique contribution to make to contemporary christological discussions. He believes that there is a "true theology which does not, or need not, pass through the Constantinian church" and that there is a clear choice between reading the Bible through Believers' Church eyes on the one hand and Constantinian church eyes on the other.

What are Constantinian church eyes? They are the eyes of the established church throughout the ages, most graphically represented by Constantine. Inevitably an established church embodies the temptation to affirm the status quo. This temptation was already apparent "in the Old Testament in the tension between prophet and priest or king," and in the same way, "Constantinianism has always tempted God's people."[21] It boils

20. Yoder, *Preface to Theology*, p. 141.
21. Weaver, "Christology in Historical Perspective," in *Jesus Christ and the Mission of the Church: Contemporary Anabaptist Perspective* (Elkhart, Ind.: General Conference Mennonite Church, 1989), p. 61.

down to rejecting Jesus' nonresistant love ethic (discipleship) as normative for Christian life and presumably replacing it with a societal norm premised on the need for coercion (although in this essay Weaver nowhere spells out what this Constantinian norm is; he speaks only of what it is not).

Weaver is concerned to show how the theological changes that occur in the development from the Gospels to Nicaea-Chalcedon should be seen as part of the gradual Constantinian shift that is taking place. The underlying theological shift is from the use of narrative to ontological (or generic) categories in defining Jesus. "Jesus is identified in terms of essential (generic) categories to which he belongs—humanity and deity—rather than in terms of the unique way he was a human being or how he specifically made God's presence known."[22] Jesus' particularity—his concrete life, deeds, and teachings—gets lost. Further, there is a narrowing down of christological images. From a diversity of New Testament christological images, the one from the prologue of John's Gospel is selected as the only legitimate way of talking about Jesus. Related to this is the fact that certain titles change their meanings. Whereas "Son of God" was initially a reference to God's relation to the world, it now designates "a relationship entirely within the heavenly realm, a relationship within the Godhead itself."[23]

As an alternative to Weaver's portrayal of early church theological development, I would like to suggest that what happened was not a narrowing of christology or a selection of one of many christologies in the New Testament but the development of a distinctively Christian doctrine of God out of the diversity of the Scriptures, a theological framework large enough to hold within itself a variety of theological emphases. It was the "heresies" that narrowed down the gospel, and it was for the purpose of protecting the Christian view of God from such a narrowing that orthodoxy was formulated. Further, Aloys Grillmeier, in his definitive study of this period, has concluded that the Nicene theologians did not change the meaning of the title "Son of God":

22. Weaver, "Christology in Historical Perspective," p. 56.
23. Weaver, "Christology in Historical Perspective," p. 58.

"Without having thought through all the implications and problems, the Fathers of Nicaea had the courage to maintain the tradition of the 'Son of God' to be found in Bible and church in all its strictness, in part with unbiblical words. . . . So much did the Fathers of Nicaea wish to remain within the framework of the baptismal kerygma, that they did not add any explanation of the way in which they themselves wanted the *homoousios* to be understood."[24]

Behind both Yoder's and Weaver's critique of the theological changes that took place in the first five centuries of the Christian church lies their legitimate concern for ethics. What occurs, as they correctly see it, is an ethical watering down of the Christian message. According to Weaver, Anabaptists take discipleship (shorthand for saying "that Jesus—his life and teaching—are normative for the Christian life") to be at the heart of the Gospel narratives. The formulations of Nicaea and Chalcedon are devoid of this ethical-discipleship dimension: "That fact should help us to understand that Nicea-Chalcedon is not a lens through which to read the New Testament, nor can Nicea-Chalcedon alone serve as the norm which tells us whether we have read the New Testament correctly."[25] Neither is there in these definitions of orthodoxy any reference to the manner of the atoning work of Christ. However, since Mennonites and others consider the nonviolent and nonresistant manner of Jesus' death crucial for people who claim Jesus as authoritative for their lives, these definitions are suspect. I share Yoder's and Weaver's concern to retrieve the ethical normativity of Jesus for Christian theology, and I lament the loss of this narrative, historical, and ethical dimension in the first few centuries. Nevertheless, I view the theological development that occurred as necessary. Some sort of a barebones theological substructure had to be created as a ground of ethics, and the framework that was constructed does not contradict the ethical claims of the New Testament.

The reasons for the theological shifts away from the New

24. Grillmeier, *Christ in Christian Tradition*, vol. 1: *From the Apostolic Age to Chalcedon (451)* (Atlanta: John Knox Press, 1975), p. 270.

25. Weaver, "Christology in Historical Perspective," p. 59.

Testament are for Weaver intrinsically linked to the gradual Constantinian shift that occurred over the centuries and reached its symbolic climax with the person of Constantine himself. Jesus was no longer taken to be normative for the life of average Christians, nor was the church thought of as a critical, prophetic minority. The emperor and responsibility for the state came to be authoritative. The Nicene council, called by Constantine and assisted in its theological formulations by Constantine, "was a matter of political expedience as well as a search for theological truth."[26] The slight hint by Weaver here that there may have also been at work among the bishops of the fourth century a search for theological truth is overshadowed by the general tenor of suspicion throughout that it is ultimately political expedience which determined the entire project of so-called orthodoxy. While alluding to the fact that Arius gained the upper hand after the Council of 325, that Constantine later threw his support behind Arius, that Athanasius (the defender of orthodoxy) was banned five times, and that in the end an Arian baptized Constantine, Weaver does not draw the obvious conclusion: that it was Arian theology rather than orthodoxy that lent itself more readily to Constantinianism. Here Weaver is less nuanced than Yoder, who acknowledges, as we have seen, that Arianism and the erosion of the claims regarding the exclusive deity of Christ were less faithful to the New Testament and could more easily be adapted to political idolatry than the claims of orthodoxy.

Weaver's conclusion is that, while Nicaea and Chalcedon have provided the church with a time-honored answer to the christological issue, it is only one and not necessarily the best answer. He argues that the answers given at Nicaea and Chalcedon are the products of a conference of people gathered together similar to a conference of Mennonites that met recently in Normal, Illinois, to discuss christology. As Mennonites pursue their contemporary search for christological clarity, he urges that they remain faithful to their sixteenth-century spiritual ancestors. Hans Denk's mystical christology, Pilgram Marpeck's external christology, and Menno Simon's suspect "un-Chalcedonian"

26. Weaver, "Christology in Historical Perspective," p. 63.

christology differ in substantive ways, but they have one thing in common: they hold Jesus' life, deeds, and teachings to be normative for Christian life. The established (or mainline) church has given up this normativity of Jesus since Constantine, and the Believers' Church needs to offer an alternative christology based on the normativity of the earthly, historical Jesus. In short, we have the choice of reading the Bible through Constantinian church eyes or Believers' Church eyes.

Both Yoder and Weaver reflect in good part the historic radical Protestant position, including the identification of the fall of the church with the Constantinian synthesis of church and state and a concomitant suspicion of the metaphysical, sacramental, and ontological language of the historic creeds.[27] There are many other contemporaries who could be cited to illustrate the same point of view. John E. Toews, for instance, has recently argued that the creeds and confessions do not help us in developing a sound doctrine of the church:

> The Christology of the creeds represents the thought and language of a particular time in history. Their theological affirmations served the churches of their era. *But the language is neither biblical nor modern, let alone post-modern.* Furthermore, as scholars have pointed out, the creeds do not offer good Christologies, nor were they intended to. The ecumenical creeds were never designed as Christologies. Instead, they answered specific and narrow Christological questions of their time, e.g. was Jesus both human and divine? They outline rules for doing Christology but not Christology itself.[28]

27. See Donald F. Durnbaugh, *The Believers' Church: The History and Character of Radical Protestantism* (Scottdale, Pa.: Herald Press, 1968), pp. 212-16.

28. Toews, *Jesus Christ the Convener of the Church* (Elkhart, Ind.: Mennonite Church, 1989), p. 5; italics mine. Toews is dean of Mennonite Brethren Biblical Seminary, Fresno, California. Although Ben C. Ollenburger is much more open to the importance of creeds than Toews is here, he makes the same point about creeds not offering us a christology but just rules for christology. See Ollenburger, "Christology and Creeds," *AMBS Bulletin* 52 (May 1989): 2. One can say this if christology is defined exclusively in terms of the work of Christ and not his being. If the being of Christ is considered to be part of christology, however— and surely it is—then the Nicene Creed does provide us with a substantive christology and not just a rule for christology.

A devaluation of the classical credal tradition is evident here. Toews implies that the creeds and Scripture are mutually exclusive categories, and that the New Testament is the only acceptable "starting point for Mennonite theological reflection" on the nature of christology and the church. Also, interestingly, there is the implication that one reason the creeds cannot be taken seriously is that they are alien to modern and postmodern thinking. I would argue that it is precisely in the modern and postmodern context, which has seen the consequences and collapse of strictly historicist and empiricist modes of perceiving the world, that the ontological and metaphysical presuppositions behind the classical creeds offer an appealing alternate way of viewing reality.

A PROPOSAL: TRINITARIAN ORTHODOXY WITHOUT CONSTANTINIANISM

There are, however, new voices being heard within Mennonite circles, individuals who are taking a second look not only at the importance of postbiblical patristic theological development but also at the Constantinian and post-Constantinian church. One of the most outspoken is Dennis Martin, a teacher at Associated Mennonite Biblical Seminaries in Elkhart, Indiana. In a provocative 1987 article, Martin distinguished between the modern linear view of history and the premodern multidimensional, multitemporal view. The former subordinates "the timeless, transcendent, traditional past to the present and future" and "rejects traditional pre-modern history in order to restore 'true history,'" locating this " 'true history' not in tradition or the mystery of the church but in a lost yet supposedly recoverable body of 'facts.' "[29] This fallacious view of history, Martin says, lies behind the Anabaptist-Mennonite *restitutionist* model of church renewal, in which a traditional, sacramental approach to history as characterized by the Catholic Church between A.D. 300

29. Martin, "Nothing New under the Sun? Mennonites and History," *Conrad Grebel Review* 5 (Winter 1987): 4-5.

and 1500 was rejected in favor of what was perceived to be a more New Testament view of the church. "They [Anabaptist Mennonites] believed that they could restore, recreate, or reconstruct that original Christian community rather than re-present or re-call (anamnesis) it. In the process they read back into the first three Christian centuries elements of their own situation."[30]

In effect, says Martin, it is "discontinuity" rather than "continuity" that characterizes history in the restitutionist model. In this view almost everything postbiblical is seen as discontinuous with the gospel. The fourth century and the Constantinianization of the church is most frequently identified as the place where the "fall of the church" occurred. Yoder suffers the brunt of Martin's critique: "Yoder distorts 'Constantinianism' by reading the 'established churches' of the post-Reformation era back into the fourth century. Nearly all the characteristics of 'Constantinianism' that Yoder adduces are more recognizable in the modern world than in the ancient or medieval world (dualism, establishment power, utilitarianism). He makes little distinction between the 'Constantinianism' of Eusebius in the early fourth century and that of Augustine."[31]

Martin defends what he calls the *reform* view of history: "It is the way the ancients understood history. It is the attitude toward history that predominated in the world of the Bible, in the world of the Greeks and Romans, and in the world of medieval Christianity. The traditional way of reform accepts the past all the way down to the present while at the same time calling for reform of institutions where they have become deformed. . . . It is an attitude that accepts institutions and has a basic attitude of trust toward the handing down (tradition) of institutions, even when it recognizes that institutions are deformed, and need reform."[32] Although Martin does not go into what this might mean in the way of understanding the theological formulations of the fourth and fifth centuries, his analysis and critique of the Anabaptist Mennonites' restitutionist ap-

30. Martin, "Nothing New under the Sun?" p. 7.
31. Martin, "Nothing New under the Sun?" p. 8.
32. Martin, "Nothing New under the Sun?" p. 11.

proach to history prepares the way for a much more sympathetic appropriation of classical trinitarian and christological formulations within Mennonite theology.

There are other voices that do indicate precisely such a new, more positive interest among Mennonites in the classical formulations of the ancient creeds, as is reflected in recent essays by Ben C. Ollenburger, Cornelius J. Dyck, and Marlin E. Miller.[33] The 1985 publication of Howard Loewen's *One Lord, One Church, One Hope, and One God* has contributed significantly to this renaissance of interest in the fourth- and fifth-century theological formulations.[34] Loewen's study suddenly brought to the attention of Mennonite readers, who had presumed that Mennonites like other radical Protestant groups were noncredal, that the various Mennonite groups have produced probably more confessions in their 465 years than any other Christian tradition. Many of these confessions, in their general structure (theology, christology, ecclesiology, eschatology) bear some remarkable similarities in their organization to classical creeds. What distinguishes them from the classical formulations and other mainline post-Reformation confessions is a heightened ethical consciousness. This concern for personal and social ethics, obedience to the life and teachings of Jesus, colors all of the articles of these confessions from beginning to end.

The radical Protestant suspicion of credal development during the patristic period is rooted, as we have seen, in its rejection of the Constantinian synthesis of Christianity and classical culture, its restitutionist view of church renewal, and its legitimate objection to the loss of the ethical. There are some valid grounds for this historic suspicion of Constantinianism and its theological legitimation. The insights of radical Protestantism in this regard ought, in my opinion, to be in the forefront of ecumenical discussion. Nevertheless, I want as a self-critical

33. Ollenburger, "Christology and Creeds," *AMBS Bulletin* 52 (May 1989): 1-3; Dyck, "C. Norman Kraus's Jesus Christ Our Lord in Historical Anabaptist Perspective," *AMBS Bulletin* 52 (May 1989): 4-7; Miller, "Christological Concepts of the Classical Creeds and Mennonite Confessions of Faith," *AMBS Bulletin* 52 (May 1989): 7-11.

34. Loewen, *One Lord, One Church, One Hope, and One God: Mennonite Confessions of Faith* (Elkhart, Ind.: Institute of Mennonite Studies, 1985).

Mennonite to propose in the final section of this essay (1) that theological orthodoxy as it developed in the first five centuries after Christ stands in fundamental continuity with the Scriptures, (2) that orthodoxy necessarily went beyond the Scriptures in developing a uniquely Christian doctrine of God, and (3) not only that classical trinitarian orthodoxy need not be identified with sociopolitical Constantinianism (it is in fact more able than alternative theologies to function as a critique of all forms of Constantinianism) but that it actually provides a necessary framework for Christian ethics.

Orthodoxy Stands in Continuity with the Scriptures

While the full-blown trinitarian formulation of Nicaea-Constantinople is not explicitly present in the Scriptures, it is there implicitly in the form of a question. The New Testament writers asked how they as early Christians could

1. remain faithful to the Jewish monotheism of the Old Testament (the one God, Yahweh, creator of everything visible and invisible, whom no one has seen, of whom no images are to be made, and who has repeatedly acted in the history of his people) and at the same time
2. acknowledge or account for the fact that this God has communicated himself to us, has been with us (Immanuel) in the birth, life, teachings, death, resurrection, and ascension of Jesus of Nazareth in an absolute sense, with the power to forgive sins and restore all things, and
3. acknowledge or account for the fact that the Holy Spirit, who descended upon the early followers of Jesus at Pentecost, is in fact the very presence and reality of God and of Jesus, giving birth to the church and uniting all believers with God, Christ, and each other.

Behind the trinitarian debates of the first few centuries lies the need to express these three separate convictions while asserting simultaneously the unity of God.

What is one to make of the claim by both Yoder and Weaver that between the Gospels and the creeds there occurred a major shift? Both (Weaver even more so than Yoder) stress the discontinuity that exists between the fourth-century theological definitions and the New Testament. They talk about the shift from the narrative mode of the Gospels to the ontological mode of the creeds as though this were a deviation from the biblical text. This fails adequately to recognize the "ontological-metaphysical" presuppositions behind biblical narrative itself. In my view the biblical kerygma is distorted if narrative (historical chronology or story telling) and ontology (generic being language) are torn asunder the way Yoder and particularly Weaver tend to do. Not only are both modes present within the biblical texts, but narrative as we have it in the synoptics (not to mention the Pauline epistles which are written earlier), I would argue, takes place within an ontological framework. In other words, the Bible does not absolutize history but places historical events within the context of ultimate reality, the way things are. The ontology of the relatively late prologue to the Gospel of John is not unlike the confessional ontology of Philippians 2, one of the earliest hymns to be found in the Christian Scriptures (likely sung or chanted well before the retrospective and narrative setting in order of events as we have them in the synoptics). Only in the modern context does narrative become pure historicism—that is, freed from cosmic and ontological moorings.

Yoder seems to equivocate in this regard. At some points, he draws direct links between the wisdom literature of the Hebrew Scriptures, the logos traditions of the Christian Scriptures (as embedded in Col. 1, Heb. 1, John 1, Phil. 2, and 1 Cor. 8), and the Greek concept of logos as cosmic rationality.[35] At other times, he talks about the shift from narrative to ontological language as a form of discontinuity, as a "moving away from the biblical center in mood, in style, in content."[36] There is, of course, a good

35. Yoder, *Preface to Theology*, pp. 123-25.
36. Yoder, *Preface to Theology*, p. 139.

deal of truth to Yoder's critical observation that with the passage of time, as we get closer to the fourth and fifth centuries, there appears to be less and less historical narrative present within the ontological framework of the creeds. The ethical gets lost. The alternative is not, however, to find a christological alternative to Nicaea and Chalcedon, as Weaver seems to suggest, but to retrieve the historical, narrative, and ethical content of trinitarian christology.

The basic point to be made here is that the ontological language of Nicaea-Constantinople stands in fundamental continuity with the Scriptures. The numerous binitarian (Rom. 8:11; 2 Cor. 4:14; Gal. 1:1; Eph. 1:20; 1 Tim. 1:2; 1 Pet. 1:21; and 2 John 1:13) and triadic references (Matt. 28:19; Acts 2:32-33; 1 Cor. 6:11; 12:4ff.; Gal. 3:11-14; Heb. 10:29; and 1 Pet. 1:2) simply confirm this basic continuity. In the words of William G. Rusch, "No doctrine of the Trinity in the Nicene sense is present in the New Testament. However, the threefold pattern is evident throughout, in spite of the fact that there is usually nothing in the context to demand it. The conclusion seems obvious; the idea of the triadic manifestation of the Godhead was present from the earliest period as part of Christian piety and thinking."[37]

The pressure of heretical groups (who threatened the truth of the biblical kerygma), the missionary impulse to explain the truth of the kerygma to the pagans, and the simple desire to know the truth of the matter propelled the church in the first five centuries to formulate what it took to be true. In the process, a Christian worldview developed that was distinct from strict Jewish monotheism on the one hand and Greco-Roman dualism on the other. What unfolded was a doctrine of God as three in one and one in three with profound implications for the Christian view not only of God but of the whole created universe and of human history. God was seen as having three modes of being: *transcendent* creator of all things visible and invisible, *historic* incarnation in human flesh in the person of Jesus of Nazareth,

---

37. Rusch, in *The Trinitarian Controversy*, ed. William G. Rusch (Philadelphia: Fortress Press, 1980), p. 2.

and *immanent* and *dynamic* presence in all of creation but particularly in the church through the Spirit.

The particular heresy that brought the issue to a head was
Arianism. The upshot of Arius's theology was that Christ was
not fully divine, shorthand for saying that the power of God in
Jesus was not really the eternal divine power itself but a lesser
power (i.e., in Jesus, God was not fully with us as humans).[38]
Both the christological debates leading up to Chalcedon and the
trinitarian debates leading up to Nicaea and Constantinople had
finally to do with the nature of our salvation, and were, consequently, deeply concerned with God's relation to the world of
human experience. To question the full deity of Christ is to call
into question the fullness of our salvation. A trinitarian christology is essential for soteriology. This is especially relevant for
Mennonites and their concern for regenerate life. The Anabaptists repeatedly spoke of regeneration as not only becoming
Christ-like but actually taking on or participating in the divine
nature itself. In this they have something in common with the
Eastern theological tradition. It was, they believed, through the
Holy Spirit that we become Christ-like, and through being
Christ-like that we partake of the divine nature itself.

The creed of Nicaea-Constantinople is the culmination of a
development that begins in the New Testament itself. What
occurred was not a corruption of the original message but an
unfolding and development of the ontological implications of the
original message. It was not just one possible line of development,
one of many other lines that might have been taken just as
legitimately. Nor was it a formulation necessary for only one
historical moment. The orthodoxy that was defined and the distortions of the truth that were identified continue to have universal significance for the Christian church. Credalization took place
more or less at the same time that canonization took place and for
more or less the same reasons: to establish norms by which to
determine what was true and what was false. The primary importance of the Nicene formulation is not each literal word (there
was no plenary or verbal inspiration) but the basic trinitarian

38. See Rusch, *The Trinitarian Controversy*, p. 17.

structure that has become theologically normative for the church. By it the church defined the Christian doctrine of God—the one God having three modes of being: Father, Son, Holy Spirit.

Classical Orthodoxy Is a Necessary Doctrinal Development beyond the Scriptures

No one disputes the fact that the language of Nicaea, Constantinople, and Chalcedon is not pure biblical language or that the doctrine of the Trinity as articulated in 381 cannot be found as such in the New Testament. I would like to propose, however, that Nicaea and Constantinople represent a necessary development of doctrine beyond the Scriptures, retaining a faithful continuity with Scriptures as far as its formal christological claims are concerned but unfortunately losing sight of the existential component of the kerygma and the ethical claims of Jesus without which all dogma becomes abstract formalism. The point I want to make at the end of this essay is that classical dogmatic formulations are in fact essential for assuring an onto-logical-metaphysical grounding for ethics—relevant especially in an age when ethics is defined primarily if not exclusively in terms of free human agency, without reference to a transcendent ground. Here I want to concentrate on what Richard P. C. Hanson has recently described as the development of a uniquely Christian doctrine of God that occurs during the patristic period.

Hanson distinguishes between the "immediate occasion" of the trinitarian development (the Arian controversy) and the "original urge or need or dynamism" that gave rise to it. The latter is more important and has to do with the development of a specifically Christian doctrine of God distinct from the Jewish doctrine of God. The New Testament just hinted at such a doctrine. "It was when Christianity emerged during the second century into a non-Jewish largely Gentile milieu that the pressure to produce a specifically Christian doctrine of God became unavoidable."[39] Why was a Christian doctrine of God so neces-

---

39. Hanson, *Studies in Christian Antiquity* (Edinburgh: T. & T. Clark, 1985), p. 239.

sary? I find Hanson's answer to this question persuasive: "If Christianity was to be more than an enthusiastic or moralizing sect making no pretensions to intellectual respectability, more than an ethnic religion . . . it was bound to produce a specifically Christian doctrine of God."[40] It was necessary "if Christianity was to be a missionary religion, a religion capable of sustaining the daring claim that it was a faith for all races and all classes and all minds, a religion for the whole world."[41] In other words, what Hanson appears to be saying is that in the first few centuries after Jesus of Nazareth came and went, a new religion was born, the Christian religion, with a new doctrine of God profoundly indebted to but ultimately different from the Jewish doctrine of God. According to Hanson, Christianity was more than a "subvariety of Judaism."

The noteworthy fact is that the fourth-century development destroyed "the tradition of Christ as a convenient philosophical device, of Christ, as the Cappadocian fathers put it, existing for the sake of us instead of our existing for his sake."[42] It was the Arians who (influenced by middle Platonist cosmology)[43] Hellenized the gospel and tended to see Christ as a "demigod" philosophically understood. The trinitarian faith of Nicaea-Constantinople, as shaped finally by the Cappadocians, was in fact much truer to the biblical Christ ("the monotheism that is part of the inner nature of Christianity and that also did justice to the ancient practice of worshipping Christ")[44] than the theological positions as articulated by most of the leading theologians from the second century onward had been.

Hanson is arguing that the development of the fourth-century doctrine of God was in fact a return to biblical origins. It was, however, a return characterized by new language and new imagery. Hanson makes the lucid point that "One of the lessons learnt by the bitter experience of the Arian Controversy was that you cannot interpret the Bible simply in biblical terms. If

---

40. Hanson, *Studies in Christian Antiquity*, p. 240.
41. Hanson, *Studies in Christian Antiquity*, p. 240.
42. Hanson, *Studies in Christian Antiquity*, p. 244.
43. See Grillmeier, *Christ in Christian Tradition*, 1:228ff.
44. Hanson, *Studies in Christian Antiquity*, p. 244.

your intention is to explain the Bible's meaning, then on crucial points you must draw your explanation from some other vocabulary apart from that of the Bible. Otherwise you will be left with the old question in another form still unanswered."[45] It may be the case, as Hanson states, that pro-Nicene theologians found it difficult to deal with a transtemporal God acting in temporal history, with the Word taking on human flesh, with "the full force of the dynamic, eschatological language which the N.T. uses of Christ and the Holy Spirit." In the words of Hanson, "They flatten and blunt this language, transposing it into ontological categories. For Athanasius, as has frequently been observed, the divinity of Christ means his ontological stability."[46]

But this charge that the dynamic element was lost in the fourth and fifth centuries is in my view open to further debate. Already in 1940 the great classicist Charles Norris Cochrane argued persuasively that it was precisely the dynamic nature of the fourth-century trinitarian schema, particularly as later formulated by Augustine, that overcame static Greek dualism and helped shape Western views of dynamic history.[47] On this matter, Hanson slips into a Yoderian kind of argument which he fails to sustain consistently. He qualifies his previous comments and speaks of the fact that the fourth-century Fathers retained nonphilosophical language when talking about the bodily resurrection, the creation of matter *ex nihilo*, and the incarnation. He concludes that "Perhaps the best way to express the situation would be to say that in all their theology there is a tension between the ideas of Greek philosophy and those of the tradition of Christian truth which they inherited."[48] The point I am trying to make, more strongly than does Hanson, is that the two (the biblical and the philosophical, the historical-Hebraic and the ontological-Hellenistic) ought not to

45. Hanson, *Studies in Christian Antiquity*, p. 247.
46. Hanson, *Studies in Christian Antiquity*, p. 248.
47. Cochrane, *Christianity and Classical Culture: A Study of Thought and Action from Augustus to Augustine* (London: Oxford University Press, 1940, 1974).
48. Hanson, *Studies in Christian Antiquity*, p. 248.

be torn asunder. They belonged together in the formation of primitive Christianity and in the theological development that occurred in the first four centuries, and they ought to be held together.

One could say that the nature of theological language itself evolved during these first four centuries as the uniquely Christian doctrine of God unfolded. Hanson traces the changing use of trinitarian imagery in the first four centuries (Logos, Father and Son, icon, ray or reflection, character as impression or stamp, stream, branch, sunbeam, and so on). Arians, interestingly, tended to be more literalistic in their use of such imagery. They argued, for example, that since sons come after fathers, the Son of God must have been produced after and be inferior to God the Father.[49] The important point for us here is that the Church Fathers and particularly the Nicene theologians (Athanasius and the Cappadocians) fully recognized the inadequacy of human language to talk about God. They were less concerned with precise literal wording and formulas than later generations (including ours) have been, and they were more concerned with the meaning and content of what was expressed.[50] In the end Basil and the two Gregories reduced their use of images and analogies to a minimum because they disagreed with the way these images had been used by previous generations of theologians. In particular they objected to the use of "the pre-existent *Logos* as a convenient *philosophical* device" to preserve the "impassibility of God."[51] They went back to the New Testament *theological* notion of Christ as Logos, as found in John 1. "The interesting and almost startling repudiation of tradition," says Hanson, "should remind us further that a process of development of doctrine can very well include a movement of pruning, almost reformation, as well as a positive evolution into something new."[52] They insisted that the Christ as Logos was both incarnate and pre-existent and that it was in this way that the transcendent God had involved

---

49. Hanson, *Studies in Christian Antiquity*, p. 260.
50. Hanson, *Studies in Christian Antiquity*, pp. 250-51.
51. Hanson, *Studies in Christian Antiquity*, p. 276.
52. Hanson, *Studies in Christian Antiquity*, pp. 276-77.

himself with human existence and experience. Although it is unfortunately true that the historical, narrative, ethical Jesus largely got lost in this theological development, it is not true that the God whom the Nicene theologians envisaged was solely a transcendent distant God who was removed from the world of human experience. The whole point of the trinitarian formulation was to express as adequately as possible that God is transcendent and impassible, that God did take on human flesh in the incarnation, and that God remains with us historically in some way. It is within the framework of these three claims that a contemporary ethic can be theologically retrieved.

Trinitarian Orthodoxy as a Necessary Framework for Ethics

We come now, finally, to the most difficult and most important aspect of this discussion: the relation of the theological developments of the fourth century to Constantinianism and to ethics in general. It is the agenda that has been set for us in this essay particularly by Yoder and Weaver. I want to support the radical Protestant suspicion of all forms of Constantinianism and its theological legitimation but to dispute the frequent assumption made by radical Protestant theologians that theological orthodoxy is necessarily always a handmaiden of Constantinianism.

Even the fourth-century connection between Constantine's political ambitions and the bishops' theological concerns at and after Nicaea are more ambiguous than some claim. Aloys Grillmeier gives us a penetrating historical analysis of Constantine's role at Nicaea. He acknowledges that Constantine's personal intervention in religious politics after his conversion in 312, and more actively in 324, "was the most momentous decision on the way towards the imperial church."[53] It was Eusebius of Caesarea, however, with his Arian tendencies, who truly espoused a political theology. "A historico-political theology emerges: the appearance of the Messiah and imperial peace, Christianity and

53. Grillmeier, *Christ in Christian Tradition*, 1:249-50.
54. Grillmeier, *Christ in Christian Tradition*, 1:251.

the empire, are bound together in an indissoluble unity by the idea of providence."[54] The Roman monarchy came to represent the heavenly monarchy. The divine Logos was seen by Eusebius and some of the bishops he influenced as embodied within the Constantinian monarchy.

This was not a uniformly held opinion, however, and Augustine decisively broke through such a view of history and the world in his *City of God*. It is this diversity of views concerning the role of the emperor in church affairs that Grillmeier emphasizes. According to Eusebius, the emperor was the sovereign even in deciding matters of orthodoxy. Others, including Constantine himself, did not view it this way. Constantine was, of course, convinced that "the well-being of the state and the unity of the church" belonged indissolubly together. But Constantine, according to Grillmeier, believed that this bond "had been created by experience of the power of the God of the Christians and his grace."[55] He had sleepless nights over the Arian controversy, and his calling and participation of the Nicene Council was to help bring unity, end heresy, and search for truth. According to his own correspondence, he saw himself not as one who dictated a solution but as a "fellow servant" of the bishops. He thought of his own intervention as "subsidiary," the final norms being the church's own canons and tradition: "In his own documents he does not claim to have directed the synod. On the contrary, the decisions were worked out by the bishops themselves, under the guidance of the Holy Spirit, in search of the will of God. The ultimate norm for the decision of the council is to be sought here, as in the apostolic traditions and the canons of the church."[56] In short, Eusebius made much higher claims for the emperor than did Constantine himself. It was Eusebius's sacralization of the emperor as "the interpreter of God and of the Logos-Christ," as someone at "the supreme summit of the visible world understood in religious terms," that accompanied later Byzantine history.

According to Grillmeier, the imperial documents between

---

55. Grillmeier, *Christ in Christian Tradition*, 1:257.
56. Grillmeier, *Christ in Christian Tradition*, 1:260.

325 and 335 suggest that Constantine did not really influence the council's theological statements significantly, that he was not even up to the theological debates going on at the time, although in time his advisors, especially the Eusebian party, seem to have increasingly found his ear. Hanson makes the point in a slightly different but complementary way. He argues that, while most of those involved in the Arian controversy (with some rare exceptions) thought of the emperor as having final authority, and while several emperors attempted to play such an authoritative role but failed because they did not have sufficient support from the church, in the end Theodosius succeeded because he was backed by the general assent of the church.[57] It was the Eusebian-type political theology in which Constantine took on divine status, became a Logos figure, an Arian-like demigod, that must be seen as the prototype of a fallen church, not the era as a whole or theological orthodoxy in particular.

Where does all of this leave us as far as our immediate proposal is concerned? The particular contribution that the theology of radical Protestantism can make to any ecumenical discussion of the fourth century resides in its suspicion of all forms of "Constantinianism"—that is, in its critique of all political theology in which theology and politics are fused, or worse, where theology functions as an instrument of political ideology. In such political theology, true theology loses its own ground; it no longer witnesses to transcendent, revelatory norms by which critically to evaluate political society and thereby sanctify finite, historical empires, nations, parties, movements, groups, and figures. That this happened during the time of Constantine and subsequent emperors cannot be denied. In fact, that this has happened throughout most of Christian history cannot be disputed. Constantinianism and so-called "Caesaropapism" must from the radical Protestant perspective be severely judged. Here Yoder and Weaver are surely right. The question is whether classical orthodoxy, as articulated in the ecumenical creeds of the fourth and fifth centuries, is contingent on Constantinianization (or the other way around). I have attempted, using

---

57. Hanson, *Studies in Christian Antiquity,* p. 239.

Hanson's and Grillmeier's historical analysis of the period, to distinguish between the two and to say that the theological development cannot be explained comprehensively solely with reference to the sociopolitical milieu in which it occurred.

It is true that the Emperor Constantine called the Nicene Council, chaired the meetings and doctrinal discussions, and allegedly contributed some of the crucial terminology. It is also possible that Constantine's own conversion and interest in creating ecclesiastical unity during the Arian controversy was motivated largely by political expediency, the desire for political unity. It does not follow, however, that the theological formulations coming out of this and subsequent councils are therefore to be rejected outright. The theological formulations of Nicaea, Constantinople, and Chalcedon cannot be accounted for exclusively in terms of their sociopolitical context. If one looks carefully at the historical events surrounding the trinitarian and christological debates, one comes to the following conclusions:

1. Nicaea itself was the culmination of a long process that began already in the New Testament (as a question to be answered), a process that gave birth to a uniquely Christian doctrine of God. It so happened that Constantine was the catalyst who brought the various groups together and played a crucial role in moving the theological development forward for whatever reasons.
2. The specific wording that Constantine is said to have provided ("of the same essence") was in fact quite ambiguous and began a heated round of debate that was resolved only at Constantinople, largely through the influence of three biblically minded theologians, the Cappadocians.
3. Athanasius, one of the chief early architects of Nicaea, was a political persona non grata during the Constantinian period.
4. The emperors and their immediate circle of advisors (e.g., Eusebius) appear to have been more inclined toward Arianism than orthodoxy. Theologically, as Yoder so astutely observes, Arianism, which allowed for demigods, was much more congenial to Constantinianism than orthodoxy.

In conclusion, I give three reasons why I believe an orthodox trinitarian theology is important for a contemporary Christian ethic. First, it provides us with the best conceptual critique of all political theology that legitimates a civil religion—that is, one in which religion or theology functions primarily as a conservative force in society, a glue that holds things together, usually sanctifying the dominant culture of an age.[58] A trinitarianism in which the one God is believed to be genuinely *transcendent* (Yahweh, of whom no graven images can be made, alongside whom there are no other gods), *historically* uniquely present in Jesus Christ (who is not simply one more demigod who can be incarnated in numerous forms, political figures, or historical movements but is truly God with us), and *immanently* present within the cosmos, nature, history, and particularly the church as the Holy Spirit (not as the human spirit, but as the Spirit that proceeds from God the "Father" and God the "Son"), is the surest way of guarding against all forms of political and national idolatry (Constantinianism). This is the basis of Karl Barth's own twentieth-century defense of a christocentric trinitarianism in the face of the "Aryan" heresies of the pro-Hitler German Christians in the 1930s.

Second, the mystery of the Trinity has throughout history inspired mystical thought and spiritual formation. In fact, as Roberta C. Bondi has so persuasively shown in her contribution to this colloquium,[59] many of the bishops who played leading roles in credal development in the fourth century themselves came from the monastic tradition and were shaped by the moral and spiritual formation at the heart of monasticism. There has been a growing recognition among Christians engaged in the struggle for social justice that if the contemporary ethical agenda is not to be reduced to human action pure and simple, and if the struggle is to have staying power, it will need to be rooted in spirituality. I would hold that the kind of spirituality that pro-

58. I'm not denying that religion, including Christianity, ought to have a priestly-sacramental function, only that the prophetic-eschatological role ought to be stronger and the sacramental role subordinate.

59. "The Fourth-Century Church: The Monastic Contribution," pp. 60-82 herein.

vides a distinctively Christian basis for moral and ethical action in the world is a trinitarian spirituality. Classical trinitarianism is not merely an abstract philosophical construct but is concerned precisely with what *God* is doing in the world in and through *Christ* and the *Spirit*. For Mennonites, who are especially concerned with the ethical dimensions of Christ's message (a nonviolent love ethic in particular), it is doubly important to ground the moral claims of Jesus and the regenerative power of the Holy Spirit in the very nature and person of God without thereby claiming to have said everything about the mystery of God that can be said.

Finally, trinitarian thinking about God is urgently needed in the face of of the contemporary environmental crisis. The threat of ecological disaster has its origin in modern assumptions about historical progress, unlimited human freedom, nature as "dead stuff" to be subdued in whatever ways we see fit, and the loss of a sense of moral responsibility to a transcendent reality for what we are doing with and on the earth. A trinitarian doctrine of God provides us precisely with three necessary ways of perceiving divine reality in relation to this world and our moral responsibility: as transcendent Creator to whom we are accountable, and who is ultimately in charge of the cosmos despite what we do; as historically self-disclosed in the being and nature of Christ (therein giving us a quite specific moral and ethical agenda); and as Spirit immediately present to us in the church but also in all of creation. No longer can the created order be seen as dead stuff at our disposal. All of creation is in some sense grounded in the very being of God.

The Trinity as Public Theology:
Its Truth and Justice for Free-Church,
Noncredal Communities

MAX L. STACKHOUSE

WHY ARE WE DOING THIS?

The formation of the trinitarian creeds in the early church involved a step of faith for the Christian Tradition that was second only to the writing, redaction, and canonization of the Holy Bible. Few Christians doubt that the doctrine of the Trinity is near the center of our confessions, our hymnody, and our liturgies, where our traditions are embodied. And these all point to the most clearly defined understandings of the true nature of the living God and the ways God relates to humanity that are available to us. But some may wonder why, at this time, the interpretation of the history, origin, and implications of this doctrine would become central to the ecumenical movement and why Christianity engaged in the formation of such a theory.

A key reason for this new interest, I believe, has to do with the fact that many feel that Christianity is on the brink of, and in considerable need of, renewal—a renewal that would rediscover the vitality of Christian understandings of God and guide the restructuring of church and society as we enter a decidedly cosmopolitan era. At the deepest level, that is what the doctrine of the Trinity does. As we call the Hebrew Scriptures the "Old Testament" and the writings from Matthew's Gospel to John's Revelation the "New Testament," we might call the great classical trinitarian creeds the "renewing testaments"—or, to reflect more accurately the biblical traditions, "covenant renewals."

Each authentic reformulation represents a recovery and recasting of the faith in the face of internal threats, external compromises, new insights, doubt, or confusion. It also provides—indeed, must provide—a model for just living in church and society. It is thus an exhilarating challenge, as well as a weighty duty, to take up these questions again in our age.

The fact that the ecumenical church is now setting about a long-term study of the ancient confessions of faith indicates both that the church has not yet fully settled all the issues connected with what our forebears did in the councils and that we may again be facing internal threats, external compromises, new insights, doubt, and confusion. That all matters are not resolved seems clear enough. The continuing debates between Eastern and Western views of filioque suggest that Tradition is not finally settled, much as the full meaning of any biblical text is not finally settled, although different traditions of exegesis interpret the same witness in distinctive ways. Nevertheless, it can be said that the trinitarian creeds are basically in accord with biblical meanings and that Scripture and creed together allow us to interpret each more clearly than we could if we had to rely on one alone. As Pastor John Robinson said in sending forth the Pilgrims to their new land, "God hath yet more truth to break forth." We today expect that truth to break forth from both Scripture and Tradition.

To be sure, we must early face the fact that many Christians in the "free churches" and among the "newer churches" in non-Western cultures are not sure whether we ought to rely on this Tradition as a source of authority. The term suggests a magisterial heritage that was a source of persecution to some and a metaphysical mode of discourse too wedded to the cultural ideas of the Greco-Roman world. Often these accusations accurately reflect particular moments of history. Sometimes confessions of faith were enforced by the power of the sword, generating a great suspicion of any direct relationship between politics and religion. But this suspicion is misdirected if it fails to understand that Tradition is less a matter of historical moments than an ongoing process of discernment, that its intellectual precipitates are formed by Christians trying to be faithful as they encounter new social, intellectual, cultural, and personal contexts of life, and that every serious theology must imply a social ethic for the ordering and conducting of public life.

For example, non-Western Christians are today finding fresh insight in the thought of such figures as Jonathan Edwards, a free-church thinker who spent many years as a missionary in a non-Western culture and stands still as one of the greatest minds in the transition from classic to modern thought.[1] He argued more than two centuries ago that the Trinity is a critically important social and philosophical-theological way of stating the truth that is present in the biblical understanding of "covenant"—one of the core notions behind both Testaments, yet one long neglected by Orthodox, Catholic, Anglican, and Lutheran theologians until modern historical study rediscovered its centrality. Following his lead today could evoke an awakening to the wider implications of the Trinity or even a Josiah-like renewal of the covenantal tradition in public affairs.

As the people of God rediscover and recast the central themes of the faith today in the context of a new global consciousness shaped by fresh encounters with the world's great religions and a concomitant ignorance of the importance of religion among secular leaders, absolutization of religion by resurgent fundamentalism, and chauvinist celebration of particular contexts by no few believers, we try to give account of the faith that is within us. But more, we shall have to show that it makes a difference in this life and in the life to come that all

---

1. See, especially, Sang Hyun Lee, *The Philosophical Theology of Jonathan Edwards* (Princeton University Press, 1989), and Krister Sairsingh, "Jonathan Edwards and the Idea of Divine Glory: His Foundational Trinitarianism and Its Ecclesial Import" (Ph.D. diss., Harvard University, 1986).

humanity believes the truths of the Trinity—a matter the world now doubts.

One of the most remarkable things about the trinitarian creeds is that they transcend their origins. The decisive debates refuse to perish with the early Arians, Athanasians, Eusebians, and the like. They continually open new horizons, and they demonstrate how to state, in terms foreign to biblical thought, basic themes about the nature of God and about the way God relates to creation that are clearly drawn from biblical materials—which are much more historical in origin and narrative in character. Indeed, one of the reasons for attempting to recover and recast the truth of the ancient trinitarian creeds is that many today doubt whether it is possible to thematize narrative and historical patterns of truth at all, although doctrines of both Trinity and covenant are transcontextual, even universal, in importance.

It has become a seldom-challenged truism today that everything must be understood in terms of its social and historical context. The difficulty comes when it is held that this is the only valid way to understand some historic claim about what is universally true and just. Not a few think that we should have done with all those quaint, old-fashioned efforts to think in universalistic ways. What the Greeks thought to be universal turned out not to be entirely so. Therefore, some say, we should learn from this that we cannot state universal transcontextual truth; we can state only the particular concrete truths of our own contextually defined experience. The advocates of this position talk of Trinity only impatiently; their hermeneutics of suspicion contains an implicit doubt about the orthodoxy and the catholicity of the classic teachings on these abstract points. Indeed, nothing could be orthodox or catholic according to this view.

On the other hand, others say that we must follow the lead of those who met in the early councils to set forth enduring transcontextual theological truth in language that included the particular temporal, spatial, and cultural insights of the biblical narratives and of all the particular churches and cosmopolitan civilizations of the ancient world from which the delegates came. The church has only a few options: to dwell in the thought world from which our particular traditions derive (and have little to say to the world in which we live today) or to adopt the intellectual life of the present (with no deeper memory or wider faith to bring to it).

Or, we can follow the lead of our forebears. That does not entail simply repeating what they said, any more than preaching a good sermon entails merely reading a long passage of Scripture. Rather, being faithful to what they did may entail identifying, defending, and preserving what they did on the one hand and assuming the responsibility of speaking to our contexts in fresh ways—as they did—on the other.

In this regard, our work together anticipates an eventual agreement of the ecumenical church in council on key questions. This in itself is of great significance, for it suggests (1) that the doctrine of the Trinity involves a logic and a comprehension that can be debated and discussed reasonably as we encounter one another beyond our particular traditions, languages, and cultures and (2) that the discernment of valid truth by drawing a community of persons into engaged dialogue embodies part of the meaning of the Trinity itself. To put it another way, following the lead of our conciliar forebears invites a modern invocation of the Spirit of Pentecost—which, if it attends, allows whole cultures to grasp the biblical message in their own terms while bringing a new birth to the church.

When we take up the ancient trinitarian formulas as valid touchstones of understanding in the contemporary church, we are saying at least that the gospel can be stated in terms other than those of the biblical record and that attention to the formation of tradition in "abstract" terms is proper to questions of salvation and necessary to the witness of the authentic community of faith. Such a view involves a direct, if quiet, challenge to all Protestants—evangelical or existential or liberal—who all too often leap from the Bible to contemporary applications, ignoring or repudiating all between then and now.

When we take up the ancient trinitarian formulas as major questions that may require contemporary reformulation or refinement, we are also asking whether we can speak both to the modern worlds of humanism and metaphysical skepticism (which claim to have left all such "speculations" and "myths" behind) and to the worlds where the great non-Christian religions have shaped philosophies and civilizations as great and subtle as those of Greece and Rome. Sooner or later we may even have to ask whether the truth of Scripture, known also in the trinitarian creeds, can be known in terms that are as different from those of the Greco-Roman world as that world was from the Scripture. We face today several complex cultures and worldviews quite as nuanced as those of the ancient Western world. Do the trinitarian creeds help us address them? And if so, how? Such a question involves a direct, if quiet, challenge to all Orthodox, Catholic, Lutheran, and Anglican thinkers who think that all would be well if we could simply get back to the "authentic" tradition as our forebears handed it to us.

As we assume the responsibilities of taking up these matters, we might do well to recognize from the outset that not every transcontextual truth issued by the councils is of equal importance. Some are quite possibly not universal, even if we have thought they were for some time. The church may have to apply what we may call the "Petrine test" in each epoch—that is, it will have to recognize, as did Peter, that it may have to repent when it denies the truth even if it knows that telling it may have adverse consequences. And, as Peter did later, it may have to acknowledge in council that the principles of inclusion and exclusion that reigned earlier ought not be taken as final.

Some councils are weightier than others and some formulations are deserving of greater attention than others. We have to discern which parts of what they said are the foundation stones on which we are today able to build the church in the faithless contexts in which many live, which serve as bridges to non-Christian faiths, which are necessary to construct a fortress against barbarous paganisms, which are landmarks for pilgrims of all ages, which are stepping-stones on which the church has moved from past to future (and whether they have been eroded by the floods of time as the church has moved on), and which mark the rock on which all humanity must stand forever if it is not to fall utterly.

Of course, some changes will take place in how we talk

about these matters, and this is so for several reasons. Some dimensions of the creeds will have to be taken up in the context of new questions. For example, questions of the relationship of *ecclesia* to *imperium* were decisive for many in the early centuries: it shaped basic perceptions of and language about the divine nature of persons in relationship.[2]

The covenantal tradition has surpassed that pattern and given rise to forms of constitutional democracy under laws that seek to assure the rights of religion, speech, dissent, and assembly—forms that both developing countries and the socialist world are seeking to emulate in one of the most dramatic revolutions of modernity, as has been suggested elsewhere.[3] In the West, meanwhile, questions of *connubium* and *commercium* seem more pressing to many believers and so they stress aspects of our forebears' formulas that appear to have been weighted in directions that we now judge to be biased against women and the poor.

We shall have to decide whether we believe that the Holy Spirit is present in the movements drawing these matters to our attention and whether we think that ethical criteria of justice can be properly used to alter previous truth claims. It may be that we should presume that if the Church Fathers were in conversation with the many who now see issues of sexuality and economic life in a new light (due in part to the gradual, if partial, actualization of Gal. 3:28), they would pray that we correct their errors.

The whole community of faith is not yet clear how it should adapt its language and practices to become genuinely inclusive, nor even as to where exactly the boundaries of gender might properly be drawn; but all who have ears to hear agree that we need to approach our modern clarifications on the basis of, at least, nonexclusivity. Careful work on this front, such as that being attempted in my communion by Barbara B. Zikmund and Susan Thistlethwaite, represents a contribution to the capacity

2. See especially the ground-breaking work in this area by George Hunston Williams, "Christology and Church-State Relations in the Fourth Century," *Church History* 20 (Sept. 1951): 3-33; and 20 (Dec. 1951): 3-26.

3. See my *Creeds, Society, and Human Rights* (Grand Rapids: William B. Eerdmans, 1984).

of the whole people of God to have a more covenantal view of the doctrine of the Trinity.[4]

Other changes may be less heated but equally important as we take up these questions in a new global situation in which we have few guides to overcome the moral and spiritual anarchy that is modulated only by modest approaches to a new cosmopolitan quest for universal standards of justice and truth. Of course, we must recognize that for many believers what we do will make little immediate difference in faith or practice (or, possibly, for their salvation, although we must leave that question to God). Those who pray to the loving, law-giving Creator of all, who contritely confess that Jesus is Lord, or who feel the presence of the Holy Spirit as they sing their hymns are likely to care very little how our discussions come out. Indeed, the noncredal churches, such as my own, are surely accurate in grasping the dispensability of "credalism" at this level. The relation between the personal love of God and having right ideas about God is not immediately clear.

Nevertheless, it may be that at entirely other levels the issues we take up may well be decisive for salvation. We should perhaps recognize at the outset that we are working at a level of theology that is only indirectly decisive for the personal faith of believers, even should we find agreement on the need for and the nature of substantive change in rather "abstract" dimensions of theological and symbolic formulation. In this area, the non-credal communities of faith may have something important to learn—especially if they are concerned to be prophetic in their social witness.

One resource that can help us see the importance of what we are doing is a major mode of postreductionist social analysis that takes religion very seriously as a critical factor in civilizations. Most of the social sciences as they developed in the last century presumed that religion could best be understood as a function of something else—psychological need, economic deprivation,

4. See Zikmund, "The Trinity and Women's Experience," *Christian Century*, 15 April 1987, pp. 354-56; and Thistlethwaite, "God Language and the Trinity," *United Church of Christ/Evangelische Kirche der Union Newsletter*, 1984.

political ideology, cultural convention, and so on. But modern cybernetics theory, as it has been adapted into social interpretation by (especially Weberian) theorists such as Parsons, Geertz, and Wuthnow, suggests that low-energy systems such as ethics and religion in fact set the boundaries for, guide, and control higher-energy systems that are primarily psychosexual, socio-political, material, or cultural in nature—if the linkages and feedback mechanisms between the low- and high-energy systems are present.[5] That is why, in spite of the fact that basic human needs and the mechanics of social organization are very much the same all over the world, societies may strikingly differ: their actions are channeled differently by divergent symbolic systems. If so, then symbolic formulas that deal with the highest possible realities are decisive for the ordering of civilizations.

If we, for example, attempt to identify the implications of the classic formulations of the Trinity for institutional life, we will begin to see that no arrangements will be satisfactory unless the following ingredients are distinctly present and intimately related:

> First, worthy power [must appear] in creative patterns of just order . . . that function to restrain chaos and death, to remind man of his proclivity to falsehood and evil, and to provide positive guidelines by which we can shape our environment. . . .
>
> Second, . . . conditions [must be present] whereby the self can experience the promise and possibility of continual renewal. Here the material conditions of physical existence must be conjoined to modes of normative ego identity so as to allow both flexibility and a relatively integrated identity within the context of ordered structures and genuine community participation. . . .
>
> Third, . . . there must be dynamic, creative movement that provides immediate contact with the cutting edge of historical development . . . and artistic creativity in the broadest sense.[6]

5. See, especially, Talcott Parsons, *Action Theory and the Human Condition* (New York: Free Press, 1978); C. Geertz, *The Interpretation of Cultures* (New York: Basic Books, 1973); R. Bellah, *The Broken Covenant* (New York: Crossroad Books, 1975); and R. Wuthnow, *Meaning and Moral Order* (Berkeley and Los Angeles: University of California Press, 1984).

6. I draw these from my earlier attempt to state something of the social

Of course, theology—even such a version as this, which tries to paraphrase dimensions of the persons of the Trinity to explicate their implications for normative social theory—is not simply part of a societal or cultural system. If it is correct, it transcends and evaluates all civilizational constructions, including organized religion, and it is moreover a normative symbolic mode of communication that may, if the linkages are present, guide the psychosexual, political-legal, material, and cultural systems in which we live.

If this is so, it means that what we do is potentially decisive for the salvation of the world in a quite literal sense. This is another way of saying something that our forebears believed but that many of us have come to doubt—namely, that theology is the queen of the sciences, and getting it right is critical for human salvation. There are no other sources from which we can draw normative models for the guidance of the common life.

For all the changes that work on the trinitarian creeds might well bring (during the next half-century, if *Baptism, Eucharist and Ministry* is any indication), the deeper question is whether there is any knowable right ordering of persons in relationship in God and in God's relationship to the world that must be recognized as reliable guides to life and thought in the midst of all the change, diversity of understanding, and novelty that is also entailed in the affirmation of the doctrine of the Trinity. It is perhaps in this question as much as in any other that the fundamental questions about the relationship of faith and order are necessarily linked to questions both of life and work and of peace and justice—inescapable dimensions of the common commitments of the whole ecumenical church.

On these issues, our efforts will come to nothing if we are not careful both historically and systematically and if we fail to recognize the intimate connection of the truth of God to the justice of God.

---

significance of the Trinity, in *Ethics and the Urban Ethos* (Boston: Beacon Press, 1973), pp. 137-38. I am indebted with respect to this to Williams, "Christology and Church-State Relations in the Fourth Century."

WHAT FREE-CHURCH ECUMENISM OFFERS

The United Church of Christ offers to discussions of these matters a set of perspectives that, as I understand them, are characteristic of many contemporary "liberal" denominations that have developed a historic stress on Christian social ethics. A chief contribution of the UCC is this: social justice questions are taken to be central to all issues posed by and to the whole community of faith. Thus, while the UCC unquestionably accepts the doctrine of the Trinity, basically in the Western form, many want to know what difference these ecumenical efforts might make in guiding the common social life. Why is it important to this vocation of the church?

The social justice question is obviously not the only question that needs to be raised, but it is possible that others might learn from our question as we try to learn from theirs. Indeed, modern challenges to the doctrine of the Trinity not infrequently have come from close encounters with philosophical or social movements that brought or accompanied or legitimated immorality in the name of the Trinity. In some cases the doctrine led to ecclesiastical or social policies that were repressive, paternalistic, and authoritarian. Leaders required confessions that demanded conscience to acquiesce to teachings that were unpersuasive to conscientious minds. Injustice and fideism promoted doubt and distrust.

Hence, Unitarianism split the churches of our forebears in New England, and it did so at a time when many theologians and more pastors failed to make a decent case for a trinitarian theology that could engage the more cosmopolitan views of the world or meet common standards of justice and intellectual integrity. As Norman Pittenger has shown, modern liberal Protestantism has been tempted again and again by the "pathologies" of a trinitarianism come apart and reduced to a single theme—deism, humanism, and spiritism. In each case, the repudiation of the classic heritage was connected with a betrayal of justice or intellectual integrity on the part of the advocates of trinitarian thought. Many today still accept his critique, even if they do not accept "process" proposals to overcome the perils he identifies.[7]

Our communion, and modern Christianity generally, does not have a single prescription for how we are to view such matters as the doctrine of the Trinity, but it does have a profound conviction that our affirmation of faith and our use of the ancient creeds must manifest intellectual integrity and be linked to social polities, policies, and programs that are marked by the quest for justice in the common life. Our stance could be formulated in this way: if a doctrine of the church is not just, it is probably also not faithful and not true! We are not obligated to hold it; we are obligated to revise it or, if it cannot be revised toward greater truth and justice, abandon it.

But justice is a complex concept. It has several dimensions. For one thing, justice reflects the moral habits by which people build lives in a community. That is, justice requires the capacity to discern, to interpret and analyze, the structures and dynamics of relationships in society. In classic thought, this aspect of justice is the part that demanded a shrewd reading of the actual situation, as we see in Solomon. Later, this was carried out with the help of "natural philosophy." In the modern world, this dimension of justice is often discovered with the assistance of the social sciences.

But justice requires more than simply the savvy awareness of how things are, how they work, and how they change: it requires an awareness that every sociohistorical context is ultimately rooted in fundamental convictions about how the world (both biophysical and social) is constituted in a moral sense. This is the view that every deep analysis of the human condition carries us to questions of ethical and spiritual meanings— "values" as they are often called today.

This dimension of justice, studied by "social ethology," identifies the values that are built into the civilizational ethos in which we humans live and move and have our being and

7. See Pittenger, *The Divine Triunity* (Philadelphia: United Church Press, 1977).

through which people experience God's love concretely in common forms of grace—families that sustain love, schools that nurture wisdom, courts that are a terror only to evil conduct, economies that support the commonwealth, technologies that work, cultures that give expression to the joys and pains of life, hospitals that heal, and regimes that establish peace. Any ultimate theory of God's truth that fails to take account of such institutions or sustain them and human commitments to them will not be taken seriously by them.

Second, justice also has the dimension of anticipation. Justice has a vision of what ought to be the good of life beyond its present social contexts. Justice wants to change things, to transform things for the better, to convert souls and societies to a larger horizon. No civilization or person is beyond need of transformation toward a greater good. Thus, justice demands a sense of divine purpose beyond every *status quo* that pretends that the way things are is the best of all possible ways and beyond every *fluxus quo* that imagines every change to be benevolent. In fact, some change brings demonic destruction. We need to know what God has promised and what God is bringing.

Christians speak of the plumb lines of novelty in terms of incarnation and resurrection. These give assurance to our hopes for the reign of God, the New Jerusalem, and the communion of the saints, all of which are only proleptically present in the ordinary contexts of life. These images of hope point toward a future beyond all that we may realistically expect. God's goodness, God's purpose, and thus all that is truly of God in both human personality and civilization will be fully and finally actualized. We can then know that all that presently exists is but a parable of things to come. This theological teleology is a necessary complement to every serious ethology, as hope is a necessary complement to love. Every creed that is to be embraced in the name of justice and truth will have to be able to sustain such visions.

And third, justice also has a dimension of constant and reliable principle. Some things are forever wrong: idolatry, murder, rape, oppression, exploitation, lying, torture, and so on. Some things are eternally right: worshiping God, telling the truth, honoring legitimate authority, protecting the innocent, defending the human rights of all, loving the neighbor, and so on. To believe this demands an act of faith; to live it is evidence of fidelity. And this dimension of justice complements both the hope of teleology and the love of ethology. This we share with the world's religions and principled humanists, for these things we know in a rough way by *justitia originalis* (which some attribute to common grace and others to natural law). This can be called the deontological aspect of justice. Non-Christians also know that standing over every civilization and over every human relationship, and serving as a standard of every hope for personal or social fulfillment, is a plumb line of duty and of rights accessible to all. None is exempt.

Christians know also that the plumb line is heavy, for we hold that not a jot may pass from God's law and that, in all things, we are to obey the spirit as well as the letter of the commandments. We also know that all humans are convicted in their hearts by this dimension of justice and that it is only by justification in an ultimate sense, and by sanctification in a proximate sense, that we can speak of fidelity to God's righteousness. Nevertheless, we are to seek those kinds of structures of personal habit and social order that enhance rather than inhibit this righteousness.

The triune, covenantal structure of justice suggests that we need a way of ordering the ethological, the teleological, and the deontological dimensions of justice. In fact, concentration on the question of justice, if it is deeply understood, adds to the sense that a trinitarian understanding of reality is essential for the ethical analysis of life and its meanings. It is not that creeds must be made "practical" or that truth must meet some test beyond itself; it is rather a way of saying that ethics is constitutive of right faith, that justice is integral to truth. In both creed and deed, the most difficult questions often arise in the effort to find an integral ordering of pluralistic elements. Like Augustine's trinitarian analogy of memory, intelligence, and will or the numerous subsequent analogies and symbols that have been developed historically to identify the possible meanings of Trinity that Gabriel Fackre has recently catalogued, the three dimensions of justice cannot be reduced to one another.[8] They are sometimes experienced as pulling against one another, because the kinds of arguments and data we marshal for each is distinct from those we marshal for the others, even if each implies the importance of the others. Yet in both the life of God and in our life with God we hold that a specific kind of unity and pluralism, of singularity and diversity, is the only realistic possibility.

And so, with regard to the justice as well as to the truth of God, we have to recognize how necessary it is to make again the case for the doctrine of the Trinity. It may well be that this doctrine will not only provide the decisive postbiblical model of how to preach the gospel in a strange land and how to embody the message in worship rightly but that it will also, as C. R. Dziczek says, provide the decisive way of uncovering and communicating, in highly symbolic language, the fundamental structure of the common social and ethical life implicit in ecumenical efforts to discuss faith, science, and the future and to embody these themes sacramentally and socially.[9]

THE TRIUNE CHARACTER OF EVERYTHING?

It is not a new idea that all of reality is, at base, trinitarian. A number of the ancient Church Fathers, both East and West, spoke of the *vestigia trinitatis*. This is the idea that since God created the world, the traces of the very constitution of God, which is trinitarian, remain in the structure of all that is. Even if all that is is fallen, it could not lose its divine constituting structure, or it could not be.

This is the metaphysical parallel to the moral *justitia originalis* which makes it necessary for all humans to understand the basic covenantal patterns of life. They are valid for both ontological and ethical reasons. Further, humans are capable, in some

8. See Fackre, *The Christian Story*, vol. 2 (Grand Rapids: William B. Eerdmans, 1988).

9. C. R. Dziczek, "The Eucharist and Ecumenical Ethics" (D.Min. thesis, Andover Newton Theological School, 1986). I am grateful to Dr. Dziczek for his help in the editing of this essay.

measure, of recognizing this deep trinitarian imprint. We humans are made in the image of God, and so we have the potential, epistemologically, to recognize that both God and the universe is trinitarian in metaphysical-moral structure—if our perceptions are rooted in accurate knowledge and actually grasp the character of things as God intended them to be, which is their deepest nature even if they are distorted in existence.

But of course, this ancient idea requires a certain confidence in the potential of humans to know such ultimate things with some degree of reliability. Such an idea is in considerable disrepute today—or so it seems. Have not Freud and Marx and other "modern masters of suspicion" demonstrated that the mind is governed by irrational forces and that what we hold to be "the way things are" is actually a rationalized construal of reality? No small number of scholars is inclined to take a reductionist psycho-sexual or sociopolitical view when accounting for human beliefs about what is real. Indeed, we are all heirs, today, of the hermeneutics of suspicion.

Even here, however, traces of the Trinity may be present. Important suggestions along this line can be found in a dialogue between Leonard Hodgson, a British theologian struggling with the relationship of faith to the psychiatric understanding of personal integration and anthropological theory today,[10] and Jan Lochman, a noted Eastern European theologian writing out of the modern Christian encounter with Marxism. The discussion, in short, is about the relationship of the doctrine of the Trinity to the understanding of modern theories of the social sciences.

Lochman calls to our attention the deep tradition of the *vestigia trinitatis* and notes that it was Augustine's adherence to this view that allowed him to draw on the triune understanding of the human self to form his analogy for explicating the trinitarian understandings of God.[11] Augustine is followed by Luther in this, and no small number of modern scholars has been

---

10. See Hodgson, *The Doctrine of the Trinity* (New York: Scribner's, 1944).
11. Lochman, "The Trinity and Human Life," *Theology* 78 (April 1975): 173-83.

aware that similarities, to say the least, can be found between Augustine, Luther, and Freud.

The evidence is rather convincing. The threefold nature of human personality—id, ego, and superego, as Freud develops it, has deep affinities with trinitarian understanding—except, of course, for the fact that id, the dynamic and spontaneous source of the human spirit, is seen as the psycho-physical source of creative energy, from which the other key dimensions of human personality proceed. In this view, ego is the mature, organized, incarnate identity, while the superego, which involves the internalization of fatherly norms as influenced by an external "reality principle," is basically derivative. It is not hard to see that, in a rather direct, if inverted, way Freud can be said to manifest the *vestigia trinitatis* in his theory. To be sure, he would not want to talk about it in these terms, for he associated religion with neurosis and Christian ideas with nonuniversal and prescientific idiosyncrasies.

Nevertheless, the kind of awareness to which this debate draws our attention would account both for the fact that Christian pastors have found aspects of Freud useful in pastoral care and for the presumed ability to apply Freudian theory cross-culturally. If Freud is dependent on some form of the *vestigia trinitatis,* it would account for the fact that secular scholars can find some evidence that seems to support his theories in all parts of the world. Of course, the accuracy of his account of the relationships of the triune parts to one another and to the whole would have to remain under discussion, and the question is open as to whether his view is defensible or not.

But Lochman is less interested in observations about the intersections of theology and psychology than he is in the encounter of politics and theology in the modern world, especially as they have developed in contemporary dialectical thinking. But even in this regard, Lochman notes that Hegel, the father of sociohistorical political thought, also seems to manifest the notion of *vestigia trinitatis.* Further, Hegel seems to be followed in this by his greatest pupil, Marx—though Marx, like Freud, would have difficulty using these terms because of his estimation of religion generally and Christianity in particular.

As I have suggested elsewhere, Hegel is the decisive heir of the attempts to set forth the meanings of the Trinity in terms of sociohistorical politics.[12] It was mediated from the radical Franciscans who followed Joachim of Fiora, through the radical Reformer Thomas Müntzer, to modern historicism by Hegel. From Hegel it passed to Marx, and from him to much of liberation theology—often with Ernst Bloch or Antonio Gramsci as further mediators.

In any case, Hegel is deeply concerned to overcome the deep gulf that seems to exist between the abstract, universalistic authority that designs the whole and the particular concrete life of humanity in the world that serves the design and the designer. Thus he turns to the priority of spirit and argues that it works in history through its relationship to matter in a dialectical logic that resolves tensions between the two to form a new organic community life with new forms of consciousness. The social manifestation of this dialectic between spirit and matter, the master-slave relationship, is also resolved in a new whole. In such arguments, Lochman points out, Hegel

> understood himself basically as a "trinitarian thinker." The claim of his philosophy to have grasped the ultimate mysteries of spirit as it comes to consciousness in history he substantiated in a trinitarian way: the doctrine of the Trinity, interpreted from a speculative standpoint, is *the* revelation of being. A philosophy which wishes to do justice to being, which desires to understand and interpret the world correctly and—as Karl Marx further concludes—which wishes to transform the world, orients its thinking about trinitarian truth: in a dialectic sort of three-step the triune God manifest [sic] himself in history. The dialectic is the rational form of this mystery and as such the Law and motor of thinking and life in our universe. The doctrine of the Trinity has a constitutive significance for our being and for our cognition.[13]

---

12. Stackhouse, "Protestantism and Poverty: An Interpretation of the Economic Implications of Reformation Views of the Trinity," in *The Preferential Option for the Poor,* ed. Richard John Neuhaus (Grand Rapids: William B. Eerdmans, 1988).

13. Lochman, "The Trinity and Human Life," p. 175.

Lochman does not pursue this in great detail, in part because he is doubtful about the whole idea of *vestigia trinitatis* as being abstract and unhistorical (as Marx might have said) and in part because the Hegelian-Marxist view seems to have a kind of ordering of the parts that he finally does not find convincing. We might point out here that this sociohistorical ordering of the triune logic took two forms. One clearly supported the Prussian Empire, and the other demanded the overthrow of every established bourgeois regime. Both involved an impersonal spirit ordered by a dynamic grounded in a new triune dialectic of scientific consciousness. In both personhood gets lost.

Lochman, like many others facing various forms of modern thought that are close to but clearly distinct from Christian trinitarian thought, turns away from the debate with these views. He turns to Barth, whom he reads through the eyes of a Christian socialism. His views on this matter are not incompatible with those worked out by Jürgen Moltmann, who helpfully extends the debates in the churches about the proper interpretation of the doctrine of the Trinity in our confessions and constantly relates the question to the notion that we are, under a triune God, to anticipate the reign of God by forming a covenantal community based on the ethological, teleological, and deontological dimensions of justice.[14]

But here we note that they, with Barth, are basically uninterested in the question of whether we can defend our trinitarian beliefs on universalistic grounds. Only a few recent scholars, such as Rolf Ahlers, have tried to show deep correlations between the triune dialectic of Hegel and an unadmitted and largely unexamined "natural theology" in Barth and a number of Barthians on this point that lives, somehow, easily with romantic elements in modern forms of socialism and often judges all questions of justice in such terms (thereby embracing, in practice, an irrational decisionism that Ahlers heatedly repudiates).[15]

14. See Moltmann, *The Trinity and the Kingdom of God* (San Francisco: Harper & Row, 1981).
15. See Ahlers, *The Community of Freedom* (Peter Lang, 1989).

Whether his arguments turn out to be widely accepted by the specialists or not, I will submit that for the most part modern Protestant theology in the wake of Barth's genius has not attempted to give arguments as to why a Christian perspective on this issue ought to be accepted. It is proclaimed in many ways, and frequently in a mood of sharp antagonism to culture and philosophy and ethics. Such a view may have served as a rallying point when Europe was passing through the dark night of Hitler, and it may have protected the consciences of Christians when they were confronted with the pretenses of omniscience presented by scientific socialism (as in eastern Europe before the recent collapse of the communist worldview), and it may have rallied the spirit of believers who were besieged by an expressive and managerial individualism without a clear normative "second language" (as in countries such as our own, if Robert Bellah's analysis of our society is correct).[16] In these situations, where people are caught up in systems that prevent them from trying to make a case for the truth of theology or of a universalistic sense of justice, God surely rejoices when they simply hold fast to things that are good and build a fortress faith against the ideological forces of emptiness and normlessness.

But with fascism defeated and with socialism revising its orientation to everything, and with a burst of Christian renewal all over the world by groups that care little about the niceties of doctrine[17]—not to mention an enormous surge of neopaganism in the West and fundamentalism in several of the world's religions—the fortress of faith has collapsed in many parts of the church. On what basis can we make a plea for the classic Christian way of stating that all that is most holy is most truly grasped by particular formulas about Father, Son, and Holy Spirit? And on what basis can we recover, adopt, reform, or adapt that which we believe in our hearts and confess with our lips?

As we have seen, modern thought that may appear to be

16. See Bellah et al., *Habits of the Heart: Individualism and Commitment in American Life* (Berkeley and Los Angeles: University of California, 1985).

17. See D. Martin, "After Catholicism: Speaking in Latin Tongues," *National Review*, 29 September 1989, pp. 30ff.

quite post-Christian or at least postmetaphysical or postmoral may actually have trinitarian elements at the deepest levels. The question that then comes immediately to the fore is whether the founders of modern thought are in fact deeply influenced by a particular view developed out of the uniqueness of Christian experience or whether Christian doctrine articulates with precision what they also found even after repudiating Christianity, something that needs theological definition if we and they are to see clearly what was, and is, and ever shall be true.

If the former is the case, any attempt to export Freud, Marx, or Barth to the cultures that are not a part of the West's historical experience would be a form of cultural or religious imperialism. Even if we come to some common formulation of the faith, we would basically be forming a cultural-linguistic convention for which no ultimate justifying arguments could be given.

But if the latter is true, then aspects of Freud and Marx and Barth would be able to find rootage in every culture. Indeed, rightly articulated trinitarian thought would allow many cultures to understand their own deepest structures better than the alternative religious opinions that are presently held by many in those cultures. And we would know that when we move toward a fresh appropriation and articulation of the faith we share, we would have guiding arguments by which we could discuss whether our efforts are closer to or farther from the mark of truth.

If we are going to pursue these issues, we shall also have to take at least one other major perspective into account. The noted Catholic thinker from India Raimundo Panikkar has analyzed major dimensions of Hindu thought and noted that at the depths of that tradition we can also find a trinitarian structure.[18] Such a finding not only tends to confirm the notion of *justitia originalis* but makes us aware that we live in a global situation today and forces us to pose fresh questions. One such question involves certain implications of the filioque. Is it possible that the Holy Spirit, proceeding from the First Person of the Trinity, but not in

18. See Panikkar, *The Trinity and the Religious Experience of Man* (Maryknoll, N.Y.: Orbis Press, 1973).

any fashion obvious to human consciousness proceeding through Jesus Christ, could be present in the world religions and leading them to a trinitarian awareness—at least as a *preparatio*, at most as a general or common *revelatio?* When we shift to non-Christian but still obviously religious understandings of triune life in areas that are not and could not have been influenced by Christian claims, how can we make arguments about the deepest meanings of the Trinity that are not dependent on, or even related to holy Scripture?

Here we come to the decisive issue beyond that of a general triune sense of the way things are everywhere. By what logic and with what kinds of evidence might we say that the Freudian or Hegelian or Marxist or Barthian or—as we suggested earlier—the feminist or now the Hindu sense of the triune character of reality is more or less correct? And why would we need specifically Christian forms of stating these matters? All in fact may well participate in and be more or less aware that the fundamental character of reality—divine, human, social, and possibly cosmic—is triune, relational, and neither totally atomistic nor completely collectivistic. And if they all, more or less, manifest the same deep structure, what difference would it make if we, and whole societies, choose one or another?

It is one of the great tragedies of modern theology that it has become entirely confessional on such points. People state their own convictions about matters, and in one sense everyone's view is equally honored, but in another sense, everyone's view is equally ignored because it is not ours. On what grounds might Lochman have argued that Freud's or Hegel's or Marx's ordering of the triune realities are mistaken and that Barth's are correct, or that all are problematic and that some other alternative ought to be considered?

There is something missing in these several views of contemporary ecumenical, noncredal, postcritical believers who want to remain faithful but are not sure that they will be honest or just if they do: they need to know how the most distinctive Christian doctrine of God is related to intellectual integrity, religious pluralism, and social justice. We already know that the dimensions of justice are triune, and we know that all modern societies are pluralistic and complex and yet have some kind of relational coherence. What is it in all this talk of the Trinity that does and can lead us beyond understandings of human psyche and social history and pluralistic values to the decisive center of all spiritual, intellectual, and social existence in and under God?

If it turns out that intrapsychic, interpersonal, and communal understandings of life are all relational, then no one is, or could be, against them, and we are saying nothing of importance. Merely to repeat these pantheistic (or sometimes panentheistic) nostrums in obscurantist language does little to guide life and thought. Nor does it help simply to confess that we have this view while someone else has another one. On these grounds, one might just as well be a Freudian as an Eastern Christian, a Marxist as a Western Christian, or a Hindu as a feminist Christian.

The questions can be simplified: What is the best way to order the triune character of life and thought? How would we know? And how can this help us understand and live rightly? These questions, which are constitutionally related to questions of the character of God and the structure of justice, are not only intra-Christian and confessional. They are, if they are anything, global and ecumenical. They are, in short, questions of public theology at the deepest levels and in the broadest sense.

A PUBLIC TRINITY

At this point we have to turn again to some of the key issues behind the development of the doctrine of the Trinity that have been neglected in at least some of the historic debates. We shall have to face the fact that key doctrinal debates were not only questions of how the unity of the church could be maintained and the truth of the faith stated in terms that made sense in a non-Hebraic context but also questions of how Christianity was to be related to the structures of power and the pluralism of cultures, religions, and philosophies in the ancient world.

Both the internal church debates with heterodox leaders and the sociopolitical context that prompted Constantine to call the council of Nicaea involved the fundamental issue of what could hold diverse, conflict-ridden, protocosmopolitan societies together when the metaphysical-moral theories that had guided the earlier religions and city-states were falling apart. We miss the point of the early debates about the Trinity if we do not see questions about the fundamental structure of God and God's relationship to humanity also as questions of God's order of justice for the order of civilization.

The theological issues, in other words, are public and not only confessional, although we make a grave error if we understand the word *public* to mean matters primarily political or governmental. Not only did the Church Fathers firmly if indirectly (by the way they articulated what the Trinity was and meant) resist the efforts to sanctify the status of the emperor and make the church merely a chaplain of the court, but they also held that what they said about the Trinity was properly to be proclaimed in public preaching, celebrated in public worship, and debated in public discourse. The Trinity they were talking about was not esoteric or privileged but public in fundamental character.

They were very aware that the public is always prior to any republic and that the latter depended on the truth and justice of the metaphysical-moral ideas that came to dominate the civilization. The thought of the leadership that formed the mind of the public was decisive for the destiny of the whole. What they held to be genuinely evangelical had also to be public in the sense that it would be genuinely cosmopolitan, genuinely ecumenical, genuinely catholic, genuinely orthodox, genuinely evangelical, and thus universally true and just. It had to be accessible to all as well as guiding for all, true for all, and just for all. It had to provide the models for the normative ordering of civilization. It was, and is, a vocation of the church even if only a few rulers and political scientists know it.

Today, however, themes such as these have been taken up by those deeply influenced by revisionist traditions that are rooted in Freud and Marx as well as by classical Christian thought. We can see many features of these new directions if we consider the new study *Trinity and Society* by the noted Brazilian

Catholic Leonardo Boff. Although his argument is rooted in a Latin spirituality that gives it distinctive nuances, much of what he argues is closely compatible with what we can today find in many ecumenically oriented Protestant churches that have been touched by the arguments of psychology, socialism, and neo-orthodoxy as well as the new awareness of a global vision. Boff, for instance, is open to the use of modern psychiatric insights, although he is attracted to Jung rather than Freud because of Jung's presumed inclusion of "the feminine," which Boff identifies with Mary at key points. He is also sympathetic to Hegel and Marx, as one can see when traces of the Joachite historicism of his radical Franciscan roots appear in his interpretation of liberation.

Nevertheless, Boff's views invite a rapprochement between ecumenical Protestantism and post–Vatican II Catholicism, in part because he approximates a mode of covenantal thinking that is antihierarchical, antipatriarchal, decidedly personalistic and communitarian. His understanding of the Christian base community is close to the "congregationalism" of the Jonathan Edwards tradition. (Admittedly, this troubles the Vatican, and it is doubtful whether a personalistic and communitarian model that could be realized in a congregation or an order is yet genuinely societal and public. Here distinctions between a communal and a societal conception of human association is decisive.)

Boff argues that the basic meaning of the Trinity is that ultimate reality—divine, and therefore also human—is constituted by loving relationships of persons in community. Not only does this deny the ultimate importance of monarchic or imperial or colonial models of relationships between God and humanity, but it makes such relationships in church and society highly questionable. In genuinely trinitarian life and thought, we can see the normative importance of persons, of mutuality, and of living in solidarity with others.

Boff rehearses the decisions of the great councils on the Trinity and shows considerable command of the classic, especially Western, doctrinal discussions on the matter (in a way that leads him to an unquestioning acceptance of filioque). These he correlates with texts from the New Testament. But he also knows that the meaning of the Trinity pertains to the human sense of relations today, for the truths of God are not pertinent only in heaven or long ago. The doctrine of the Trinity, he points out, is most important when it strengthens faith, when it re-presents the mystery of truth, and when it promotes loving social participation in the common life—now, in this life.

We might ask why he did not try to be more searching about the Eastern positions generally and filioque specifically (since some also stress the intimate relationship between theology and human community, and he is seeking a broader view). We might ask why he did not quote any Protestants on these matters except Barth and Moltmann (especially in view of some free-church developments in his own context). We might argue that some aspects of his view of human nature owe more to Aristotle than to a biblical anthropology. We might be very troubled by his neglect of the idea of covenant, a failure that leads him to see most of Jahwism as simply monarchical and to lose a sense of the prophetic power of the deontological principles of right and wrong that must always be a part of any fundamental theory of the defense of personhood and viable society. But we would have to acknowledge that he is on the brink of the kinds of questions that need to be asked.

Many Protestants quickly identify with him, although recent evidence developed by David Martin and a team of researchers suggest that the "Protestantization" of the Latin American church is one of the most dramatic events of the century, far outstripping any liberation developments. To take a step beyond this useful work, we have to recognize that his perspective is not yet genuinely "public." It is highly contextual, as are many Protestant, North Atlantic, liberal, European, and Eastern perspectives. The difference is that he so wants his views to be contextual that he loses his cosmopolitan vision.

To be more pertinent to the broader public questions he begins to raise, and to be more faithful to what the ecumenical councils did, we shall have to ask what their fundamental questions were. And while we have to note that they were legion, we can no longer doubt that among their questions were some that had to do with several public theological, social, and ethical issues:

1. Is ultimate reality personal or impersonal? (If it is impersonal, it is not theistic and hence not ethical.)
2. If it is theistic, are there many gods or only one or two? (Polytheism, monotheism, and dualism are the basic options.)
3. What is the social significance of right doctrine? (Whether "right" is or can be reliably known is the question.)

The Church Fathers believed that the internal life of the church, the well-being of the whole society, and the relationship of the community of believers to political, economic, and legal principalities and powers were at stake.

The masterly work of George Hunston Williams on christology and church-state relations in the fourth century has clearly indicated what some of the decisive symbols of the trinitarian debates meant for social life. Writing from a free-church perspective, he shows that the authors of the great creeds developed a dynamic view that invites continued reappropriation and reapplication to guide new civilizational situations. They set forth a doctrine of the Trinity that (1) was open to the reality of life in a moral universe; (2) was able to link the tensions of unity, plurality, and duality together; and (3) demanded the recognition that theology knows enough of ultimate things to set forth structures and patterns that can inform civilization, establish peace, and sustain humanity.

Further, they set forth this doctrine in a symbolic way that was open to further discussion and refinement. It was more than a stroke of genius; one can only suggest that it was inspired. For they allowed Christianity to sing the Lord's song, even in a strange, cosmopolitan, and postbiblical land, in a way that did not prescribe how everyone had to sing every note but that was nonetheless able to say No to any number of false notes and wrenching dissonances. The whole maintains a harmony that can be, and has been ever since, sung with different accents and rhythms, in many keys and arrangements.

This is what makes it genuinely open. In the end it does not tell us exactly how we have to believe in a positive way, but it does contain clues that allow us to reject untrue or unjust options. And this is why, in understanding the Trinity, we are necessarily introduced to a great number of heresies. To put the matter in other, more contemporary terms, the doctrine of the Trinity is a marvelous cybernetic model, for it points to the answers of the most ultimate questions and yet remains open to new symbolic input and genuine feedback. It warns against and finally denies validity to immoral or amoral views of ultimate reality and to relationships of the one and the many that tend to destroy meaning and justice and civilization.

FINALLY: THE ISSUES TODAY

If we are to be faithful to this legacy today, we will continue to wrestle with the depths of the implications of what they did, but we will do so by alerting ourselves to the critical issues that are before us. We have to take up the questions of Trinity in the context of a new global dialogue of religions and anthropologies, such as those of Freud and Marx as already mentioned. I do not mean simply the formal discussions held between representatives of various faiths at international conferences, however important these are. I mean the basic wrestling with the contending commitments about the nature and character of all that is holy that takes place in our spiritual lives as concretely lived out in our families, our schools, our jobs, our laboratories, our courts of law, and our factories and marketplaces.[19]

In all places, we are struggling today with senses of meaning that are not certain of their roots. And in a day of democracy rather than the rule of an emperor, we engage in all arenas in a fateful inevitable struggle for the hearts and souls of those, from all walks of life, who will make decisions about the future. We struggle, in other words, not with Constantine but with the

19. On this, see, for example, Christos Yannaras, *The Freedom of Morality* (Crestwood, N.Y.: St. Vladimir's Seminary Press, 1987).

lawyers and managers and engineers and workers and politicians and doctors and teachers and artists and journalists and military officers on whom we depend, with whom we live, and through whom the church shapes the cosmopolitan civilization.

Today all must be involved in identifying and exemplifying those features, structures, dynamics, and qualities of that triune holiness critical to the future. All are now prophets, priests, and politicians in a democratized and thus potentially covenantal society who, like bishops of old, properly claim magisterial and teaching authority in the worlds where we enact our faith—worlds not always eager to face the implications of a reclaimed and recast claim about ultimate truth and justice.

We might remember, in this regard, that it was in the shadow of Hitler that Erik Peterson wrote one of the major studies of the twentieth century alerting us to the perils of certain views of monotheism.[20] His study triggered a great deal of new work on the Trinity. But totalitarian barbarism is not the only form of monotheism we face. The "soft" forms of Unitarianism that broke with the biblical traditions and the "hard" forms of Islam that claim to have a subsequent revelation represent forms of antitrinitarianism that are very much a part of what Christianity faces, leaving aside those forms of "centrism" that singularly focus on Jesus or the Spirit.[21] These lead to very different kinds of theories of justice and truth, and hence of church and society.

Pastors know that tendencies in these directions can be found in nearly every congregation, however many times the creeds are said. And scholars know that, in veiled forms, these options are present in every community of discourse. In the face of such realities, not only we, but the whole world, have to think through once more whether G. K. Chesterton had it right when he wrote,

> Unitarians (a sect never to be mentioned without a special respect for their distinguished intellectual dignity . . .) are often reformers

20. Peterson, *Monotheismus als Politische Problem* (Bütersloh: Gerd Mohn, 1978).

21. See H. R. Niebuhr, "Theological Unitarianisms," *Theology Today* 40 (July 1983): 150-57.

by the accident that throws so many small sects into such an attitude. But there is nothing in the least liberal or akin to reform in the substitution of pure monotheism for the Trinity. The complex God of the Athanasian Creed may be an enigma for the intellect; but He is far less likely to gather the mystery and cruelty of a Sultan than the lonely god of Omar or Mahomet. The god who is a mere awful unity is not only a king but an Eastern king. The *heart* of humanity . . . is certainly much more satisfied by the strange hints and symbols that gather round the . . . image of a council at which mercy pleads as well as justice, the conception of a sort of liberty and variety existing even in the inmost chamber of the world. . . . It is not well for God to be alone.[22]

Chesterton neglects, in his analysis of monotheism, other forms of neopagan monisms that are currently the rage in New Age spirituality. In these, the divine is fully resident in or identical with the cosmic forces. The human task is to tune in to them by attending to the "real self" or to "natural vitalities." It turns out that neither the Gnostics nor the Druids are entirely gone. They are alive, present in our churches, and overtly opposed to aspects of Christianity—sometimes in praise of the "integrity of creation," as if it were not fallen, broken, alienated from its Creator, and in need of salvation by a Creator who alone has integrity—marked by plurality.

All these various forms of theological unification introduce a cosmic monotony into the common life. In the final analysis they cannot account for the rich complexity of ethology, and they thus attempt to contain it—either by an interpretation of diversity that so relates everything to one ultimate reality that the variety becomes only a fraudulent appearance, or by a demand for conformity enforced by the sword. It fails also to reckon with the first dimension of justice.

But the contraries to these deifications of singularity and unity are no less present. No small number of covert polytheisms flourish in the modern world. Long ago it was well understood that every people had its own gods and that every

22. Chesterton, *Orthodoxy* (1908; London: Collins-Fontana, 1961), pp. 133-34.

function in life—planting, singing, fighting, loving—had its own deity. Today people speak little of gods in this connection, but every culture, subculture, gender, and lifestyle is presumed to have its own inviolate values, and every discipline and craft has its own creeds, codes, and cults. The sovereignty of each of these is challenged only at the cost of vilification or excommunication, and attempts to draw them into a more disciplined and more integrated pattern are met with screams about the violation of the sacred.

In this kind of world, many have grave doubts as to whether any universal sense of justice or truth exists—or, if there is, whether anyone can know it with any security. Perhaps ultimate reality is so constituted that one can only have a perspective—with each perspective being of equal ultimate value to every other. If this is the case, no one can call wrong any effort of one power or perspective or deity to triumph over another or all others, for the genius of some may be precisely to subdue lesser potencies. Ironically, the relativism of this sort of pluralism is the prologue to the subordination of others where it does not lead to the radical monotheism that Chesterton feared.

It helps little to turn to "henotheism," the nineteenth-century name given to those religions which, believing that there are many ultimate centers of power and authority, nevertheless chose one for their own. It is important to say that Christ is *my* Lord, even if that does not mean that Christ is *the* Lord. It is a matter of indifference whether one speaks of the Lord Jesus or Lord Shiva or Lord Buddha, but each must have his or her own deity or the ideal of civilized tolerance is itself undercut, for there is no normative vision that binds me to a pluralism with unity that includes the neighbor at the level of religion or theology.

Nor does it help justice or truth to claim as do the Hindus, East and West, that these are actually all manifestations of the one, true, central "Oversoul." We have to ask, for it is not a settled question, whether all paths lead to the same mountain and all rivers flow into the same sea. The evidence that this is true is hard to find. Besides, this intended inclusive pluralism turns out on analysis to be an extremely dogmatic monistic view that is not tolerant at all. Civilizations formed on this basis tend either to fall into incoherence (as each person or group follows its own path) or to demand, under the surface, a hierarchy of being from which few can break (since some are further along the path than others).

In all these celebrations of multiplicity, deontology is denied. No great and common singularity of moral principle obtains that applies equally to the high and the low. In a sound doctrine of the Trinity, one that recognizes the power of variety, diversity, and plurality, there nevertheless remain both the ultimate centrality of the Godhead (the basic notion that the first Person of the Trinity is both Creator of all and the Source of universal righteousness) and the awareness that the reality of the Trinity is present in all three persons.

And so on we could go. The dualisms worked out in Taoism and Zoroastrianism and Manicheism, although quite distinct, are with us also. They have parallels and advocates in every age and among all religions. The tendencies to find good and evil in everything in equal proportion, to see complementary opposition as the root principle of all, to seek the balance of everything in an immobile harmony, to seek the utter defeat of the wicked by the sword of saintliness, to try to separate the pure from the defiled by force, or to read the whole world in terms of male and female or bourgeois and proletariat (as, in spite of their latent traces of trinitarianism, the heirs of Freud and Marx are inclined to do)—all lead to polarizations or dominations.

No teleology of whole justice is possible if reality is ultimately dualistic, for either the two principles will have equal ultimacy or one will overcome the other and thereby destroy the very basis of reality. Nothing novel can proceed from anything in a way that would represent freshness of equal importance to the originating pair. The inherent capacity of narrative creativity and dynamic inspiration is undercut.

Against that view, the doctrine of the Trinity tells us that no polarity is final. Another option is yet possible beyond every apparent antinomy. It alters the way we understand and respond to any initially contrasting pair. This is true despite the fact that a subordinate dualism (in the context of Trinity, Christ is of two natures) may actually reflect the mutually implicative identity required by some aspect of the larger whole, to prevent it from being understood in reductionist terms.

If not dualism, why not quaternity? Ah, but that falls into a dualism of dualism. Why then not a pentagon of gods or persons, or a pentatonic view of the world? And seven has often been treated as a holy number, as has nine (but, of course that is a trinity of trinities). Or what about sixes and eights? But then we are quibbling over the number of centers in diversity beyond dualism (if we are not lapsing into a de facto polytheism). Neither five, nor six, nor seven, nor any other number is required by evidence or logic to convey differentiated, nondualistic plurality. No, there is something fundamental about the Trinity, as the ancient advocates of *vestigia trinitatis* recognized.

Yet this epistemological propriety needs the vitality of dynamic and living actuality to come alive, just as it needs explicit formulation to be clearly recognized and direct refutation of false options to gain clarity. Thus we find it proper to speak of "creation" and "begetting" and "breathing" and "death" and "life" and "church" and "communion." The drama traced in moral and metaphysical terms recognizes relational interaction in the midst of formal epistemic requirements, and thus invites sociohistorical participation on a universal scale.

By way of contrast, it does not help to deny conflicting theisms by attempting to treat the universe atheistically as a nonpersonal, and hence nonmoral, set of phenomena or relationships in flux and flow. The Buddhists long ago worked out the implications of this dispirited view—which is quite rampant in the scientism of some modern naturalists and among both pragmatic and process philosophers today. It ultimately means living in a void of meaning, constancy, and justice—a void that must either separate itself from the people or admit into its midst cant and magic and myth and idols for which it has utter contempt but which it must tolerate rhetorically to cover its own metaphysical-moral nakedness.

Each one of these options has been proposed as a basis for life and thought, worship and civilization. They have failed because they are inadequate, because they are fundamentally flawed. The doctrine of the Trinity does not seem to be thus flawed, although the esoteric and quaint ways in which it is presently discussed makes it distant from the communities of faith and civilizations of the world that embrace or do not resist it.

The main point is perhaps clear: we may well have to take up such major contenders for the basic understanding of the nature of ultimate reality as presented here and show that each of them meets a grave difficulty in providing the intellectual, ethical, and sociopolitical model to guide complex and pluralistic cosmopolitan life. Of course, if the doctrine of the Trinity in its most careful form cannot meet the test here posed to other great visions of the nature of divine reality, then Christians should have to be prepared to give it up. That would be one of the greatest imaginable shocks to the faith.

We have to countenance this possibility because it is surely not possible to prove in any final way the truth of the Trinity. No knock-down arguments attend this doctrine. Nevertheless, part of what may be implied by the "mystery" of the Trinity is that we believe that it cannot be refuted in these ways. It is likely to be left standing after we follow the paths of the *via negativa* against the present world religions and pseudofaiths, invite them to exercise the same efforts against us in open conciliar debate as our forebears criticized heresies in their midst (and took the risk of being attacked by them), and ourselves apply the Petrine test to our own beliefs. In any case, questions of justice, with all their ethological, teleological, and deontological dimensions, will be decisive to these debates.

Even if they cannot confirm the doctrine of the Trinity, it is likely that they can refute many false alternatives. Such arguments do not deny that there is truth in each of the great options we face. Had they nothing to commend them, no one would believe them, and we would not have to take them seriously enough to criticize them. Not only the world religions, but modern secular philosophies of psyche and history also have much to offer; they commend themselves to us, demand that we be in dialogue with them and that we recognize insights from which we can learn. But such arguments as these suggest that, in the final analysis, trinitarian thought can and should attempt to show how the great strengths of these alternative traditions are lacking in themselves, even if aspects of their views can be incorporated and related to contributions made by others. Thereby the adherents of the great religions and philosophies of humanity can find ways to be drawn into a covenant and enabled to live in the cosmopolitan civilization of the future, mutually corrected by one another.

Should we follow this way of looking at the matter, we would have to be prepared to modify the ways we speak of the Trinity. For example, it could be suggested, on the basis of my own church's efforts to wrestle with the relationships of Christians and Jews after the Holocaust, that we will not resist dropping the filioque, but will do so for reasons that have less to do with certain ancient purely doctrinal debates between Catholics and Orthodox Christians and less with the social histories of groups backing one or another view (as John Romanides has documented)[23] than with the fact that we believe that the Holy Spirit has been and is present among the people of God's initial covenant with Israel, without the conscious awareness of the presence of the second Person of the Trinity, having proceeded directly from the Father.

In a parallel position, many ecumenical Christians believe they can recognize a similar procession or "spiration" in other of the world religions. It may well be that believers in the great non-Christian faiths too will have to come to grips with the christological reality and that until they do, their doctrines are likely to remain incomplete. But that does not deny the real presence of the Holy Spirit, inspired from God the Father, in their midst and among people who hold to other faiths.

I am not, in these pages, setting forth in any detail what a restatement of the doctrine of the Trinity for our age in the context of present questions might finally entail. I have been content to suggest the kinds of issues that may well be at stake as we begin to talk about the issues and prepare ourselves and our publics to discuss them. But more, I have suggested in quite

23. See Romanides, *Franks, Romans, Feudalism and Doctrine: An Interplay between Theology and Society* (Brookline, Mass.: Holy Cross Orthodox Press, 1981).

concrete terms how it is that what we do may well have direct pertinence for the salvation of the world. By taking on questions of this scope ecumenically, we are most faithful to the best of our traditions. Let us pray that we make no grave blunders and that we find the courage to face the intellectual tasks of our global age in a way that is faithful, true, and just. It is a sobering responsibility; it prompts us to careful work but with a cosmic vision.

Faith to Creed Consultation
Summary Statement

INTRODUCTION

We have sought to explore issues that would lead to a common understanding of the social and historical context for the development of the Nicene-Constantinopolitan Creed. We came together as representatives of diverse Christian communions with many personal and scholarly perspectives on this period in our common history. We also attempted to hear the various voices within the period itself and to move closer to shared understanding of the fourth-century expression of the apostolic faith as confessed in the creed.

I. THE CREED IN ITS FOURTH-CENTURY CONTEXT

Considering the creed in its fourth-century context broadened our understanding of its meaning.

- Monastic spirituality with its triad of prayer and worship, faith and theology, and ethical practice in daily life was an integral part of that context. This context must be seen as part of the meaning of the creed.
- The complex theological ferment from 325 to 381 included a struggle to develop sound teaching in trinitarian ter-

minology. The creed was elaborated in the context of these developing trinitarian terms in a dynamic process of conciliar debate, consensus in the church, and subsequent retrospective appropriation.

- Before and after Nicaea, various similar local creeds were used in the churches. They were used in the process of Christian formation in the catechumenate and baptism, which entailed basic ethical as well as doctrinal instruction. Creeds were meant for personal profession of faith as well as for corporate reaffirmation of faith in the act of worship.
- A conciliar tradition already existed before Nicaea. Bishops of particular churches met regularly to resolve issues.
- In the need to interpret Scripture to explicate faith, the creed served as a bridge, expressing the truth of Scripture in contemporary fourth-century terms.

II. PERSPECTIVES THAT SHAPE OUR APPROACH TO THE FOURTH CENTURY

In our discussions we became keenly aware that we tend to import into the fourth century questions that are at the center of our own traditions' life and history.

- Many issues regarding creeds and confessions, their status and function, seem to reflect the experience of the Reformation and Counter-Reformation period more than that of the early church.
- Christian groups that have experienced persecution and domination at the hands of other Christians in control of political power sometimes read the fourth century in terms drawn from those experiences.
- Churches that regard themselves as in direct continuity with the conciliar process that formed the creed tend to see the fourth century through the model of development toward the fully realized structures and theology that came afterward.

Our understanding of the creed's content and character is strongly colored by our own current ecclesial contexts.

- Those for whom the creed today plays a regular and integral role in liturgy, personal prayer, baptism, eucharistic celebration, and instruction tend to perceive its nature in the fourth century quite differently than those for whom the creed is known primarily as a historical document or a source for theological and doctrinal study.
- Experience of an ecumenical context, whether of worship with other Christians or of study and discussion such as we have enjoyed in this meeting, changes our perspective on the fourth century and the creed in the fourth century.

Most of us have implicitly or explicitly learned a perspective toward the fourth century context of the creed as part of our own ecclesial identity. Becoming mutually aware of these perspectives and of the realities in the fourth century that each of them both illuminates and obscures is one necessary step toward a common explication of the creed.

III. CREED, CHURCH, AND EMPIRE

Different perspectives on the development of church life in the fourth century, and especially of the Nicene-Constantinopolitan Creed, seemed to be influenced by different assessments of how faithful believers thought God wanted them to relate *ecclesium* and *imperium*. A major issue was to what extent and in what ways these developments were the product of the church and to what extent and in what ways they were the product of the temporal powers, specifically of the Roman *imperium*. The relative influence of each of these forces also seemed to be evaluated differently. For some the greater the influence of the *imperium*, the more negative their evaluation of the creed. For others, the amount of imperial influence had relatively little effect on their estimate of the creed's value. Still others viewed the political authority as a providential part of God's nurturing of the church.

Similar questions and evaluations concerned the extent to which the creed and related developments were issues only for an elite group in society and/or the church or for the common people as well. Related questions were raised concerning the extent to which these developments furthered the aims of the imperial power (e.g., did the evolving Nicene-Constantinopolitan Creed help Constantine and his successors unify the Empire?) and the extent to which they may have strengthened the church to resist imperial power. Once again, however, the relation of the church to imperial power was evaluated differently. The church's recognition of, alliance with, or use of imperial power was valued positively by some and negatively by others.

Finally, there were different perceptions at to whether with the conversion and rule of Constantine a shift took place in the life of the church, and if so how great a shift took place. Some saw it as involving a far-reaching reversal of the relationship of the church to society. Others saw it as a more continuous outgrowth of developments of the preceding centuries whereby the gospel further permeated the world. In general those who saw the Constantinian period as a radical shift tended to evaluate it negatively, while those who saw it as a more natural outgrowth tended to evaluate it positively.

IV. ETHICAL DIMENSIONS OF THE CREED

Questions were raised concerning the ethical implications and presuppositions of the creed.

For some participants, its lack of explicit ethical content is what would stand in the way of their being able to affirm the Nicene-Constantinopolitan Creed as a common expression of the faith. For some of these there was the issue of whether the gospel, in which the ethical commitment is central, was not marginalized or distorted in the process of the formation of this creed or in the place it held subsequently.

Still other participants represented an emerging openness within several traditions including that of the radical Reformation to the trinitarian orthodoxy of the Nicene-Constantinopolitan Creed as an essential theological framework and grounding for a political and social ethic.

Others in our group viewed the creed as part of and connected to an emerging theological-ethical tradition as the church faces a complex culture.

V. LANGUAGE, GENDER, AND CREED

A major discussion took place on language and gender. We recognized that many things that trouble us today were normal and taken for granted in the fourth century, such as the use of male imagery in the creed. The significance of language and gender, of great importance today, is a concern within and among the churches. The following considerations and views figured in our conversation:

- The language and thought categories of the creed (and the fourth century) were formative for the church. Many believed that they have kept women in powerless places and today impede women from hearing the gospel as a saving word.
- Jesus, Paul, and the monastic thinkers lived by paradigms different in part from the prevailing uniform religious norms about them, especially regarding women's place and value. That encourages us in seeking an alternative rather than a uniform vision of the "way things should be."
- We know relatively little about the implicit and explicit effects of early Christian theology and christology on how women were viewed and valued. We need to examine early Christian texts *on their own terms* in order to see how our problem is and is not related to their views and presuppositions.
- The creed is a distinctive way of expressing who this God we worship is. It is problematic to change the historical words of the creed's text or references to the Trinity. It is also problematic that women lack the direct gender-affiliation to God afforded men.

- Speaking of God as father is normative; not speaking of God as mother is not normative, though we disagreed on the desirability of this usage in public worship and prayer.
- It is a matter of concern to both women and men whether males are ontologically and iconically related to God in ways women are not. Churches and Christians find and validate their different normative views in the traditions of this and earlier eras or in a revisionist, contextual reading of this era.

VI. ADDITIONAL ISSUES

We agreed that there were several issues that did not receive extensive attention but were significant and required more work.

- Although we explored many of the divisive issues that have arisen in relation to the creed, we did not give as much attention to the specific nature of the unique and authoritative status that the creed received and the process that led to this status. The nature of this special status and function deserves more historical and theological discussion.
- We recognize the need for more discussion of the way the creed does and might function in our churches today.
- We acknowledged that there are many groups whose perspectives on the creed would enrich our discussion but that were not represented in our consultation, including Pentecostals and traditional black churches.
- Another topic that requires further work is the normative character of the creed and the extent to which this character attaches primarily to the paradigmatic, cognitive, propositional content on the one hand and the extent to which it attaches to a covenantal and ecclesial participation on the other.
- We recognize the need for further study of the specific conciliar context that produced the creed, particularly with reference to its social, political, economic, and ethical dimensions.

- Some representatives of traditions identifying with the radical wing of the Reformation wondered whether the more ontological categories in the creed themselves have distorted the messianic particularity of Jesus and whether there might be alternative modes of theologizing that preserve the discipleship ethic as integral to christology.

CONCLUSION

We all acknowledged the power of this creed to bring us into conversation with each other concerning issues of central importance to our faith: how to talk to God, trinitarian ethics, the relation of the church to temporal powers. Even in our disagreements we experienced the capacity of the creed to unify us by directing our attention to the faith we share.

Participants

Dr. Roberta C. Bondi	United Methodist Church
Dr. Charles Brockwell	United Methodist Church
Rev. Dr. Charles Bruggink	Reformed Church in America
Dr. David Bundy	United Methodist Church
Dr. David Daniels	Church of God in Christ
Rev. Dajad Davidian	Armenian Church of America
Rev. O. C. Edwards	The Episcopal Church
Dr. Thomas Finger	Mennonite Church
Rev. Fr. Thomas Fitzgerald	Greek Orthodox Church
Dr. Paul Gritz	Southern Baptist Convention
Rev. Dr. S. Mark Heim	American Baptist Churches USA
Rev. Dr. E. Glenn Hinson	Southern Baptist Convention
Prof. Eduardo Hoornaert	Roman Catholic Church
Rev. Thaddeus Horgan, S.A.	Roman Catholic Church
Dr. Rosemary Jermann	Roman Catholic Church
Rev. James Jorgenson	Greek Orthodox Church
Fr. Krikor Maksoudian	Armenian Church of America
Rev. Dr. Melanie May	Church of the Brethren
The Very Rev. John Meyendorff	Orthodox Church in America
Rev. Dr. Lauree Hersch Meyer	Church of the Brethren
Dr. James Reimer	Mennonite Church
Dr. Paulo Siepierski	Brazilian Baptist Churches
Dr. Max Stackhouse	United Church of Christ

Rev. Dr. Robert G. Stephanopoulos	Greek Orthodox Church
Dr. Mary Tanner	Church of England
Dr. J. Denny Weaver	Mennonite Church
Dr. Timothy Wengert	Evangelical Lutheran Church
Dr. George Williams	United Church of Christ